IVORY, HORN
and BLOOD

IVORY, HORN
and BLOOD

Behind the Elephant and Rhinoceros Poaching Crisis

RONALD ORENSTEIN

FIREFLY BOOKS

A FIREFLY BOOK

Published by Firefly Books Ltd. 2013

First Printing

Publisher Cataloging-in-Publication Data (U.S.)
Orenstein, Ronald.
    Ivory, horn and blood : behind the elephant and rhinoceros poaching crisis / Ronald Orenstein.
[216] p. : col. photos. ; cm.
Includes sources and index.
Summary: A crime story that, for most, is unseen and takes place thousands of miles away and in countries that few will visit. But like the trade in illegal drugs, the trade in elephant tusks and rhinoceros horns has far-reaching implications for the world economy, as it is destabilized by this organized crime, corruption and violence.
ISBN-13: 978-1-77085-227-3 (pbk.)
1. Elephants — Effect of poaching on. 2. Rhinoceroses — Effect of poaching on. 3. Poaching. I. Title.
364.164 dc23   SK36.7.O756Iv 2013

Library and Archives Canada Cataloguing in Publication
Orenstein, Ronald I. (Ronald Isaac), 1946-
    Ivory, horn and blood : behind the elephant and rhinoceros poaching crisis / Ronald Orenstein.
Includes sources and index.
ISBN 978-1-77085-227-3
    1. Poaching. 2. Ivory industry. 3. Rhinoceroses. 4. African elephant. 5. Asiatic elephant. I. Title.
SK36.7.O74 2013   333.95'9668   C2013-901238-9

Published in the United States by
Firefly Books (U.S.) Inc.
P.O. Box 1338, Ellicott Station
Buffalo, New York 14205

Published in Canada by
Firefly Books Ltd.
50 Staples Avenue, Unit 1
Richmond Hill, Ontario L4B 0A7

Cover: Gareth Lind, LINDdesign
Interior design and typesetting: Interrobang Graphic Design Inc.

Printed in Canada

The publisher gratefully acknowledges the financial support for our publishing program by the Government of Canada through the Canada Book Fund as administered by the Department of Canadian Heritage.

To the memory of my father
CHARLES ORENSTEIN
November 1, 1916 – October 18, 2012

Acronyms

AEAP: African Elephant Action Plan

AEC: African Elephant Coalition

AEF: African Elephant Fund

AfESG: African Elephant Specialist Group (under IUCN)

ASEAN-WEN: Association of Southeast Asian Nations Wildlife Enforcement Network

CACA: China Arts and Crafts Association

CAMPFIRE: Communal Areas Management Programme for Indigenous Resources (Zimbabwe)

CAR: Central African Republic

CARPE: Central African Regional Program for the Environment (under USAID)

CITES: Convention on International Trade in Endangered Species of Wild Fauna and Flora

COMIFAC: Central African Forest Commission

DEA: Department of Environmental Affairs (South Africa)

DENR: Department of Environment and Natural Resources (Philippines)

DRC: Democratic Republic of Congo (formerly Zaire)

EIA: Environmental Investigation Agency

ETIS: Elephant Trade Information System

GEF: Global Environment Facility

ICCWC: International Consortium on Combating Wildlife Crime

IFAW: International Fund for Animal Welfare

IUCN: International Union for Conservation of Nature

KWS: Kenya Wildlife Service

LAGA: Last Great Ape Organization

LATF: Lusaka Agreement Task Force

LRA: Lord's Resistance Army

MEA: multilateral environmental agreement

MIKE: Monitoring the Illegal Killing of Elephants

NBI: Philippines National Bureau of Investigation

NDF: Non-Detriment Finding (under CITES)

NGO: non-governmental organization

PAPECALF: Plan d'Action sous-régional 2012–2017 des pays de l'espace COMIFAC pour le renforcement de l'Application des Législations Nationales sur la Faune sauvage [Sub-regional Action Plan for the strengthening of the implementation of national laws on wildlife] (under COMIFAC)

PIKE: Proportion of Illegally Killed Elephants

SACIM: Southern African Centre for Ivory Marketing

SADC: Southern African Development Community

SAHGCA: South African Hunters and Game Conservation Association

SCAT: smoothed continuous assignment technique

SRT: Sumatran Rhino Trust

SSC: Species Survival Commission (under IUCN)

SSN: Species Survival Network

TRAFFIC: Trade Records Analysis of Flora and Fauna in Commerce

UNEP: United Nations Environmental Programme

UNODC: United Nations Office on Drugs and Crime

USAID: United States Agency for International Development

USFWS-FL: US Fish and Wildlife Service Forensic Laboratory

WCO: World Customs Organization

WWF: World Wildlife Fund / Worldwide Fund for Nature

ZAWA: Zambian Wildlife Authority

Contents

FOREWORD

BY IAIN DOUGLAS-HAMILTON, OBE

As Ron Orenstein's book goes to press the killing of elephants in Africa for ivory has intensified to new heights. Elephants are fewer in number than they were in the previous ivory crisis of the 1970s and 1980s. I have never witnessed such a demand for ivory in the 48 years I have studied them. The prices for ivory to the poacher and, in ever increasing increments, to the final buyers in the Far East exceed all previous records. Demand for ivory is driving the illegal killing and exceeds all possible supply. If demand is not reduced the elephants will be largely eradicated.

Already populations have been exterminated in places like Comoe National Park in the Ivory Coast and in the Affole Mountains of Mauritania, both of which had thriving elephant populations when I started the first Pan-African Elephant Survey in 1975. There has been a horrific roll call of incidents in the last few years. Bouba N'Djida in Northern Cameroon was attacked by horsemen from Sudan allied to the notorious Janjaweed, and half the elephants were killed in a few days. Minkebe National Park in Gabon lost 11,000 elephants, Tsavo, Samburu and Mara are under attack in Kenya, and in East Africa nine out of ten populations are in decline. The Central African Forest Elephants have lost 62 percent of their numbers in one decade. All of this and far more is recorded in papers, reports and scientific publications.

The sheer weight of the destruction is overwhelming, but the statistics give no idea of the individual suffering, wounding and bereavement that accompany them. The rhino situation is even worse, with far higher prices for rhino horn and escalating killing in what formerly were the most secure havens. For these species to survive we need champions to tackle the poaching on the ground, to lower the demand, and like Ron to fight in the high corridors of power, at treaties like CITES, for political will and for united international action to counter these disasters.

Ron is one of those Westerners who care deeply for elephants and rhinos that still live somewhere "out there," far away on other continents. Where Ron is exceptional is that he has made it a lifetime mission to secure their future with the skills he has at his command, an eloquent, tireless and legally ency-clopedic knowledge. Those who ask the question "What can I do to help?" should read his book and learn of the endeavors of so many highly motivated conservationists. The future of these endangered creatures is often decided by policies forged in the remote assemblies of CITES, far from flesh and blood struggles. Though Ron has experienced the dust of the field he is known as a redoubtable warrior, always on the side of the animals, within the halls of the CITES Conferences of the Parties, where the rules are hammered out that de-termine how species may survive the relentless international and often crim-inal trade.

As a bewildered field person arriving at CITES for the first time I first met Ron as a guiding hand on the floor of a debate of CITES CoP 1987, and for many Conferences since. He is an unfailing source of legal advice in the laby-rinthine complexities of this huge living, working treaty that has to cater to so many endangered species and conflicting human responses.

As Ron's book goes to press at this crucial time, it will help people under-stand the history, background and current situation of elephants and rhinos. Ron is helping arouse the world to understand how we can secure a future for these species. Their fate is in human hands. The policies we adopt to save wildlife are generated from our sentiment and our understanding of the facts. We are the ultimate destroyers or guardians of wild creatures' existence. Ron's book tell stories of how we can save them.

Iain Douglas-Hamilton, OBE
Samburu, Kenya
March 2013

INTRODUCTION

For the worst possible reasons, elephants and rhinoceroses are front-page news today. From symbols of their ecosystems and magnificent standard-bearers for conservation they have become poster children for the worst excesses of organized wildlife crime. Horrifying stories of the current poaching crisis and the illegal trade that feeds on it have appeared in the *New York Times* and *National Geographic*, and on the BBC and the Australian Broadcasting Network.

The present crisis is the outcome of some 40 years of history, some of it acted out in nature and some in the debating halls of international politics. This book is an attempt to take you through that history, to explain how we and the animals got into this mess, and to suggest some ways to get out of it.

My own work, and my role in this story, has been away from the field, at international meetings where the rules that may decide the fate of both rhinos and elephants are fought over, seemingly endlessly. The inspiration for my work, though, has come from moments in the elephants' and rhinos' world. I have wandered close to wild African Savanna Elephants, who warned me away with outstretched ears and lowered trunks. I have ridden on the back of an Asian Elephant into the *terai* grasslands of Nepal's Chitwan National Park, where I came face to face with a Greater One-horned Rhinoceros. I have floated close to Pygmy Elephants in a longboat on Borneo's Kinabatangan River, and I have shared a cup of tea with the remarkable Dame Daphne Sheldrick on her front porch as her orphaned baby elephants gamboled on the lawn below me. I have walked almost up to placid Southern White Rhinoceroses in South

Africa, and been chased by a Black Rhinoceros (fortunately I was in a vehicle at the time).

One of the problems in writing a book of this kind from a desk in Canada, far from the scene of much of the action, is that accurate information about illegal activities in remote and, often, dangerous places can be hard to find. In many cases it may not exist. Sometimes the people who know are too frightened to speak out. In March 2012, the IUCN African Elephant Specialist Group (AfESG) sent out a questionnaire on poaching levels and dynamics to elephant researchers and managers across Africa, but more than half of the respondents asked not to be named or quoted.

Peer-reviewed studies in recognized scientific journals probably provide the best source of accurate, unbiased data. Unfortunately, they take time to write, review and publish. Information from the scientific literature is rarely available for the most recent events.

Stories in the news media contain mistakes or exaggerations, contradict each other in reporting the same event, and may miss crucial points. Government reports may be self-serving, particularly if issues such as incompetence, mismanagement or corruption are involved. International bodies such as the Convention on International Trade in Endangered Species of Wild Fauna and Flora (CITES) are dependent on governments for their information, and their own reports may suffer in consequence.

Non-governmental organizations (NGOs) are often in a better position to get the real story. They may have considerable expertise at their disposal. Some send in their own investigative teams, often undercover, to talk directly to the actors and stakeholders on the ground. However, NGOs, most of which are activist organizations with strong views on what have become some of the most polarizing issues in the field of wildlife conservation, may have (or be accused of having) their own biases. These are often directly opposed to the biases of governments, which, in their turn, often vehemently deny the allegations NGO reports contain. China, for example, has suggested that NGO investigators may be mistaking carved pieces of mammoth ivory or resin (colophony) for elephant ivory.

In one recent case, a group of researchers studying ivory markets in Vietnam had to write a rebuttal to a press release announcing their own report. In their view, the release misrepresented their data by emphasizing high prices for a few items, leading other organizations to seize on these figures and claim trade values for ivory in Asia that were considerably higher than the analysis in fact showed. This sort of thing not only exaggerates a crisis but risks luring unscrupulous persons into the trade with the hope of even bigger profits than are, in fact, available. This is one of the reasons why I have been reluctant to quote more than a few estimates of market price for ivory or rhinoceros horn in this book, dramatic though those estimates may be.

Fortunately, I have received invaluable help and advice. I am grateful to Edward Alpers, Pat Awori, Jason Bell-Leask, Rene Beyers, Paul Bour, Thea Carroll, Erika Ceballos, Bryan Christy, Rhishja Cota-Larson, the Earl of Cranbrook, Naomi Doak, Iain Douglas-Hamilton, Ofir Drori, Susie Ellis, Richard Emslie, Gemma Francis, Grace Ge Gabriel, Jeffrey Gettleman, Kathleen Gobush, Terese Hart, Mark Jones, Winnie Kiiru, Mike Knight, Pete Knights, Chrysee Martin, Esmond Martin, Luc Mathot, Ryan McAllister, Vivek Menon, Tom Milliken, Judy Mills, Edna Molewa, Colman O Criodain, Patrick Omondi, Julian Rademeyer, Ian Redmond, Mary Rice, Alfred Roca, Amelia Reiver Schussler, Chris Shepherd, Céline Sissler-Bienvenu, Belinda Stewart-Cox, Brent Stirton, Alice Stroud, Bibhab Kumar Talukdar, Allan Thornton, Will Travers, Michael 't Sas-Rolfes, Mark Simmonds, Lucy Vigne, Sam Wasser, Shelley Waterland, Alexia Wellbelove, Edwin Wiek, Sean Willmore, Chris Wold, Meng Xianlin and Li Zhang. Special thanks to my long-time colleague Susie Watts, who dealt patiently with my frequent Skype requests for rhino information. The electronic clipping services african-elephant and asian-elephant, kept up to date by Melissa Groo of Save the Elephants, have been invaluable sources of news stories from around the world. Others arrive on my computer through the private mailing list of the Species Survival Network (SSN). I am grateful to Ann Michels and my other SSN colleagues for seeing that they get there, and to Humane Society International, an SSN member, for sending me to CITES meetings around the world.

Thanks, too, to Lionel Koffler, Elizabeth McCurdy, Nicole North and Michael Mouland of Firefly Books for their patient encouragement.

A special thank-you to my good friend Iain Douglas-Hamilton for his Foreword, for his valuable advice, and for the stellar work he has done and continues to do on behalf of Africa's elephants. Iain's decades in the field, and his unique combination of authority and personal charm, have made him the leading figure in elephant conservation. I am honored to have his words in this book. Besides, Iain's wife, Oria, who co-founded Save the Elephants with him, is a cousin of the creator of Babar. You can't have better credentials than that. I hope he will consider his Foreword a return for making me lug a suitcase of enormous elephant radio collars from Toronto to Nairobi many years ago, and for dragging me into the former African Elephant enclosure at the Toronto Zoo, where the matriarch of the group kept trying to squash me against the enclosure wall.

Of course my greatest thanks must go to my family, including (first and foremost) my wife, Eileen Yen Ee Li, who shared her long experience of how Asian governments work. My stepson Davin Marcus Raja taught me how to set up two computer monitors at a time (invaluable for dealing with online references), and my brother-in-law Clyde Benson supplemented my meager knowledge of high-powered weaponry.

This is, of necessity, a short book, but one that covers a lot of ground. As it is primarily about the ivory and horn trade, I have said very little about such vital concerns as the establishment and management of protected areas, the transport and sale of live animals, and the crucial issue of human–elephant conflict. I urge those looking for more detail to pursue the references, most of which are readily available on the Internet.

The issues of trade in ivory and rhinoceros horn have evoked intense and often emotional debate. I have been one of the debaters, and I make no apologies for leaning towards my own point of view. Though I owe a special debt to my SSN friends and colleagues and I have been proud to serve on the SSN Board since its formation, I am writing this book in my own capacity. The viewpoints it contains, as well as any errors, are mine.

Portions of this book dealing with the 1989 ivory ban and its aftermath have been adapted, in part, from text I wrote for *Elephants: The Deciding Decade* (Key Porter, 2nd ed., 1996) and *Elephants: Majestic Creatures of the Wild* (Weldon Owen, 2nd ed., 2000).

PART ONE

WHAT HAPPENED?

CHAPTER ONE

THE LIVING ELEPHANTS

Elephants and rhinoceroses are morphologically unique and ecologically crucial. Included among their number are the largest living land animals. They once dominated much of the planet. They are symbols of human culture, and beacons for the wilderness. They are also, alas, the targets of our greed and credulity. Today, elephant ivory and rhinoceros horn have become currencies of war.

Rhinos and elephants share more than humanity's fatal attraction for their horns and tusks. As giant plant-eaters — *megaherbivores* — they play, or once played, vital roles in their ecosystems. Few other large animals have as great an effect on the shape of their environment and the variety of plants and animals that live there. The traces of their passage, and of the passage of their fossil relatives around the world, can become permanent fixtures of the landscape.

Probably only human beings and beavers have the elephants' capacity to alter their surroundings. Elephants in search of minerals are thought to have excavated, or at least greatly enlarged, entire cave systems on Mount Elgon in western Kenya. Elephants in the African savannas clear brush, knock over trees and trample paths to waterholes, creating a patchwork of habitats that can support more species of animals and plants than either a grassland or a closed-in woodland. Rainforest elephants, by feeding on fallen fruits and depositing their seeds in piles of nutrient-rich dung, are important regenerators of growth and dispersers of forest trees. Ecologists have dubbed elephants *keystone* or even *super-keystone species*, as central to the functioning of their ecosystems as a keystone is to the structure of an arch.

Elephants are the last survivors of the once vast order Proboscidea, a group that included mastodons, mammoths and the peculiar deinotheres. They are members of a broader group of mammals whose other living representatives include such unlikely creatures as seacows and hyraxes, the elephants' closest cousins, and such oddities as aardvarks, sengis (elephant shrews) and golden moles. There are two or, more likely, three living species, but humans certainly encountered others in the past. Cave paintings, carved artifacts and other evidence testify to our species' familiarity with the Woolly Mammoth (*Mammuthus primigenius*). The last mammoths, isolated on remote Wrangel Island off the Arctic coast of Siberia, survived until around 1650 BCE, more than 5,000 years after their continental cousins disappeared. In 2012, a team of Chinese scientists proposed that another extinct elephant had survived into historic times. Up until about 3,000 years ago there were elephants living in northern China. It was always assumed that these were the living Asian Elephant (*Elephas maximus*), but their few surviving teeth seemed to show features more typical of African elephants. Bronze figures from the period clearly show animals with two finger-like extensions at the tip of the trunk, as in living African elephants, rather than one as in the Asian Elephant. Ji Li and his colleagues now suggest that the North Chinese animals were not Asian Elephants but the last survivors of a straight-tusked elephant (*Palaeoloxodon*) that was thought to have vanished some 7,000 years earlier. Not everyone agrees, and it is possible that the crucial teeth may prove to be Asian Elephant molars after all.

DNA studies support the long-held assertion, put forward among others by my late friend and collaborator and dedicated elephant expert Jeheskel (Hezy) Shoshani, that there are two species of African elephant: the widespread and well-known African Savanna Elephant (*Loxodonta africana*) and the smaller, rounder-eared African Forest Elephant (*Loxodonta cyclotis*) of the rainforests of West and Central Africa. IUCN's African Elephant Specialist Group is still reluctant to accept the division, on the grounds that it is not yet possible to draw a clear line between the ranges of the two populations, and there is some limited hybridization. It nonetheless appears that broad recognition that there are two species of elephant in Africa is only a matter of time. A suggestion that West African Forest Elephants should be recognized as yet a third species has not been supported by the genetic data.

Recently, Nadin Rohland and her colleagues found evidence that Savanna and Forest Elephants may have been separated for longer than anyone suspected.

We now have the rather astonishing ability to compare DNA not just from the living elephants but also from two long-extinct species: the Woolly Mammoth and the American Mastodon (*Mammut americanum*), a much more distant relative that can serve as a standard for comparison (in technical terms, an *outgroup*). Rohland's study compared DNA from the cell nuclei of all five species.

The results confirmed that Asian Elephants and Woolly Mammoths are indeed close relatives, closer than either is to the African elephants. They probably diverged from each other, evolutionarily speaking, anywhere from two to five and a half million years ago. The surprise was that the Savanna and Forest Elephants appear to have been separated from each other for just as long — almost as long as human beings have been separate from chimpanzees. As Michael Hofreiter, one of the co-authors of the study, put it, "This result amazed us all."

Elephant society may have existed in something like its present form for millions of years. A six- to eight-million-year-old Miocene trackway in the United Arab Emirates, possibly made by a four-tusked fossil elephant relative called *Stegotetrabelodon syrticus*, appears to show the passage of a family group much like those of its modern cousins.

Most of what we know about living elephants in the wild comes from the African Savanna Elephant. Pioneering, decades-long life history studies by Cynthia Moss and Joyce Poole, population analyses and radio-tracking programs by Iain Douglas-Hamilton and revelations about elephant communication by Katy Payne have been built upon by their students and successors. These include George Wittemyer, who has analyzed Savanna Elephant social structure in depth, and Caitlin O'Connell, who has studied elephant communication in the arid lands of Namibia. Their research has painted an indelible picture of a species with startling similarities to our own.

Newborn elephants spend years under the care and tutelage of an extended family of sisters, cousins and aunts before taking their place in a complex social hierarchy that binds mothers and their infants into family groups, family groups into herds, and herds into clans. They keep in touch via long-distance communication: infrasonic vocalizations, too low for us to hear, that travel through the ground and under ideal conditions can be picked up by other elephants over six miles (10 km) away. Individuals can recognize each other's vibrations from well over half a mile (1 km) away, and may be able to do so over two and a half times that distance. Males leave their social units at maturity but may band together outside of their periods of reproductive excitement, or *musth*. Family groups are guided by matriarchs, elders whose ability to make leadership decisions — how to react to the presence of lions, for example — improves with age and experience.

Perhaps most perplexing, and disturbing in the light of their fate at our hands, is the behavior elephants show towards their dead. African Savanna Elephants often show a great interest in the bodies, and even the bones, of dead members of their own species, stepping on them, holding bones or tusks in their mouths, and sometimes carrying them for a considerable distance. They do this, apparently, regardless of whether the carcasses are of members of their own family, though they may defend one of their own dead calves for days. Forest Elephants may do the same, but we have much less evidence to go on.

Savanna Elephants in Amboseli National Park, Kenya, presented experimentally with the bones and ivory of their own and other species, displayed significantly more interest in the elephant remains. They reacted particularly strongly to ivory, perhaps because the act of feeling each other's tusks is a part of normal elephant social interaction. The experimenters, Karen McComb, Lucy Baker and Cynthia Moss, were cautious in their interpretation, noting only that "while the behaviors described here obviously differ fundamentally from the attention and ritual that surround death in humans, they are unusual and noteworthy." Iain Douglas-Hamilton and his co-authors, in describing the reaction of elephants in Samburu, Kenya, towards a dying matriarch, were less circumspect: their subjects' interest was "an example of how elephants and humans may share emotions, such as compassion, and have an awareness and interest about death."

Forest Elephants stay, by and large, hidden in their rainforest realms. What little we know about them suggests that they live in smaller groups and cover less territory than Savanna Elephants. Most of our knowledge comes from studies by Andrea Turkalo and Mike Fay of groups that gather at relatively open clearings, called *bais*, in the Central African Republic. The bais, where the elephants gather to consume mineral salts, are of critical importance, but the elephants resort to them largely by night, perhaps to avoid exposing themselves to poachers by day. Those who would follow their paths through the forest usually depend on such indirect indicators of their presence as the arrangement and density of their piles of dung.

Forest Elephant tusks are narrower and less bulky than those of the Savanna Elephant, but their ivory has long been prized for its hardness and faint pinkish tone. Perhaps as a result of these features, though equally as a consequence of its unfortunate distribution through some of the most lawless and war-torn areas of Africa, the Forest Elephant has been hard hit by today's poaching crisis. In 2012, the Wildlife Conservation Society published survey results showing that Forest Elephant populations over a 10,400-square-mile (27,000 sq km) area of the Republic of Congo had fallen by more than half, from 13,000 animals to 6,300, in the five years from 2007 to 2011.

A massive overview of Forest Elephant populations published in 2013, drawing on 80 surveys covering over 8,000 miles (13,000 km) and involving 91,600 days of fieldwork, revealed "a widespread and catastrophic decline," with numbers falling by 62 percent between 2002 and 2011. Over much of their range, Forest Elephants may have been totally exterminated. In the Democratic Republic of Congo, once a Forest Elephant stronghold, 95 percent of the forests are almost empty of elephants. Today Gabon may be the only country with substantial numbers, and even there only 14 percent of the forests retain high-density populations.

The Asian Elephant's relationship with humans has been far more ambivalent. It is the living evocation of the Hindu god Ganesha, who has borne the head of an elephant ever since Lord Shiva, in a fit of rage, struck off the original. The Asian Elephant has been a part of Asian society, as a work animal, a war mount and an object of ritual, for at least 3,000–4,000 years, and perhaps, based on rock paintings in India dating to 6000 BCE, for far longer. When Siamese delegates returning in 1858 from a royal audience in London compared Queen Victoria, "in her eyes, complexion, and above all her bearing," to a "beautiful and majestic white elephant," they meant it as the highest of compliments.

What the Asian Elephant never became, in all those centuries, is truly domesticated. Working Asian Elephants have almost never been bred in captivity. Aside from the sheer difficulty involved, raising an elephant for the ten years or more it needs to mature into an animal capable of work is not economically feasible. Instead, generations of elephant handlers have captured young elephants in the wild and trained them to live with and work for human beings.

It is a myth, by the way, that African Elephants cannot be tamed. At least some of the animals that crossed the Alps in the service of Hannibal were African Savanna Elephants from the vanished population of North Africa. Until very recently an Elephant Domestication Centre, the brainchild of King Leopold II of Belgium, operated near Garamba National Park in the Democratic Republic of Congo. Its few remaining inhabitants offered visitors rides into the forest when the eastern DRC was still more or less on the tourist route.

Asian Elephants are very different creatures from their African cousins. They have smaller ears, rounded instead of swayed backs, a single "finger" at the tip of the trunk, a high bony boss on the top of the skull, and a number of anatomical distinctions including number of toes and the structure of their teeth. Usually only the males have tusks, a fact that may have contributed to making African, rather than Asian, Elephants the chief targets of ivory poachers even when the markets are in Asia. The social lives of Asian Elephants center on family groups of females and young, though these are smaller than in the African species. Although family groups do join together in larger units, they do not appear to organize themselves into the clear-cut, tightly interlinked hierarchical structures of Savanna Elephant society.

Given the attention surrounding the two African elephants, it may be a surprise to learn that the Asian Elephant is a far rarer animal. Its total population, about 43,000–44,000 animals, is less than one-tenth of that of the two African species combined. A further 25,000 or so are in captivity, most of them work animals in Asia. Asian Elephants are divided into either three or four subspecies: the Sri Lankan, Sumatran and Mainland Elephants (*E. m. maximus*, *E. m. sumatranus* and *E. m. indicus* respectively), and the smallest, rarest and almost certainly valid fourth subspecies, the Bornean Pygmy Elephant (*E. m. borneensis*). Borneo's elephants comprise some 2,000 highly inbred animals, almost entirely confined to the East Malaysian state of Sabah, where they are increasingly hemmed in by forest destruction and the expansion of oil palm plantations. In January 2013, 14 Pygmy Elephants were found dead in the Gunung Rara Forest Reserve in Sabah, the victims of possibly deliberate poisoning.

The Bornean Pygmy Elephant is something of a mystery. There is no tradition of elephants as wild animals in Borneo. Because its population is localized and relatively tiny, and no subfossil remains are known from anywhere on the island, it was long thought that it must be the descendant of escaped animals from the Asian mainland. Genetic studies established, however, that Bornean and mainland elephants have been separated for a very long time, perhaps as long as 300,000 years.

The Earl of Cranbrook and his colleagues proposed an interesting solution by following up documentary sources that some elephants had long ago been a diplomatic gift from the Sultan of Java to the Sultan of Sulu, and the local tradition that some of the naturalized Sulu stock were later released in northeastern Borneo. Elephants have been extinct on Java for some 800 years. Bornean Pygmy Elephants may, in fact, be the last survivors of the otherwise extinct Javan Elephant, saved to preserve friendly relations between two powerful sultans.

CHAPTER TWO

THE LIVING RHINOCEROSES

Though naturalists once grouped them together as "pachyderms" — animals with thick skin — rhinoceroses and elephants are not particularly close relatives. Rhinoceroses are *perissodactyls*, odd-toed hoofed animals, and their closest relatives are horses and tapirs. Rhinoceroses are adaptable creatures. Rhino species are able to thrive on herbivorous diets consisting of everything from soft aquatic plants to coarse browse and the toughest grasses. For millions of years, they were an evolutionary success story — until we came along.

Like elephants, rhinoceroses once roamed in numbers over much of the world, in a far greater variety of shapes, sizes and lifestyles than we see today. Some fossil rhinoceroses were small, delicate and quite horse-like. Some apparently lived in the manner of, and rather resembled, hippos. The largest of them all, *Paraceratherium* (also known as *Indricotherium* and, formerly, as *Baluchitherium*), from the Oligocene of central and eastern Asia, was a towering, hornless behemoth vaguely resembling an obese giraffe. Measuring over 16 feet (5 m) at the shoulder, it was the largest land mammal that ever lived. Even today, the largest rhinos are second only to elephants on land: a White Rhinoceros (*Ceratotherium simum*) can reach almost 6,000 pounds (2,700 kg), and the Greater One-horned Rhinoceros (*Rhinoceros unicornis*) can reach over two tonnes.

At the end of the Miocene, some five million years ago, a period of global climate change probably killed off most rhino lineages, including almost all of the rhinoceroses of North America. Only two lineages survived. Early humans in Europe encountered a descendant of one of them, the Woolly Rhinoceros (*Coelodonta antiquitatis*), and painted its image on cave walls. Another extinct rhinoceros, *Elasmotherium* — an enormous creature thought to have carried a huge single horn on its forehead — may have survived long enough on the steppes of central Asia to give rise to tales of legendary unicorn-like beasts, including the Chinese *ki'lin*.

Rhinoceroses were long believed to be mostly solitary, asocial creatures, though the White Rhino, like elephants, may associate with others of its own kind and has been shown to communicate with ultrasonic vibrations. Black Rhinos may gather in social groups, particularly at night. Footage of their interactions was screened for the first time by the BBC in 2013. Though they are more social than we once thought, rhinos lack the complex social structures that dominate elephant life. Though rhinos can be noisy creatures, scent, including the smell of their urine and feces, may be more important in rhinoceros communication than sound.

Though they lack the elephants' toolkit of trunk and tusks, rhinoceroses affect their environment through sheer size. The White Rhinoceros uses its wide mouth and thickened lips to crop grasses with lawnmower-like efficiency. Rhino "grazing lawns" are favored feeding grounds for other, smaller herbivores, not only for their nutrient value but because they provide excellent views of any would-be predators. Greater One-horned Rhinoceroses perform the same function in riverside grasslands in Asia. Like elephants, rhinoceroses contribute to the spread of a number of plants, devouring their fallen fruits and dispersing their seeds elsewhere. Rhino "middens" may form natural nurseries for defecated seeds.

Five species of rhinoceros — the name, in Greek, means "nose horn" — survive today. They live in habitats ranging from the rainforests of Borneo to the deserts of Namibia. Two live in Africa: the White, or Square-lipped, Rhinoceros and the Black Rhinoceros (*Diceros bicornis*). Both carry two large horns, their chief weapons of offense and defense. Black Rhinos sometimes use their horns like giant spaghetti forks, to twist, break off and bring down browse within reach for themselves and their young. The anterior horn is the larger, usually stout and thick in the White and drawn out into a narrow spike in the Black. In some Black Rhinoceroses this horn can be 4.3 feet (1.3 m) long. The three Asian rhinoceroses have horns too, but they are much smaller and are, surprisingly, not the animals' main weapons. Instead, brawling Asian rhinos rely on two large, sharp tusks in the lower jaw, absent altogether in the two African species.

The White Rhinoceros is not really white, any more than the Black Rhinoceros is black. Both are gray. Their habit of wallowing in mud — a favorite activity that may shield their skins from the heat of the sun, protect them against biting insects and other external parasites, and, perhaps, even help them communicate scent signals to other rhinos — can give them a range of apparent colors that has more to do with the local soil than with their actual hues. It is, apparently, not true that the White Rhino owes its name to a misunderstanding of the Dutch word *wijd*, "wide," referring to its broad, squared-off upper lip — the mark of a grazing animal, quite unlike the pointed, prehensile lip of the Black Rhino, a browser.

An animal of savanna, woodlands, desert and scrub, the Black Rhino's choice of browse includes plants with sap that is toxic or irritating to other animals. The widespread Tamboti (*Spirostachys africana*) and the Damara Milk Bush (*Euphorbia damarana*) of Namibia, both dangerously toxic to humans, are rhino favorites. Black Rhinos have long had a reputation as surly, ill-tempered beasts, though this may be a function of their inquisitiveness and their poor eyesight. (I have been charged by one. It was an unnerving experience.)

Zoologists traditionally recognize four subspecies of Black Rhinoceros. One, the Western Black Rhinoceros (*D. b. longipes*), has recently been poached into extinction (see p. 120). Though Black Rhinos once numbered in the tens or even hundreds of thousands, according to the latest population figures there are only 5,055 left — and even that, as we shall see, is more than twice the number that remained in the mid-1990s. There are two subspecies of White Rhinoceros, the Southern (*Ceratotherium simum simum*) and the Northern (*Ceratotherium simum cottoni*), first made known to science in 1903. Today, thanks to decades of intense conservation efforts, mostly in South Africa, Southern Whites have increased to a degree that they now account for the overwhelming majority of rhinoceroses in the world — 20,405 animals at last count. The northern subspecies has gone in the other direction. Today its last confirmed wild population is apparently extinct, and the handful in captivity will almost certainly be the last of their kind (see p. 121).

The Sumatran Rhinoceros (*Dicerorhinus sumatranus*) appears to have changed little from ancestors that lived forty million years ago. It is the closest living relative of the extinct Woolly Rhinoceros. The smallest, at about

1,320–1,540 pounds (600–700 kg), and hairiest of the living species, it is the only Asian rhino with two horns. A shy, elusive and increasingly rare denizen of hill forests, it reveals its presence to researchers only through occasional sightings of muddy tracks on forest trails, or as images on remote camera traps. Though they once ranged widely over Southeast Asia, Sumatran Rhinos probably survive today only in eastern Borneo (*D. s. harrissoni*) and in three national parks in Sumatra (*D. s. sumatranus*). Unfortunately, one of the most concerted efforts to save the Sumatran Rhino ended up, in Eric Dinerstein's words, as a "conservation debacle." The Sumatran Rhino Trust (SRT) was formed in the 1980s to breed the species in captivity, originally in zoos in the United States but, after a number of protests, in a separate breeding program in Malaysia. Alan Rabinowitz described the result in a scathing analysis:

> In 1993, the SRT was dissolved after five years and a cost of more than $2.5 million. Virtually none of the money went to improving the protection and management of wild rhinos in existing protected areas. This program, along with the similar efforts in Sabah and Peninsular Malaysia to catch doomed rhinos for breeding, were expensive failures resulting in the capture of 35 rhinos and the deaths of 12 rhinos between 1984 and 1993 … As of 1993, the surviving 23 rhinos (14 females, nine males) were being held in 10 separate areas in Indonesia, Peninsular Malaysia, Sabah, the United Kingdom, and the United States … Because adult males and females were never together in the same place for a significant amount of time, there have been no births from captive Sumatran rhinos to date, except for one female who was pregnant when captured.

Since then, we have learned a good deal about how to keep, and breed, Sumatran Rhinos in captivity. Three calves have been born at the Cincinnati Zoo in Ohio. One has now been returned to Sumatra, where he has sired a calf of his own in a reserve funded by essentially the same organizations that made up the SRT. Most of the rhinos involved, though, may have bred more successfully if they had been left in the wild with properly managed reserves to protect them. The wild population is now so diminished that some sort of semi-captive management must be considered as a possible option (see p. 123), though a better approach may be to establish a wild population in a controlled area where the rhinos can behave naturally and there may be less risk of disease. The Sumatran Rhino remains one of the most endangered large mammals on earth.

Rarest of the rhinos is the Javan or Lesser One-horned Rhinoceros (*Rhinoceros sondaicus*), now reduced to a tiny population in Ujung Kulon National Park, at the western end of Java, in Indonesia, where they are very difficult to observe. What little we know of their behavior comes, mostly, from footage recovered from video traps. The most recent video trap data puts their numbers at, minimally, 22 males, 13 females and five juveniles: 35 in all, though there may be as many as a dozen more, as the traps were not placed throughout the park. Even this is a slight increase from the 25 estimated to be present in 1967. Like the Sumatran, the Javan was once far more wide-ranging — more so, in fact, than any other Asian rhinoceros. It ranged from Assam east to Vietnam, and southward through Indochina, Myanmar, Thailand and the Malay Peninsula to Sumatra, Borneo and, of course, Java. The last of the continental animals, the final survivor of a remnant population recently discovered in Vietnam, was killed by poachers as recently as 2010 (see p. 119). There were plans to move some of Ujung Kulon the rhinos to Way Kambas National Park on Sumatra, where they once lived, but the surviving numbers are so low that the journey was judged too risky. More recently the International Rhino Foundation, in association with Yayasan Badak Indonesia and the Indonesian Ministry of Forestry, has been exploring the idea of transferring some animals to a much nearer reserve, in the Honje Mountains of West Java. This would involve not moving the animals but restoring rhino habitat in the area between the Honje Mountains and Ujung Kulon in the hope that rhinos will cross to their new homes on their own. Javan Rhinos might still be translocated to Sumatra in the future.

The Javan Rhinos in Ujung Kulon may have benefited from one of the greatest natural disasters in recorded history, the explosion of the nearby island of Krakatau in 1883. The animals not only survived the ensuing tsunami but increased in numbers as the primary forest destroyed by the waves gave way to successional-stage trees that provided them with better browse. The Ujung Kulon wilderness might not even exist today if the eruption had not devastated human settlements in the region, effectively emptying a corner of one of the most densely populated islands in the world.

The third Asian rhino is the "unicorn" of the ancients: the Greater One-horned, or Indian, Rhinoceros of northeastern India and Nepal. It is the only one that is holding its own in any numbers, though it is still one of the rarest mammals on the Indian subcontinent. Surveys as of June 2012 revealed an overall population of 3,264 (2,730+ in India and 534+ in Nepal), up from 2,800 in January 2007. The Greater One-horned Rhino lives in the *terai*, alluvial floodplains at the base of the Himalayas where the grasses reach eye level by the end of the rainy season, even for a tourist riding on elephant-back. Its most important strongholds are Royal Chitwan National Park in Nepal and Kaziranga National Park in Assam, India. Thanks to effective conservation measures in its two home countries, its numbers continue to rise, though there was an upsurge of poaching in 2013 that has seen 12 rhinos killed in Assam in the first two months of the year alone, 10 in and around Kaziranga (one rhino was killed in Manas National Park, and another when it wandered out of Orang National Park). By contrast, only 21 Assamese rhinos were poached in the whole of 2012.

The Greater One-horned is the most "armored" of the rhinoceroses, its skin thrown into great folds and embossed with rivet-like carbuncles (the Javan has them too, but not so strikingly, and it lacks the great dewlap dangling from the throat of its larger cousin). Greater One-horned Rhinos are both grazers and browsers, shifting their preference (and their habitat) from grassland to forest with the seasons. They are particularly fond of a species of wild sugar cane (*Saccharum spontaneum*). Like Black Rhinos, they use their prehensile upper lip to strip tender leaves from the cane stems.

The Greater One-horned, by the way, is the rhinoceros in Albrecht Dürer's famous woodcut of 1515. Dürer never saw the animal (his rather fanciful depiction is based on a written description and a sketch). It was the first rhino to reach Europe in over a thousand years. The animal was a gift from the Sultan of Gujarat, Muzafar II, to Alfonso d'Albuquerque, governor of Portuguese India. The governor passed it on to Dom Alfonso I, King of Portugal, who intended to present it to Pope Leo X (after an unsuccessful attempt to involve it in a fight with an elephant, which wisely fled the scene of combat). Unfortunately, the ship carrying the rhinoceros to Rome was wrecked off the Italian coast, and the poor beast, shackled to the deck, was drowned.

CHAPTER THREE

IVORY AND LUXURY

I vory has been adorning humans and causing elephants to be destroyed for thousands of years. It is beautiful, durable and relatively easy to shape into anything from tiny beads to intricately carved whole tusks. We have long treasured ivory for far more than simple beauty. At various times and in various cultures, it has been a symbol of power and wisdom, its possession marking its owner as a person of wealth and status. For some African peoples, ivory is a symbol of chiefly authority. For centuries, though, the chief markets for ivory have lain outside that continent.

Ancient Egyptian demand for ivory may have contributed to the disappearance of elephants from the eastern Sahara by about 2750 BCE and from the central Sahara by 2000 BCE. Trade from north and east Africa and, as African supplies grew harder to come by, India, supplied a vast and lavish taste for ivory in the Roman Empire. In the *Saturnalia* of Lucian of Samosata (c. 120–180 CE), a priest prays for "the usual thing, please — wealth, plenty of gold, landed proprietorship, a train of slaves, gay soft raiment, silver, ivory, in fact everything that is worth anything." The emperor Gaius, better known as Caligula, reputedly built an ivory stable for his favorite horse, Incitatus. Some sources say it was a marble stable with an ivory manger, and others say it was just decorated with ivory. Perhaps none of it is true. In any case, Nero's tutor Seneca is said to have owned five hundred tripod tables with ivory legs. By the 7th century CE, the elephants of North Africa had been driven to extinction.

Western demand for African ivory declined following the fall of the Roman Empire, but by the 10th century major markets had emerged in India and China. Asia was running out of its own elephants, and their ivory could not be supplied fast enough to satisfy the demand. By the mid-17th century, the Portuguese had been trading in ivory out of the Congo for over a century. The Dutch and English competed for the ivory trade in West Africa, depleting the herds along the Guinea coast. Though the trade declined by the 1780s, rising demand in Europe drove the price upwards tenfold over the next century and a half. New hunting grounds were exploited in the interior of the continent, and a complex trade network transported tonnes of ivory to the coast every year. In some areas being an ivory porter became a prestigious occupation.

By the latter part of the 19th century, if not earlier, the trade in Central Africa was intricately interwoven with the trade in slaves, to the horror of European explorers like David Livingstone. Ivory had become a mass-market item, used for everything from delicate sculptures and fine jewelry to piano keys and billiard balls. The smooth touch of ivory to the fingers of a pianist or the familiar click as billiard balls collided could be reproduced by no other substance. As historian Edward Alpers put it, "For all intents and purposes, ivory became the plastic of the era."

For much of the 20th century, the largest ivory market in the world was in Japan. Japanese have signed their names for centuries with personalized signature seals, or *hankos*, traditionally made of wood with a plate of metal at the tip. Well-made hankos are prized possessions, and seals made of precious materials are particularly valuable. As Japanese society became more affluent in the 1960s and 1970s, the most prized material for signature seals was ivory. At first, ivory was used only as a printing plate, but later only a hanko made from pure ivory — long a status symbol for the elite — would be acceptable. At least half of the ivory entering international trade during the poaching crisis of the 1970s and 1980s went to make signature seals for the Japanese market.

Before 1920, when large-scale imports of African ivory first became available in Japan, Japanese carvers made hankos from the ivory of Asian Elephants. Asian Elephant ivory, known as *togata* in Japan, is still regarded as the finest for carving, combining the best qualities of the two African species. *Hard ivory* from the African Forest Elephant is next in preference, followed by the *soft ivory* of the Savanna Elephant. A hanko carved from ivory from the heart of a tusk is held to be of higher quality, and one containing the core of a tusk is considered particularly auspicious (and is correspondingly expensive).

Ivory hankos are still in demand, but Japan's place as the world's leading customer for ivory, both legal and illegal, has been taken by China. China's surging affluence has allowed indulgence in a seemingly bottomless market for wildlife products, from medicinal plants to turtles and tiger bones. Africa, where China has invested massive amounts of money and deployed hundreds of thousands of workers, has become a major source for ivory in particular. Though other Asian countries, especially Thailand, have been implicated as major markets for smuggled ivory, it is the enormous demand for ivory among China's newly wealthy, as both a luxury item and an investment vehicle, that is destroying the world's elephants today.

A survey by the International Fund for Animal Welfare (IFAW) found that 70 percent of Chinese (based on a survey of 1,253 people in six cities) believe that ivory — *xiang ya*, "elephant's teeth" in Mandarin — comes from tusks that simply fall out of an elephant's mouth and then grow back. Sellers encourage this idea. *Vanity Fair* journalist Alex Shoumatoff asked a dealer in Guangzhou, a center of the ivory market, if they had to kill the elephant to get the carved tusk he was being offered. "No," the dealer told him. "After you get the ivory, teeth grow again, just like human teeth."

It just ain't so. There is almost no practical way to gather ivory from wild elephants and leave the animals alive. Tusks are, of course, teeth (elephant ivory is highly compressed dentine; mature tusks have no enamel). Like adult human teeth, once they're gone, they're gone. Furthermore, you can't just lop off the tusk and let the animal go. The root of an elephant's tusk penetrates some two-thirds of its length, so cutting off any more than the tip could expose the animal to serious infection. Elephants with naturally broken tusks and exposed nerves can be maddened by the pain. I have seen footage from Zimbabwe of a bull with a broken tusk that relieved its apparent agony by savagely attacking anything that came near.

Removing an entire tusk — sometimes necessary in captive animals with dental problems — is a complicated and difficult operation. The root of the tusk penetrates deep into the skull. Extracting it normally requires a power winch, takes several hours, and leaves a gaping hole in the animal's face that may require months of post-operative veterinary care.

The only way to remove ivory safely and easily from a living elephant is to cut off the tip of the tusk, ahead of the point where the root cavity ends. This has long been a way to get extra value from domestic elephants in Nepal, Myanmar, Thailand and Cambodia. Thailand exported tusk tips to China, where they were made into ivory scent holders, as long ago as the 13th century. In Myanmar and Thailand, which have large populations of domestic elephants, pruned tusk tips from domesticated male elephants are an increasingly valuable source of ivory.

Tips, which are solid, are often worth more than ivory from the hollow portion of the tusk. The price of tusk tips in Thailand rose from less than $100 per kilogram to $350–$1,200 per kilogram between 2001 and early 2008. One 200-gram polished tusk tip from an Asian Elephant, offered for retail sale at an antique shop in Vietnam in 2008, carried a price tag amounting to $1,863 per kilogram — high even for a tip, and far higher than the going price for raw ivory at the time (an average of seven prices for small ivory in Vietnam, without the tips, was $791 per kilogram). In Myanmar, the legal sale of tusk tips has been identified as a serious loophole in that country's wildlife legislation.

Tip pruning hardly seems practicable for wild elephants. They would have to be immobilized during the process, and poachers, who want every bit of ivory they can get for their efforts, are highly unlikely to be satisfied with tips alone. This does not mean that harvesting ivory without killing wild elephants is impossible. Rowan Martin, one of the most vocal opponents of the international ivory ban and a strong believer in legalizing the trade, proposed years ago that if an elephant population is large enough a substantial amount of ivory can be gathered from the carcasses of animals that have died naturally. Tusks grow throughout life, and older elephants lay down more dentine per year, so natural-mortality ivory could yield the largest, and most valuable, tusks available. In 2012 Martin and his colleagues, in a study commissioned by the CITES Secretariat, proposed again that natural-mortality ivory could provide the basis for a legal and sustainable ivory trade, but in an Africa overwhelmed by poachers Martin's proposal may be, at best, naive (see p. 171).

Tusk tips from domesticated animals aside, then, elephant ivory comes from dead elephants. With the limited exceptions of some of the stockpiled ivory sold as part of "one-off" sales to Japan and China and tourist souvenirs carved in Zimbabwe and Namibia (see p.82), ivory that is less than 20 or 30 years old almost certainly comes from animals that were killed by poachers. If we are talking about the raw ivory flowing out of Africa and, to a lesser extent, Asia today, forget about the "almost." Every pair of tusks smuggled onto the market represents the death of an elephant. Usually, but according to some reports not always, the animal dies before a poacher hacks or chainsaws away half of the animal's face.

Ideally, poachers want the largest tusks possible, both because this maximizes the return per kill and because the highest-quality ivory comes from the interior of the larger tusks, where it is protected from cracks, staining and erosion. The biggest bulls and, for African elephants, the elder matriarchs, are the first to go. Their loss, and the loss of the matriarchs in particular, leaves a gaping hole in the complicated structure of elephant society.

As poachers turn to younger animals, family groups lose their remaining caregivers, leaving a population of wandering orphans whose chances of survival are slim. Even young elephants may be hunted down in their turn, and because they carry smaller tusks, poachers may need to kill more of them to make up their ivory quota. In the 1980s, one of the chief pieces of information that showed the effect then-massive poaching was having on elephant populations was the appearance, and eventually the dominance, of smaller and smaller tusks on the ivory market.

That the ivory trade — or, to be fair, the extensive and highly organized criminal activity that constitutes the international ivory trade today — is devastating to elephants in both Asia and Africa is beyond argument. What to do about it, unfortunately, is not. Many of us believe that keeping legal ivory off world markets, as was done in 1989, worked for years and remains an essential part of any answer. Others argue that legal trade is necessary to drive poachers out of business, and to provide income to poor people who must live, to their cost, with enormous and dangerous beasts. The debate has lain at the heart of efforts to protect elephants and rein in their killers for decades. Today, it rages as furiously as ever.

CHAPTER FOUR

NOT AN APHRODISIAC

The rhino's "horn" is not, in fact, a true horn, with a bony supporting core like the horns of cattle or antelopes. Instead, it is an outgrowth of the skin, rather like your hair or fingernails. It is largely composed of the protein α-keratin, arranged (as it is in our own hair and in such things as horses' hooves and whale baleen) in a series of threadlike tubules or filaments. The filaments are set in a matrix of calcium, melanin and more keratin in a somewhat gelatinous state. Like your hair, the horn grows, in a series of pulses, throughout life, replacing itself as wear, use and exposure to ultraviolet radiation erode its outer surface. The horn of the White Rhino, for example, grows at a rate of up to 2.75 inches (7 cm) per year.

Rhinoceros horn is strengthened, particularly at its core, by a dense concentration of calcium deposits, which make it more resistant to wear, and granules of melanin pigment, which protect it from the eroding effects of ultraviolet radiation. As it grows, the weaker outer surface wears away and the tip becomes honed to a point while the strengthened core remains relatively untouched (the animals assist the process by rubbing their horns against trees, stones and the ground). Surprisingly, the horn can contain a significant amount of water — from 20 to 40 percent by weight. A fully hydrated horn may be more elastic and resistant to fracture. Scientists impressed by the horn's structure have suggested that if we could figure out how to make keratin assemble itself in the way it does in a rhinoceros, it would vastly improve our ability to produce tough, fracture-resistant composite materials for our own use.

All this has nothing to do with why humans have valued rhinoceros horn for so long. Rhinoceros horn, like ivory, is beautiful and easy to carve into such things as Japanese *netsuke* (kimono toggles) and, in Victorian and Edwardian times, sword, walking-stick and gun handles. However, in the eyes of many of the people who have wanted it, rhino horn is not a luxury as ivory is, but a medical necessity, its value affirmed by centuries of tradition.

Why do people want rhinoceros horn, and why are they willing to pay such enormous prices to get it? For many years the answer in the West was that the Chinese valued it as an aphrodisiac. Many still believe this today. That is why you still see suggestions that flooding the Chinese market with Viagra would solve the rhino poaching problem. Unfortunately for this idea, the aphrodisiac story is just that: a story. Esmond Martin, who has followed ivory and rhino horn markets around the world, showed years ago that, except in a few places in India, rhinoceros horn was not valued as an aphrodisiac at all. Apparently it never had been. Even in India it was used rarely, though that may have been the consequence of high prices and laws preventing its sale.

Martin found no reference to aphrodisiac properties in any of the references to rhinoceros horn in the comprehensive *Chinese Medical Dictionary*. "In the course of extensive interviews with over 200 Chinese pharmacists, traders and doctors," Martin wrote in his 1982 book *Run Rhino Run*, "I became all the more convinced that this is a completely unfounded myth created by Europeans." He found that Chinese men did use a number of animal products for their aphrodisiac properties, including pig's kidneys, horse penises, deer antlers and the dried sexual organs of tigers soaked in brandy (after six months' soaking, the brandy was ready to drink before sexual intercourse). Martin himself thinks that the rhino story may have originated with Indian traders purchasing horn along the East African coast for sale into China, who told the story to curious, and gullible, European questioners.

The real reasons for the demand for horn are much more complex. The late fifth-century BCE Greek historian Ctesias, court physician to Queen Parysatis of Persia and her son Artaxerxes II, reported that a drinking cup made from the horn of an "Indian ass" — apparently the Greater One-horned Rhino — had the power of detecting any poison poured into it. This appears to have been a very widespread belief. Chinese noblemen regularly presented magnificently carved cups made from rhinoceros horn as birthday gifts to the emperor. Less elaborate cups were used from Central Africa to Eastern Asia to detect and even neutralize poisons, possibly with some success — strong alkaloids may well have reacted with the keratin in the horn, producing the bubbling effect that was supposedly the sign of poison.

In medieval Europe, where rhinoceroses were largely unknown, belief in the poison-detecting properties of rhinoceros horn was transferred to the mythical unicorn. Marco Polo accepted that the rhinoceroses he saw in Sumatra in 1292 were unicorns, but he admitted they were not in the least like the creatures of European fancy. He correctly noted their fondness for mud. Unicorn's horn, known as *alicorn*, was a priceless treasure, but in Europe it usually came not from a rhinoceros but from the male Narwhal (*Monodon monoceros*), an Arctic whale whose long, straight, spirally twisted tusk can be seen on the foreheads of unicorns in countless European tapestries, drawings and paintings.

Rhinoceros body parts have been endowed with other magical properties. C.A.W. Guggisberg reported in *S.O.S. Rhino* that in parts of Southeast Asia, "Rhino blood is supposed to facilitate the departure of the soul of a dying person and to ensure its happy arrival at whatever place it may be bound for. Before the last war, a pound of brown paper soaked with rhino's blood fetched as much as five shillings. The hunters extricate the bladder and take great care not to spill any of the urine, which is considered as an antiseptic and also serves as a general charm against disease, ghosts and evil spirits. For this purpose it has to be placed in a vessel and hung over the door." In Assam today, or at least until recently, people sometimes wear rings containing flakes of rhino horn on the inner surface, touching the wearer's skin, to protect against disease and ward away spirits.

Throughout much of eastern Asia, rhinoceros horn (and, to a lesser extent, its skin, meat, blood and urine) has been valued as a part of traditional medicine. According to the *Divine Farmer's Materia Medica* or *Shen Nong Ben Cao Jing*, written during the Han Dynasty (206 BCE–220 CE) but recording traditions supposedly dating to 2600 BCE, rhinoceros horn (*xi jiao*) "mainly treats the hundreds of toxins, *gu* influx, evil ghosts, and miasmic *qi*, kills lip-hooking [a poisonous herb], *zhen* feather [the poisonous feather of a legendary bird], and snake toxins, eliminates evils, and prevents confusion and oppressive ghost dreams." The famous herbalist and naturalist Li Shizhen (1518–1593), author of the *Compendium of Materia Medica* (*Bencao Gangmu*), considered the most complete book about traditional Chinese medicine ever written, prescribed rhino horn for everything from fever and snakebite to "devil possession."

Its "cooling" properties are reported to make rhinoceros horn effective, usually in combination with various herbal medicines, in treating a wide range of "hot blood" conditions, and in particular to purge toxins and reduce convulsions and dangerous fevers (though in Chinese medicine reducing "heat" is not necessarily the same thing as lowering body temperature). At least in Taiwan, "fire" horn from the Asian rhinos has been considered to be more powerful and effective, and more useful for serious illness or emergencies, than the more readily available "water" horn from Africa. In the early 1990s Asian horn reportedly fetched prices five to nine times as high as African, though today this may no longer be the case. In Vietnam some traditional practitioners believe that rhinos in eastern Asia eat medicinal herbs, making their horns more valuable for treatment. Traditional pharmacists sold rhino horn as a powder, sometimes cut with powdered Water Buffalo horn. A pharmacist who could afford a rhino horn treated it as a treasured possession, to be dispensed in tiny quantities. According to one study of pharmacies in Taipei in the early 1990s, "a rhino horn has always been regarded, especially by the traditional Chinese medical community, as an exotic, semi-mystical object of considerable life-giving properties which, in some family-owned pharmacies, was handed down from generation to generation."

Western medicine regards keratin as pretty much useless for anything except hair treatments in beauty salons. Cancer researchers do use keratin as a diagnostic marker for epithelial tumors, and it is possible that it may have some sort of regulatory role in tumor formation. Rhinoceros horn, even in its traditional role as a fever reducer, seems to be no better than keratin from any other animal. In a double-blind study of children in Taiwan, rhinoceros horn, though it did have a slight fever-reducing effect, performed less effectively than acetaminophen. A single, perhaps anomalous, 2011 study did report that rhino horn fared better than acetaminophen in reducing fever — in rabbits.

Rhino horn has been shown to have some ability to reduce inflammation. It has also been shown to have sedative and anticoagulant properties, at least for mice, though Yak (*Bos grunniens*) and Water Buffalo horn worked just as well and synthetic drugs worked even better. One study showed that if you inject mice with acetic acid, they writhe less if you treat them with rhinoceros horn. Don't try this at home.

In short, there doesn't seem to be any convincing research showing that rhino horn has the unique medicinal properties traditionally ascribed to it. Even when it has some effect, the same or better results can be obtained using readily available alternatives. Nonetheless, for many, trust in the curative properties of rhinoceros horn may stem not from the kinds of results that can be tested but from beliefs surrounding the power or potency of the animal itself, or from a general conviction that the underlying principles of traditional medicine are neither amenable to scientific testing nor comparable to Western medical practice.

At the southwestern tip of the Arabian Peninsula, in Yemen, rhino horn has been valued for another purpose altogether. From at least the 5th or 6th century BCE until very recently, a *jambiya* — a forbidding broad-bladed dagger with a hooked tip — was an essential part of the traditional dress of a Yemeni man of status. It was normally not used as a weapon but was displayed — in a position that depended on class and social station — in front at the waist. For at least 750 years, and probably for centuries longer, the finest and most prestigious *jambiyas* have had a handle made of rhinoceros horn, decorated with strips of silver and hand-made Yemeni gold coins. A rhinoceros horn handle became more valuable with age and repeated handling, as it developed an amber translucence and a unique patina, or *sayfani*.

After the fall of the Yemeni monarchy in 1962, the social distinctions that had reserved the *jambiya* for the upper classes relaxed. Though anyone with the purchase price could now wear one, a *jambiya* with a rhinoceros horn handle remained a powerful symbol of status and wealth. After the end of an eight-year civil war in 1970, a surge in the standard of living in North Yemen, now separated from a Marxist regime in the south, brought the price of a rhino horn *jambiya* to affordable levels for a great many more Yemenis.

As a result, from the 1970s to the mid-1990s Yemen became the largest single consumer of rhinoceros horn in the world (North and South Yemen reunified in 1990). At least 6,600 pounds (3,000 kg) of horn was imported into North Yemen per year during the 1970s, amounting to some 40 percent of the global market. Almost all of the horn came from Africa; the horns of Asian rhinos were both smaller and (because of their supposed higher potency in the medicine market) considerably more expensive than those of their African cousins.

North Yemen banned the import of rhinoceros horn in 1982 in response to international pressure from conservationists. Imports fell sharply, but this had less to do with the essentially non-existent enforcement of the law than with the facts that North Yemen was experiencing a drastic economic decline, putting rhino horn beyond the reach of at least some craftsmen and consumers, and that Africa was literally running out of rhinos. Black Rhinoceros populations had fallen from about 65,000 animals to about 15,000 between 1970 and 1980.

By 1986, when the Black Rhino population had fallen to fewer than 4,500, almost all of the rhino horn purchased by the largest merchant in Sanaa, the Yemeni capital, was being smuggled into the country from Sudan by Sudanese with family connections in Yemen (a single Yemeni family dominated the business). Horn from other countries in eastern and southern Africa reached Yemen via the United Arab Emirates or Burundi, where Ian Parker saw a consignment of some 700 horn pieces ready to leave the country. The price for rhino horn, however, was now so high that *jambiya* craftsmen were turning more and more to other materials, from wood and plastic to Water Buffalo horn and camel nails.

Until recently, when a steep rise in horn prices forced Yemeni buyers out of the market, the trade continued even though the Grand Mufti of Yemen had issued a *fatwa* in 1992 stating that killing rhinos for their horns was not allowed by Islam. The price of a rhino horn dagger handle continued to rise in the Sanaa markets through the late 1990s. Yemen joined the CITES Convention (see p. 53) in 1997, but rhino horns continued to enter the country in reduced numbers from Kenya, Tanzania, Uganda and other African countries. Some were probably taken from the vanishing Northern White Rhinoceroses of Garamba National Park in the Democratic Republic of Congo, and others from the soon-to-be-extinct Black Rhinoceros population of Cameroon (see p. 120). From the late 1990s until the middle of the next decade, when anti-piracy efforts slowed down its operations, the chief entrepôt for horn smuggled into Yemen was the tiny African country of Djibouti. Djibouti had become a major source of contraband goods, shipped by boat across the narrow inlet at the southern end of the Red Sea that separates the Horn of Africa from the Arabian Peninsula.

By 2001, though, the market had apparently collapsed. Lucy Vigne and Esmond Martin, who had been surveying the Yemeni markets since 1978, reported for the first time that no new rhino horns were being carved into *jambiya* handles in the Sanaa souk. The main reason for the end of the horn carving industry appears to have been that the price simply went up higher than most Yemenis were prepared to pay. Even customers who could afford a *jambiya* with a rhinoceros horn handle preferred to buy an older one, regarded as more prestigious and valuable.

Vigne and Martin initiated a public awareness campaign with the encouragement of the Yemeni government, supplying schools and the media with posters, leaflets and a video on the plight of the rhinoceros (including copies of the 1992 *fatwa*). They encouraged buyers to select daggers with handles made from alternative materials, including high-priced agate handles for the prestige market. The combination of rising prices and public awareness appeared to do the trick, assisted by a flood of cheap plastic handles from China and changes in fashion. Yemeni men are now more likely to wear Western trousers than the traditional robe, and, as one artisan commented, you can't wear a *jambiya* over trousers.

Rhino horn nonetheless continued to be smuggled into Yemen. Vigne and Martin found in 2007 that the price of horn had risen alarmingly, by 40 percent. Though the number of rhino horns going into Yemen has remained comparatively low, they seemed to be coming almost entirely out of East Africa. That meant that the trade into Yemen was probably still having a serious impact on local rhino populations, and it may have been responsible for the killing of some of the last wild Northern White Rhinos.

It is possible that the Yemeni trade has now subsided, if a 2010 report can be believed. If so, what was once the greatest single threat to the survival of African rhinos would appear to be out of the picture. Instead, the main market has shifted eastward, to feed the traditional medicinal demand for horn in China and a suspected demand among the wealthy for horn as an investment asset that may prove to be larger than we realize. More suprisingly, a new growing and well-documented market has emerged in Vietnam. We will turn to the Vietnamese market, considered the greatest threat to rhinos today, in a later chapter.

CHAPTER FIVE

WHAT MAKES POACHERS POACH?

The answer to the question this chapter poses may appear to be self-evident: a combination of poverty and social disruption at one end of the smuggling chain coupled with affluence, greed and ignorance at the other. For regulators, conservationists and law enforcement officers trying to decide where to place their often minimal resources, this answer is not good enough.

Perhaps it is stating the obvious, but poachers, whatever drives them to poach, are breaking the law — or, at least, some law, somewhere. The media often confuse matters by talking about "illegal poaching," as though there were such a thing as legal poaching. Poaching is the illegal hunting of wild animals, whether the animals themselves are protected by law or, in the traditional definition, the poacher is trespassing on land where hunting is restricted or prohibited. In the case of elephants and rhinoceroses, we have both: poachers are killing protected animals, and they are invading protected areas such as reserves or national parks to do it. Part of the question, then, is what drives poachers to crime.

Particularly in the context of postcolonial Africa, we may first have to ask whether the laws that the poachers break should have been imposed in the first place. Laws that keep people from traditional subsistence hunting grounds, for example, can breed resentment and invite lawbreaking. However, even if we are talking about the taking of small game for meat rather than the hunt for ivory or rhinoceros horn, the large-scale poaching going on in Africa today is not about subsistence hunting. It is unquestionably a commercial enterprise. Poached bushmeat is, likely as not, going to feed a taste for exotic wildlife in urban restaurants. Far from being the last resort of the hungry, bushmeat poaching robs local hunters of traditional sources of protein. The killers of elephants and rhinoceroses deny local peoples the opportunity to earn much-needed tourist dollars and may be destroying an important part of their cultural heritage.

Tourism, though, is not a likely option in many parts of elephant or rhinoceros ranges. Poaching may be one of the few available sources of revenue. In Gabon, a simmering combination of poverty and resentment is driving elephant poachers into the forest. Gabon, an oil-rich country with a relatively good conservation record, holds perhaps half of the remaining Forest Elephants in Africa. Its president, Ali Bongo, gained world attention in June 2012 by personally setting fire to a pyramid of 10,000 pounds (4,500 kg) of stockpiled ivory, following the example of former Kenyan president Daniel arap Moi in 1989 (and of further burnings since). Trouble, nonetheless, is brewing there. A 2011 survey assisted by the United States Fish and Wildlife Service revealed that the once-pristine Minkebe National Park in Gabon's far north had been invaded by hordes of poachers and workers from a nearby open-pit gold mine. President Bongo sent a military unit to evict thousands of miners and poachers from the park and began an intensive program to root out the rest. In early 2013 the Gabon government revealed that the poachers, allegedly from neighboring Cameroon, had killed more than 11,000 elephants in Minkebe alone — about two-thirds of its population — since 2004. Most were probably killed in the past few years.

Not far from Minkebe is the Baka village of Bitouga, a pocket of dire poverty in this otherwise wealthy country that *New York Times* reporter Jeffrey Gettleman visited in 2012. Gettleman painted a picture of desperation: "Bitouga's people live in rough clapboard houses with floors of dirt. They do not have any electricity or clean water, which villagers say is a scandal in a country with a per capita gross domestic product of $16,000, one of the highest in Africa. The children here eat thumb-size caterpillars, cooked in enormous vats, because there is little else to eat. Many men have bloodshot eyes and spend their mornings sitting on the ground, staring into space, reeking of sour, fermented home-brew." Hunters in Bitouga admitted to Gettleman that they would kill elephants for the right price — about $50. Well-dressed middlemen organizing elephant hunts, including corrupt civil servants in nearby towns, can co-opt hunters into ivory poaching "for as little as a sack of salt."

The desperately poor local hunter driven into poaching by pure need, selling ivory or rhinoceros horn on an opportunistic basis to visiting middlemen, is certainly part of the poaching picture. So, however, is another type of poacher altogether: well armed, well paid, trained to almost, or actual, military efficiency and willing to kill, or to risk being killed, in pursuit of his quarry. There is, of course, a middle ground: I remember being told, many years ago, by French zoologist and elephant expert Pierre Pfeffer, about a gang of ivory poachers in Chad who were able to escape from park rangers because they had bicycles and the rangers did not.

The key factor determining whether poaching is a small-scale local enterprise or a highly organized professional operation is price. Large, heavily armed poaching gangs with vehicles for road and air transportation, connected to sophisticated smuggling operations with access to international markets and the ability to either outsmart government officials or make them look the other way, don't just appear out of thin air. The higher the value of smuggled goods at their end markets, the more attractive they will be as investment vehicles for criminal syndicates with the ability to outspend, and the sophistication to outsmart, the law enforcement agencies trying to bar their way. That is as true for the illegal wildlife trade as it is for the drug trade.

This has been true for both ivory and rhinoceros horn. The two great ivory poaching surges, the one that led to the international trade ban in the 1980s and the one going on right now, have been marked by skyrocketing prices and increasingly sophisticated organization in the illegal trade. The current involvement of criminal gangs in the rhinoceros horn trade, and their ability to co-opt even respected south African wildlife professionals, has almost certainly been stimulated by the enormous rise in prices for horn reportedly being paid in Vietnam and perhaps elsewhere (see p. 88).

Large-scale, military-style ivory poaching has been bound up with genuine full-scale war. The huge flow of weapons into the continent during the post-independence civil wars of the 1960s enabled the first major poaching crises of the 1970s and 1980s. Poachers now had the firepower, and in many cases the organizing ability, to slaughter elephants and rhinoceroses on a scale never seen before. In Angola, Jonas Savimbi funded his UNITA rebellion by shipping ivory out through South Africa in return for shipments of arms. It is said that Savimbi personally presented a life-size ivory replica of an AK-47 to Prime Minister P.W. Botha of South Africa as a token of appreciation for his support. In January 1996, a judicial enquiry chaired by Mr. Justice

M.E. Kumleben confirmed publicly that during the 1980s South Africa's military had traded arms to the guerrillas in Angola in return for shipments of many tonnes of smuggled ivory and rhinoceros horn. There were rumors that it did the same for RENAMO guerrillas in Mozambique, but the Kumleben Commission was unable to confirm them.

It is no surprise that recent rhinoceros poaching has concentrated in South Africa, home to the vast majority of surviving rhinos. A prevalence of poachers, though, is not just a matter of the hunters going where the animals are — the poacher's equivalent of Willie Sutton's famous (but, alas, apparently apocryphal) comment that he robbed banks because "that's where the money is."

Why has the illegal ivory trade focused so strongly on African, rather than Asian, elephants? There are more elephants in Africa, Asian females normally lack tusks (though some bull Asian Elephants carry substantial tusks indeed), and the ivory trade has been primarily African-based for centuries. Perhaps the greatest factor, though, is the failure of nationhood in a number of African countries. Lawlessness and political instability, coupled with easy access to high-powered weapons, have allowed gangs of poachers to roam with impunity from country to country, killing as they please.

Lack of resources for anti-poaching activities can be a large enough obstacle to law enforcement — witness the story of the bicycle-less Chadian rangers (page 47). Far worse, though, has been a failure of governance at levels from local to national, ranging from simple unwillingness to act or lack of political will to outright corruption and complicity. As far back as 1976, the late David Sheldrick blamed the high levels of elephant poaching in Kenya's Tsavo National Park on, as Iain Douglas-Hamilton reported, "a combination of factors which included the ready market for trophies, the absence of any arrests of illicit dealers despite their well-known identity, the apparent protection offered to crooked ivory traders by influential people, a general disinterest in any form of elephant protection by those in authority, and a lack of suitably trained officers to carry out anti-poaching duties." Kenya has vastly improved since then, though it still has its problems.

During a single two-day period in January 2013, two Tanzanian police officers were arrested in the Serengeti District for illegal possession of ivory, while two more, in the Karagwe District, were murdered by villagers, apparently after a deal to buy poached ivory went sour. In December 2012, Zambia's Tourism and Arts minister Sylvia Masebo fired the director general of the Zambian Wildlife Authority (ZAWA) and four senior officials for alleged corrupt practices in awarding hunting concessions, and she canceled all safari hunting licenses for five years. In early January she announced that unauthorized foreign aircraft had been flying in and out of the country to smuggle animals. This followed the announcement the previous June that more than three tonnes of elephant tusks had gone missing from the vault at ZAWA headquarters (see p. 128). There are many such stories.

In some Asian countries, including Myanmar and Sri Lanka, armed security and military personnel have been implicated in ivory poaching. Poaching has generally not, however, reached the large-scale, organized, quasi-military level that it has in Africa. Most Asian poachers, in places like southern India or the Cardamom Mountains of Cambodia, are locals operating individually or in very small groups, using traditional weapons or crude firearms. In recent years, though, specialized poachers, skilled at killing with such weapons as a crossbow firing a poisoned dart, have been imported into elephant areas in India.

Poaching gangs in parts of India have been operating for years. In the 1980s and 1990s, a notorious gang under the leadership of a brutal south Indian brigand known as Veerappan (Koose Muniswamy Veerappan Gounder, 1952–2004) not only killed elephants but murdered a large number of rangers and policemen. Veerappan himself, despite his reputation in some circles as an Indian Robin Hood, was wanted in three Indian states for the killing of hundreds of elephants and well over a hundred people, not to mention other criminal activities, including the kidnapping of a major Indian film star. He was finally killed in a shootout with police. In 2006, another experienced poacher, Imbali Jose, who had taken over Veerrapan's territory, died of kidney failure while hiding from police at his home.

On a local scale, poaching levels may reflect such practical matters as access to roads, allowing poachers to penetrate remote areas, and the availability of vehicles, from logging trucks to helicopters, to transport the ivory (and, to a lesser extent, rhino horn) out again. A 2012 analysis of poaching in the Tsavo Conservation Area in southeastern Kenya found that "the best predictors for elephant poaching were density of elephants, condition of vegetation, proximity to ranger bases and outposts, and densities of roads and rivers." The Okapi Faunal Reserve in the northeastern Democratic Republic of Congo (DRC), one and a half times the size of Yellowstone and once home to a thriving population of African Forest Elephants, provided Rene Beyers and his colleagues with a microcosm of the spatial and social features that make some areas relatively safe for animals and others, often nearby, very dangerous indeed.

Forest Elephants are not easy to find, much less count (see p. 20), especially over a huge area like the Okapi Reserve, and their numbers must often be estimated indirectly. Beyers' study measured the density of elephant dung piles on the forest floor and found that it had declined by 48 percent. The study concluded that Forest Elephant numbers in the reserve had fallen from an estimated 6,439 to 3,288 between 1995 and 2006. Most of the missing elephants were probably poached by rebel militias between 2002 and 2004. These results are probably quite accurate: at least 23 tonnes of ivory were taken out of the reserve and surrounding areas during the decade, enough to account for more than 3,400 dead elephants.

The eastern DRC has been a land of lawlessness and war for decades, and the elephants in the Okapi Reserve have gained no favors by being in the middle of it. Beyers' report provides a stark summary of the effects on wildlife of the 1995–2006 civil war:

> DRC's conflict led to widespread lawlessness. Government institutions were disrupted or taken apart, or oriented to facilitate illegal extraction and taxation (such as the national police and military). Institutions such as the national parks service, whose mandate is the protection and control of natural resources, were the focus of attack and harassment. Thus, the collapse of wildlife conservation and enforcement during the conflict was profound. Staff ceased normal operations or moved out of protected areas, and many were killed. Hunting increased and was partly linked to the proliferation of small arms. Militias and military occupied protected areas. The exploitation of elephants for ivory and meat was used to provision insurgents or the military, and to generate revenue to fund further expansion of resource takeovers.

With this as a background, it is amazing that there were any elephants left by the end of the conflict. Things weren't always this bad: though poaching in the reserve was "rampant" from the late 1970s to the early 1980s, as it was almost everywhere in Central Africa, after the 1989 ivory ban (see p. 61) it stopped almost completely until the outbreak of war in 1996. That period of peace ended when, according to Beyers, "military and rebel factions moved into the area, looted park headquarters, disarmed park guards, brought in hunters, and opened markets around the reserve for bushmeat and ivory."

That gives us a general picture of poaching in the area. Beyers and his colleagues, though, looked more closely at how poaching had affected the reserve on a spatial scale. They found that a number of factors made parts of the reserve safer than others. Burgeoning road systems penetrating forests in Central Africa give poachers access to their victims, and Forest Elephants have been found to be unwilling to cross roads outside of protected areas. Charles Yackulic and his colleagues found, in a recent survey of five Central African national parks (also based on dung counts), that the chance that a forest location would be devoid of dung (and, presumably, elephants) was closely linked to what percentage of the area within a 28-mile (45 km) radius was within 12 miles (20 km) of a road or settlement. Beyers' results in the Okapi Reserve did not show a strong relationship between roads and the absence of elephants, perhaps because a road crosses the center of the reserve, where elephants congregate to avoid the riskier boundary zones.

In the Okapi Reserve, poachers tended to avoid better-guarded areas. Elephants were in greater numbers closer to the guard post at park headquarters and were also more numerous in the interior of the park than they were near the more accessible park boundary. The point about the guard posts is crucial. Even during wartime, committed forest wardens (and the organizations that help them do their work) make a difference: "[D]espite massive declines in numbers, our study has shown that the commitment of highly motivated government field staff, and the continued support by international organizations to provide some protection on the ground, made a difference for their survival. ... Two elements were critical in the survival of these protected areas: first was the continued presence by committed staff, while second was the continued funding by international NGOs." Unfortunately, the situation in the Okapi Reserve has deteriorated since Beyers' study, culminating in a horrific act of violence in 2012 (see p. 117).

The poacher, whatever his income or status, represents only the bottom end of the supply chain. For both ivory and rhinoceros horn that chain may be very long indeed, with the real powers controlling it, and the real money being made, at a considerable distance from the poacher himself. To quote Indian conservationist Vivek Menon, "A poacher remains at the wrong end of the ladder, of minor relevance and a pawn in the game."

Dealing with the kingpins who actually control the trade involves dealing with end markets, and the transit routes through which ivory or rhinoceros horn travel to reach them. Particularly for ivory in Africa, domestic markets may play an important role in the trade, and in recent years much attention has been focused on trying to bring these markets under control. However, for much of the trade the supply route stretches across borders, and even across continents. This has shifted the focus of the debate over what to do about elephant and rhinoceros poaching into the global arena, and particularly into the purview of an international treaty specifically designed to deal with cross-border wildlife trade and its consequences for conservation. It is to that treaty that we turn next.

CHAPTER SIX

CITES AND THE FIRST IVORY CRISIS

The Convention on International Trade in Endangered Species of Wild Fauna and Flora is best known by its acronym: CITES (pronounced "site-eez"). It was through CITES that international commercial trade in Asian Elephant ivory was banned in 1975, international commercial trade in rhinoceros horn has been banned since 1977, and African Elephant ivory has been barred from commercial trade, with a few highly controversial exceptions, since 1989.

Calls for an international approach to the growing problem of illegal trade in wildlife go back to the early 1960s. IUCN floated the idea of such a treaty at its conference in 1963, and the 1969 version of the United States *Endangered Species Act* directed the government to convene an international ministerial meeting to conclude "a binding international convention on the conservation of endangered species."

The final text, conflated from drafts prepared by the United States, Kenya and IUCN, was signed by 88 countries at a plenipotentiary conference in Washington, DC, on March 3, 1973. CITES entered into force (that is, became legally binding on its signatories) on July 1, 1975, 90 days after its tenth signatory, Canada, had officially ratified its text. Today 178 countries are Parties to CITES. Very few countries involved in the international wildlife trade (including the massive global trade in timber and fish) remain outside CITES today. The Preamble to the Convention recognizes "that international co-operation is essential for the protection of certain species of wild fauna and flora against over-exploitation through international trade."

CITES is not an international endangered species list, nor does it have a central body that makes its decisions. Those who ask, "Why are such-and-such species listed under CITES when there are still a lot of them around?", "Why doesn't CITES take some action or other?" or "If CITES is protecting a species, why can I still buy it or products made from it?" misunderstand the Convention's structure. This chapter offers a simplified account of CITES' major features; those wanting to know (a lot) more can download *The Evolution of CITES*, by former CITES Secretary-General Willem Wijnstekers, from the CITES website.

CITES requires its signatories to regulate international trade (and only international trade, not domestic trade, possession or local sale) in species of animals or plants placed on one of three lists, or Appendices. Appendix I is for species "threatened with extinction which are or may be affected by trade." Appendix II is for species "not necessarily now threatened with extinction" (they might even be abundant) but which may become so if their trade is not regulated. An additional provision allows the listing of so-called "look-alike" species that are difficult to tell from Appendix II species listed on their own merits. In part this is to forestall unscrupulous traders who try to avoid the treaty by labeling their specimens as similar but unlisted species. Species on both Appendices require an export permit to be traded across international borders. An export permit is supposed to be issued only if the Scientific Authority of a CITES member country (one of two bodies each Party is required to set up, the other being the Management Authority, the body that actually issues the permits) certifies that the export will not be detrimental to the survival of the species. This is the so-called Non-Detriment Finding, or NDF.

Species on Appendix I are protected by a further requirement: the export permit cannot be granted without an import permit from the importing country, and that import permit cannot be issued if the import is for primarily commercial purposes. This is the feature of the Convention that allows CITES to impose commercial trade bans. The long-standing bans on trade in most elephant ivory and all rhinoceros horn were initially achieved by transferring their bearers from Appendix II to Appendix I.

Decisions about which species to list, and on which Appendix they are placed, are made by the Conference of the Parties (CoP), a sort of general assembly of the member countries that now meets every three years. However, changes and additions (and deletions) can happen only if a member country submits a proposal, no matter what the world's scientists, conservationists or wildlife traders think. This makes listing an ad hoc, and highly political, process. It has certainly proved so for elephants at least.

There is another species list, Appendix III, but this operates a bit differently. Appendix III is for species whose trade individual member countries feel they cannot control without help. Species are listed on Appendix III unilaterally, without a vote. Only the country that lists them needs to issue import permits. Other countries with the same species need only issue a Certificate of Origin showing that the specimen being exported did not originate in the listing country. African elephants first made an appearance under CITES on Appendix III, placed there by Ghana in 1975 (effective, like almost all CITES listings, 90 days later, on February 26, 1976). They were not voted onto Appendix II until the First Meeting of the Conference of the Parties (CoP1), a year later.

One further, crucial wrinkle: listings on the Appendices may be subject to annotations, qualifying riders that can restrict the scope of a listing to certain countries, or delay the date it comes into effect, or restrict commercial trade to certain products only. It is impossible, at least for animals, to list only certain parts rather than the whole animal on the Appendices, but annotations, in effect, allow you to do the same thing. They have been much used for both elephants and rhinoceroses.

CITES has its fervent supporters and equally fervent naysayers. The latter group either claims that CITES isn't tough or effective enough or argues that its top-down, internationalist approach and apparent emphasis on trade bans are out of touch with "modern" ideas of sustainable use and local ownership of resources. Its adherents (and I am one) point out that international trade is, like it or not, a global phenomenon. Trade in wildlife, including illegal trade, is big business, and in order to deal with its excesses an international instrument like CITES, properly deployed, is absolutely necessary, despite its admitted imperfections.

Few issues have polarized its advocates, and its enemies, so much as the ivory trade. The Asian Elephant was placed on Appendix I in 1973, and there has never been any serious suggestion that that should change. African elephant species (including both Savanna and Forest Elephants) were far more numerous, however, and in a number of countries in Africa the ivory trade was legal. Poaching had become a serious problem in West, Central and East Africa by the start of the 1970s, but in the countries of southern Africa — in South Africa, Botswana and Zimbabwe in particular — poaching was negligible, and elephant populations were large and growing. There were so many elephants in these countries, it was claimed, that the problem was not too much killing but too little. Left on their own, burgeoning elephant populations were outgrowing their habitat and destroying it in the process: knocking over trees, demolishing brush and creating a landscape that was not only less available to other species but singularly unattractive to tourists coming to experience the African wild.

Much of this problem had arisen because growing human populations had cut elephants off from their traditional migration routes. In the past, elephants in the southern savannas were continuously on the move, never in any one place long enough to devastate the habitats through which they passed. Under normal circumstances, habitat modification by elephants can actually increase the capacity of the land to hold other species (see p. 17). Elephants in the south, hemmed in by human settlement, were forced to restrict their migratory ways but could not give up the habitat-modifying behavior that gave them access to food and water.

The response to this, in places like South Africa's Kruger National Park, was culling: the deliberate killing of elephants in an attempt to keep their numbers at acceptable management levels. What "acceptable" meant, of course, depended on one's philosophy of wildlife management. The South African view (shared by East African game wardens like Ian Parker) assumed that savanna ecosystems were stable and should be kept that way, rather than being allowed to cycle naturally through periods of relative feast or famine. Allowing elephants to modify their surroundings past a certain point would result in permanent damage.

More recent studies show, however, that savanna ecosystems are quite resilient. They suffer less, and recover faster, from the effects of elephant disturbance than had previously been thought. If so, intensive elephant management, including culling, may be neither necessary nor desirable. South Africa, which had aimed since 1967 at keeping the elephant population of Kruger National Park between 6,000 and 8,500 animals, placed a moratorium on culling in 1995 after an intense public debate. Instead, it instituted a new management policy involving control of elephant movements. The moratorium was lifted in 2008, but thus far no further culling has been done.

Culling in South Africa, whatever one might think of it, was not random slaughter but a carefully managed, precise and very expensive operation (the same cannot be said of the "culling" going on even now in Zimbabwe, which is based on probably overinflated population figures and is believed to be a cover for earning money from sport hunters and poachers). It is no wonder that southern African countries looked upon the ivory amassed from culling operations as a valuable, and indeed essential, source of revenue for conservation and wildlife management. They saw legal international trade in ivory as a necessity, and a sovereign right. As long as African elephants were retained on Appendix II, legal trade in this ivory, and in ivory from other sources including confiscation from poachers, natural mortality or control of "problem" animals, could go ahead.

Concerns had been raised at the 1981 CITES meeting that illegal ivory trading had reached "a significant level," particularly involving countries that had not yet joined the Convention. However, while launching the Fourth Meeting in Gaborone, Botswana, in 1983 the Botswanan president commented that "it is encouraging to note that CITES does not prohibit or discourage legalized trade in wild fauna and flora but rather that it aims at controlling the trade so as to ensure the sustainable utilization of the resource." The preamble to a resolution on trade in worked ivory noted that "The African Parties further believed that the endeavours by some Parties to control the trade in worked ivory are an unnecessary negative influence on the value of ivory and overlook the status of the African elephant as agreed at the IUCN meeting of the African elephant and rhino specialist group held in 1981."

By now, though, the situation farther north in Africa was growing steadily worse. Ivory prices had been on the rise since 1969, and ivory would reach nine times its 1960s value by the 1980s. This exponential rise in price, coupled with the huge inflow of weapons into the continent, provided poachers with the motive and means to slaughter the herds. Corruption was a major contributor. Craig van Note of Monitor International provided some particularly egregious examples to a United States congressional committee in 1979 (note that the Central African Empire is now the Central African Republic, Zaire is the Democratic Republic of Congo, and their horrifying 1979 leaders are long gone):

> In the Central African Empire, Emperor Bokassa has a personal monopoly on the ivory trade. He sends his army out into the countryside to slaughter huge numbers of elephants. ... Emperor Bokassa maintains his monopoly by a simple expedient. Anyone found dealing in ivory in his country other than himself is shot. ... Thousands of elephants died in just one area of Zaire last year after being poisoned. ... According to a source in Kisangani, corrupt government

officials diverted 20 tonnes of pesticide that was to have been used for spraying the coffee plantations in the province. ... The pesticide was poured into the waterholes in the marshy areas where the elephants came to drink. Within days, thousands of elephants were poisoned. ... The poached ivory was delivered to Kisangani, where the corrupt government officials chartered aircraft to fly it to Kinshasa. One hoard of ivory was so large that when it was loaded aboard a DC-3, the plane could not take off. Several tonnes of ivory had to be removed. The ivory was flown from Kinshasa to France. Millions of dollars were paid to the traders by investors in Europe and the Far East. The money went largely into the Swiss bank accounts of Zairian Government officials.

Despite furious denials by a number of governments (including Kenya's), poaching had been increasing through the 1970s and had, by now, reached alarming levels. As the 1980s progressed, it was increasingly clear that African Elephant populations were in free fall across much of the continent. There was, nonetheless, still disagreement among elephant experts as to whether this was the result of poaching, as Iain Douglas-Hamilton and others believed, or of habitat loss, as Ian Parker insisted.

With the scientific picture still ambiguous, countries supporting the ivory trade continued to argue at CITES that, with the proper controls in place, the legal sale of ivory could continue while the poachers' ivory could be denied access to the market. In 1985, CITES adopted an ivory quota system. Only countries with scientifically based management programs would be allowed to export ivory legally, a sustainable limit would be set on the number of tusks that could be sold, and all tusks had to be marked before they could be exported. An Ivory Control Unit (extensively funded, as it turned out, by ivory trade kingpins in Hong Kong) was established within the CITES Secretariat to oversee the system's operation.

It didn't work. As *The Economist* (which referred to CITES as "utterly powerless") reported in July 1989, "Rather than bother with the paperwork to get a quota authorization, most traders found it simpler to smuggle." Favoring countries with good management programs meant nothing when smuggled ivory was moving freely from country to country. A marking system for whole tusks was of little use after the ivory had been cut up, and the CITES export permits that "legalized" the shipments (and the pieces cut from each tusk) could be — and were — stolen, forged or acquired by bribery. Amnesties for countries with huge stockpiles of illegal ivory, arranged through the Secretariat as an inducement to join CITES, made matters worse. One of the recipients, Burundi, was the source of vast amounts of ivory that left Africa during the late 1980s. It had precisely one elephant of its own.

The trickle of legal ivory simply merged into a flood of contraband, the vast majority going to the chief ivory carving centers in Hong Kong. Dealers in smuggled ivory became expert at disguising shipments and avoiding CITES restrictions. Once the ivory had been carved, it became impossible to distinguish legal supplies from contraband. At the 1987 CITES meeting IUCN reported that at least 78 percent of the ivory traded as "legal" around the world originated from elephants killed by poachers.

It was estimated that half of Africa's elephants were killed between 1979 and 1989 — some two hundred elephants every day. By 1989, elephant populations in East Africa had declined by 80 percent or more. The global population was estimated at 609,000, a far cry from the estimated 1,300,000 of only a decade before. A massive study released that year by the specially convened Ivory Trade Review Group (ITRG) finally proved that the primary cause was poaching pressure. The stage was set for what the foes of the trade hoped would be the final battle.

CHAPTER SEVEN

THE
IVORY BAN

I n May 1989, the East Africans, whose herds were in dire straits and whose wildlife-related tourism (the chief source of income for Kenya at least) was in serious jeopardy, called for the transfer of all African elephant populations to CITES Appendix I. The proposal was sponsored by a record seven countries: Kenya, Tanzania, Somalia, Gambia, Hungary, the United States and Austria. Conservation and animal protection groups worldwide began intensive lobbying for an end to the legal ivory trade. In June both IUCN and the World Wildlife Fund (WWF) came out in favor of a ban. Within days, unilateral import bans were instituted by the United States, Canada, the European Economic Community and others to prevent a mass slaughter during the 90-day waiting period before the Appendix I listing, once passed, could take effect.

By now the issue had become a *cause célèbre*. The supposedly impartial CITES Secretariat lobbied heavily for continued trade. Richard Leakey, newly appointed as director of Kenya's wildlife department, launched a vigorous public campaign in favor of a ban. In July President Daniel Arap Moi of Kenya attracted world attention by publicly setting fire to 26,500 pounds (12,000 kg) of confiscated ivory worth some $3,000,000. Meanwhile, international diplomatic efforts were underway to try to forge an agreement between the East African countries and the southern countries, vehemently led by Zimbabwe, that opposed an Appendix I listing for their populations. Despite these efforts, a compromise worked out in July at a meeting in Botswana had collapsed by the time the CITES parties met in October.

The Seventh Meeting of the Conference of the Parties to CITES opened in Lausanne, Switzerland, on October 9, 1989, attended by delegates from 91 countries and a host of observers. Authorities on the African Elephants, including Iain and Oria Douglas-Hamilton, Cynthia Moss, Joyce Poole and David Western, attended to argue the case for Appendix I. The meeting became the focus of world media attention. At one point three hundred Swiss schoolchildren marched through the Palais de Beaulieu, demanding that the delegates save the elephant.

The two sides were still far apart. Supporters argued that, as ivory from all over Africa was being mixed together indistinguishably during shipment, only a ban on all African ivory would work. Rowan Martin, speaking for Zimbabwe, argued that putting all elephants on Appendix I amounted to punishing southern Africa for its good elephant management because countries such as Kenya had failed to control poachers. IUCN and WWF proposed a compromise that would have left the elephants of Zimbabwe, Botswana and South Africa, which were admittedly healthy and even increasing, on Appendix II but would have instituted a two-year moratorium on trade. This was rejected by the southern Africans, who demanded that the other parties to their customs union, including Mozambique (which was in a state of civil war) and Angola (which was not a CITES party), be included. Zimbabwe insisted that the parties accept a marketing scheme that it proposed to set up with its neighbors, and its position became even more intransigent as the meeting progressed.

Meanwhile, some Central African countries, including Gabon, announced that if southern African countries were to receive special treatment merely because of their proximity to Zimbabwe, they would seek an exemption for themselves as well. Other countries feared that the CITES rules would make it impossible to return the elephant to Appendix II and restore legal trade, even if populations recovered. By the end of the first week, there seemed little chance that the proposal would receive the two-thirds majority necessary for passage.

At this point Ruth Mace, Mark Stanley Price and I suggested a new compromise: transfer all African elephant populations to Appendix I but institute specific criteria under which any African country could apply to have its population downlisted to Appendix II. A Panel of Experts, with strong African representation, would then survey that country's elephant populations, its anti-poaching controls and the degree to which it could control ivory smuggling through its territories. If the country received a satisfactory assessment from the panel, the CITES Parties could vote to downlist its population, allowing it to begin trading in ivory once more. Our suggestion was taken up by the proposal's sponsors and was formally introduced by Somalia as an amendment.

In spite of attempts by the Secretariat to prevent the Somali amendment from coming to the floor, it was the amended proposal that was overwhelmingly adopted by the Parties, by a vote of 76–11, with four abstentions. During the remainder of the meeting, a working group, chaired by former Kenya Wildlife Conservation and Management Department chief Perez Olindo, met to develop the details under which the new rules would operate. On October 16 and 17, all African elephants were transferred from Appendix II to Appendix I, effective January 18, 1990. International commercial trade in ivory had been banned.

Immediately after the vote, Botswana, Zimbabwe, Mozambique, Malawi and Burundi announced that they would enter reservations against the listing, a procedure by which Parties can refuse, within 90 days of a final vote, to recognize an amendment to the CITES Appendices. Mozambique and Burundi did not, in fact, file reservations, but after the meeting the other countries were joined by Zambia, China and the United Kingdom, which entered a six-month reservation on behalf of Hong Kong to permit it to sell off its stocks of largely poached ivory.

Ivory prices had begun to fall even before Lausanne, following the various unilateral bans. After the CITES meeting the ivory market went into rapid collapse. Prices in Africa fell as low as $2 per kilogram. Ivory, particularly in Western countries, became practically unsellable. In Japan, demand for ivory decreased significantly after an initial surge, and by November 1990 production had fallen by two-thirds. Hong Kong was unable to dispose of more than a fraction of its stocks, and China, its carving industry nearly bankrupt, withdrew its reservation early in 1991. In eastern Asia, according to Esmond Martin and Daniel Stiles, "The number of ivory craftsmen ... plummeted ... from about 2,200 in 1989 to fewer than 300 in 2002." Eastern Asian businessmen blamed the loss of trade on "the activities of Western conservationists and journalists, which have resulted in a significant drop in Western buyers, who previously were the principal customers."

Sales in the West did not stop altogether, and ivory items, particularly antique pieces, remained on the market. Most importing countries still had stocks of ivory, both raw and worked, and the ban did not stop people from owning, buying or selling ivory items as long as they did not try to take them across an international border. A 2004 study by Martin and Stiles found over 27,000 ivory items in shops in Germany, France, the UK, Spain and Italy, mostly from ivory legally imported before the 1989 ban. The market, however, appeared to be in decline, and vendors saw no future for new ivory. In the United States, Martin and Stiles found in a 2006–2007 survey that "the country consumes an estimated less than one tonne of raw ivory annually, down from seven tonnes a year in the late 1980s." Poaching fell drastically, declining in some countries by as much as 90 percent; oddly enough, the one country where it increased significantly was Zimbabwe, where poaching levels tripled in the first months after the ban.

The ban had worked.

That is not to say that illegal trade stopped, or that elephant populations rebounded immediately — an unlikely result anyway, given that elephants have a 22-month gestation period. Kenya's population did rebound, by a thousand animals a year, in the years after the ban. There continued to be incidents: 63.5 kilograms of ivory pieces, disguised as painted wood and bound for China from Zaire, were confiscated in the Brussels airport in August 1994. In August 1996, Michael Fay discovered the carcasses of up to two hundred dead elephants, poached over perhaps a year or more, near a national park in northern Congo. Illegal ivory continued to flow, though in diminished quantity, into places like Hong Kong and Japan. Western tourists continued to bring back ivory souvenirs from trips abroad, perhaps under the impression that they were legal (an impression frequently disabused when they arrived at Customs; tourist souvenirs made up the bulk of ivory seized in the United States between 1996 and 2002). People could still be fooled. CITES does not ban trade in antique ivory, which qualifies as "pre-Convention," and according to a 2004 IFAW report on ivory sales in Britain, "At least two incidents investigated by police have uncovered new ivory being carved to 'look antique' for sale through antiques outlets — either with, or without, the knowledge of the end seller."

The ban had positive financial consequences for several African countries, which were now able to spend less money on continuous anti-poaching activities. Elephant conservation nonetheless continued to be extremely expensive. Although an African Elephant Project Database soon became filled with a lengthy wish list of necessary conservation actions in 30 nations throughout the continent, the international donors for whom the database was intended, by and large, kept their wallets in their pockets. (The United States, an honorable exception, established an African Elephant Conservation Fund in 1988 that continues to donate substantial sums to elephant conservation.) African countries could be forgiven for assuming that, once the politics was over, they were on their own.

The failure of the international donor community to follow through was shameful, but the initial success of the ban was considerable. Its success, at least in the early 1990s, was (as the businessmen Martin and Stiles had interviewed well knew) made doubly sure by massive media attention, coupled with NGO publicity and education campaigns. The reality of the poaching crisis was brought home to anyone who might think of buying ivory without being aware of its cost. In the West, ivory changed — for most people — from a desirable luxury item to a substance whose use had become associated with lawlessness, waste, cruelty and the destruction of a beloved and iconic animal.

According to the arguments of its opponents, it shouldn't have been a success. History has repeatedly proven that banning a popular and desirable commodity is more likely to drive the trade underground, and hand a monopoly for its sale to criminals, than to stop people from using it. The Prohibition amendment in the United States hardly resulted (except, briefly, after its first passage) in people giving up alcohol — instead it made bootleggers rich, and it was never proven to have had a long-term effect on the number of alcoholics. Nor has it been proven that the War on Drugs has prevented users from procuring the substances they want, and the cocaine barons of South America have become billionaires in spite of, or perhaps because of, its costly exertions. Why should a ban on ivory (or, for that matter, rhino horn) be any different? *The Economist* was convinced, a few months before the 1989 vote, that "a ban will drive the ivory trade underground, making it as hard to police as cocaine smuggling from the forests of Latin America."

We can stubbornly assert, taking a leaf from Galileo, that nonetheless the 1989 ban did work — at least as long as it was strictly observed. Explaining why, though, requires us to admit that a trade ban, and even trade regulation short of a ban, requires certain supporting circumstances if it is to have any real chance of success.

Any ban must be backed by the political will, resources and commitment needed to make it stick. The higher the price of the commodity, the more critical this becomes and the more difficult the trade is to control, but it can be done. In 2003, Esmond Martin and Daniel Stiles showed that increased law enforcement was helping to kill the ivory industry in Taiwan, where the industry was dying, and in South Korea, where it was already dead. For a commodity in international trade, that need for enforcement applies to producer countries, consumer countries and the points along the supply chain. This paradigm applies as much to the ivory trade as to the drug trade.

The key factor, though, may be the attitude of the consumer. Ivory is not cocaine. Its buyers in Japan and the West were not lining up in back alleys or meeting with dealers in the john. They wanted legal ivory, purchased through legitimate outlets. In that regard ivory was less like a drug than it was like an automobile. Though it is certainly possible to find a buyer for a "hot" car, most people in the market for an automobile want to make a legitimate purchase. The best way to make illegal ivory sellable was to convince customers that the product they were buying was, in fact, legal. Crooked dealers had to be able to launder their goods onto the legal market.

That is exactly what ivory smugglers were doing before the ban took effect. In the late 1980s, ivory with attached CITES permits had a market value four times higher than ivory alone. The permits that "proved" that the ivory they were attached to was legal were worth three times more than the ivory itself. Closing the legal markets, effectively making laundering impossible because there was no longer such a thing as newly imported legal ivory, was catastrophic for the illegal trade.

Once again, though, the evidence of history is that legal trade does not facilitate illegal trade but undermines it. Take away the smugglers' monopoly, keep prices under control, and the black market should wither and die — but that, too, depends on a number of assumptions. Can a legal, sustainable trade put enough ivory on the market at a lowered price to deprive illegal dealers of their customers? On the other hand, does the presence of legal ivory create more demand? If that demand rises high enough, might customers still turn to illegal sources, especially if they believe that they are buying legal stock?

That is what happened before the ban. Opponents of the trade argue that that is what happened again less than a decade later, in 1997, and again, with even worse results, in 2008, when a partial, temporary legal ivory trade was restored. The 1989 ban may have been a success, but as we shall see, it did not hold.

CHAPTER EIGHT

RHINOS UNDER FIRE

I It has become a truism that CITES has failed the world's rhinoceroses and that trade bans have done little or nothing to stop the flow of illegal horn. All rhinoceros species were listed on Appendix I by 1977, with little initial result. In 1987, a CITES Resolution, now repealed, admitted "that the efforts of the Parties, the Secretariat and other interested agencies have failed to stem the flow of illegal trade in rhinoceros products, particularly horn." It urged member countries to prohibit all internal and international sales and trade in rhino products except for "legitimate hunting trophies" with "appropriate full CITES documents," and to destroy "all government and parastatal stocks of rhinoceros horn" in return for "compensatory funds from external aid sources." A replacement resolution adopted in 1997 noted that the call for destruction "has not been implemented, and is no longer considered appropriate by a number of Parties." The national bans were slow in coming.

And yet, populations of the Greater One-horned Rhinoceros, East and South African Black Rhinoceros and, particularly, Southern White Rhinoceros are now higher than they were 20 years ago. Does that mean CITES has worked after all? Or are there other factors in play?

Around 1960 Black Rhinos could boast an estimated population of 100,000 animals, despite decades of legal trade involving the death of tens of thousands of animals. From 1849 to 1895, 11,000 kilograms of horn may have been exported from East Africa per year, amounting to a take of 170,000 rhinos. There were about 2,250 Northern White Rhinos in 1960; today, in the wild, there are none left. The Southern White Rhino, today by far the most numerous of its kind, in 1948 numbered only 550 animals — a handful, but well above the estimated 20 to 50 that remained at the end of the 1800s. A handful of Javan Rhinos, and numbers of Sumatran Rhinos, survived on the Asian mainland. Sumatran Rhinos probably numbered over a thousand during the 1950s; there were still an estimated 800–1,000 of them by the early 1980s. In its best-known haunts in the Chitwan Valley of Nepal, the Greater One-Horned Rhinoceros probably numbered more than 1,000 until the early 1950s.

In terms of sheer numbers, the most gut-wrenching tale is the decline of the Black Rhinoceros from the 1960s through the 1980s. When I first visited Africa in 1966, almost any conservationist you could have asked would have been far more concerned about the survival of the White Rhinoceros. An on- slaught of poaching, particularly during the 1970s, changed that picture with appalling rapidity. Numbers fell to 65,000 by 1970, 14,785 by 1980, 8,800 by 1984, 3,665 by 1987 and 3,450 by 1991. In 1992, after a 28 percent decline in a single year, there were only 2,475 left. The Black Rhinoceros had earned, in the words of Nigel Leader-Williams, "the dubious distinction of showing the fastest known rate of decline of any species of large mammal."

Poachers slaughtered every one of the thousands of animals that roamed the vast spaces of Kenya's Tsavo, then shifted south through the Selous in Tanzania to the Luangwa Valley of Zambia, where they had killed all of its es- timated 4,000–8,000 rhinos by the end of the 1980s. In 1970 there were Black Rhinos in 18 African countries, but by the early 1990s poaching had swept them from the Central African Republic, Ethiopia, Malawi, Somalia, Sudan and Uganda. Eighty-seven percent of the handful left in 1992 survived in only four countries: Kenya, Namibia, South Africa and Zimbabwe. By 1989, after heavily armed poachers rampaged through its national parks, Kenya retained only 2 percent of the rhinos it had had in 1970.

In Zimbabwe, the country with the highest remaining number of Black Rhinos by the end of the 1980s, the population crashed from a supposed 1,400 in 1991 (probably an overestimate) to only 430 a year later. Zimbabwe's rhinos fell, largely, to gangs of poachers raiding across the border from Zambia, a major hub for the illegal horn trade. Zambian poachers had wiped out most of their own rhinos by the early 1980s. After killing the animals in border areas along the Zambesi, they penetrated farther and farther, on longer poaching expeditions, deep into Zimbabwean territory. Tom Milliken and his colleagues, who chronicled the slaughter of Zimbabwe's rhinos, re- ported that "One poacher rather incredibly traveled on a public bus with his

AK-47 through communal lands adjacent to Matusadona National Park with no interference."

The Black Rhino had become the victim of forces at both ends of the market chain. In Africa, the emergence of newly independent countries in the 1960s gave local dealers a chance to break a monopoly on the horn business that had long been held by Indian traders. At the market end, a major trigger, at least in the 1970s, seems to have been the end of the civil war in North Yemen in 1969. Yemeni workers were now free to travel to Persian Gulf countries in search of higher-paying jobs, and they were ready to spend their newfound wealth on rhino-horn *jambiyas*. Yemen soon became the largest consumer of rhino horn in the world (see p. 41), and prices for horn rose sharply in both producer and consumer countries.

Horn continued to flow into China, Hong Kong, Taiwan and other eastern Asian markets. Much of it, apparently, was in the form of horn chips discarded by *jambiya* carvers in North Yemen, purchased by enterprising dealers and sent on to medicine markets farther east. From 1982 to 1986, according to the Ivory Trade Review Group (see p. 59), China imported 10,621 kilograms of African rhino horn (and 433 kilograms of the much higher-priced horn from Asian rhinos). The combination of a more fluid selling market in Africa and a host of newly affluent buyers looking for horn had become toxic, for the Black Rhinoceros in particular.

While Black Rhinoceros populations were collapsing in Africa, the Greater One-horned Rhinoceros was having problems of its own in India and Nepal. The population in Nepal's Chitwan Valley crashed even before the Black Rhino went into free fall, from an estimated 1,000 animals before 1950 to only about 100 by the mid-1960s. People had flooded into the region following successful malaria-eradication programs in the late 1950s, taking over land once occupied by the rhinos. Among the immigrants were experienced hunters, and poaching increased as rhinoceros habitat decreased. By 1968 there were only some 95 rhinos in the whole of Nepal.

The Nepali government responded by establishing the Royal Chitwan National Park in 1973, now a major tourist attraction (I was one of its first visitors in the year it was established), and replacing a poorly equipped rhino patrol with a division of the Royal Nepalese Army, beginning in 1976. The Royal Bardia National Park, established in 1988, protected another population farther west in the Nepal *terai*. Under military guard, the rhinos began to increase and poaching levels to fall. Although there was some serious poaching in the early 1990s, there was very little poaching in Chitwan, and none in Bardia, from 1994 to 1997. Horn prices on the world market remained stable, though high, during the mid-1990s, and that certainly helped, but Esmond Martin also credited stiffer penalties enacted in 1993 and the development of an effective anti-poaching and intelligence network, including rewards for informers and funding from outside organizations, around both parks.

In Kaziranga National Park, the chief stronghold of the Greater One-horned Rhinoceros in India, numbers overall rose from 366 animals in 1966 to about 1,552 in 1999. From 1989 to 1993, Kaziranga nonetheless lost at least 266 rhinos, more than 15 percent of its population, to a surge of poaching. Poachers shot the animals with everything from semi-automatic weapons to muzzle-loading sawed-off shotguns loaded with homemade lead slugs. They trapped them in concealed pits studded with sharpened bamboo stakes, and when the opportunity arose, they electrocuted them with wires slung over a nearby power line and left to dangle in the rhino's path. About the only techniques they didn't use regularly were spearing the animals, as poachers sometimes did in Nepal, or strangling them with a steel wire noose, a method more commonly used in Africa.

Back in Africa, the Northern White Rhinoceros continued its fatal decline (see p. 121). The story of the Southern White Rhinoceros, though, was proving to be very different. The apartheid regime in South Africa, with its lines of defense against the frontline states to the north and east, was largely proof against incursions by poachers. The surviving rhinos, under strict protection since the early years of the 20th century, slowly increased to 437 animals in 1953, then to 600 in 1960. They were confined to two adjacent game reserves in what is now northern Kwazulu-Natal, Umfolozi and Hluhluwe (now combined as Hluhluwe-iMfolozi Park).

In 1961, South Africa embarked on an intensive — and expensive — plan, dubbed "Operation Rhino," to put the Southern White Rhino on a better footing. It was spearheaded by Ian Player, brother to golfer Gary Player and, at the time, Warden of Umfolozi. Besides protecting the animals from poachers, the chief component of the strategy was to establish new rhino populations by translocating rhinos from the growing numbers in Umfolozi and Hluhluwe to reserves elsewhere in the country, including in its largest protected area, Kruger National Park.

Numbers rose to 1,800 by 1968 and then mushroomed upward. Translocated rhinos went to other countries in southern Africa and, in 1984, even outside the subspecies' natural range to Kenya and Zambia (animals were also sent to zoos in a number of foreign countries with the idea of building up a breeding nucleus). By 1992, the year the Black Rhino reached its lowest ebb, there were 5,790 wild Southern White Rhinoceroses, 5,297 of them in South Africa — a remarkable reversal of fortune, and a tribute to South Africa's wildlife managers. The situation of the Southern White Rhino continued to improve through the 1990s, as it has, in terms of sheer numbers, to the roughly 20,000 animals alive today.

The South African management program for the White Rhinoceros was not without its controversies. South Africa has a great number of game ranches, and numbers of White Rhinos were sold into private hands. This was an unorthodox idea at the time, but one that considerably increased the number of sites where rhinos could be established. Keeping rhinos on one's property can be an expensive proposition, and in order to provide private owners with an incentive to buy, and keep, the animals, the decision was made in 1968 to allow limited sale of rhino trophy hunting licenses. Whatever the merits of these approaches, they were to play a part in a bizarre scam that overtook some Southern White Rhinos in the new century (see p. 103).

The extermination of the Black Rhino in places like Tsavo had shown that as long as rhinos were free to roam over vast open spaces, there was no way to protect them. Conservationists focused their efforts on gathering rhinos into small, concentrated groups where they could be under close guard. Southern White Rhinos were already largely confined to small to medium-sized, mostly fenced areas, with the exception of the population in the Kruger. In the late 1980s, Kenya followed suit, placing its Black Rhinos in fenced sanctuaries, often on private land. By 1998, 28 percent of Kenya's 420 Black Rhinos were in private hands. By the early 1990s, Black Rhinos in South Africa and Namibia were also being allowed on private nature reserves. Zimbabwe established a system of Intensive Protection Zones, fenced areas within larger national parks or on other government land, and a generally successful custodianship scheme that transferred about 190 Black Rhinos from heavily poached areas in the Zambesi Valley to private ranches.

In the 1980s, the amount of horn landing on world markets seemed to decline. Nigel Leader-Williams, in his 1992 study of the global trade, reported that only three tonnes of horn per year came onto world markets between 1980 and 1985, compared to eight tonnes per year during the 1970s. Prices fluctuated during the decade, falling in some cities and then rising again from

1988 onwards. Were CITES controls making a difference? Or did Asian market countries already have such large stockpiles of horn — over four tonnes in China alone — that they could afford to import less? It is very difficult to say, but even Leader-Williams — no great admirer of CITES — had to admit that "CITES, other national bans and most other efforts have succeeded in slowing, but not in halting, the rhino horn trade for medicines in the far east."

Unexpectedly, after the low point of 1992, poaching levels also began to fall. Black and Greater One-horned Rhinoceros numbers started to recover — so much so that Esmond Martin and Lucy Vigne could write in 1997 of a "spectacular" reduction in poaching since 1993, and conclude that "Black Rhinoceros conservation is finally working."

The greatest credit for the difference surely deserves to be given to the rangers and game officers who risked their lives to protect rhinos on the ground. The anti-poaching patrols run by the Royal Nepalese Army, Operation Stronghold in Zimbabwe, the Endangered Species Unit established in 1989 in South Africa, and the newly reconstituted Kenya Wildlife Service — difficult and dangerous operations, every one — did much to bring poaching under control. Anti-poaching was serious business: in a number of countries, including Kenya and Zimbabwe, anti-poaching squads operated under controversial shoot-to-kill orders, and frequently they came under fire themselves.

Stiffer penalties for poaching, including increased fines and prison terms, helped to deter poachers in Namibia, South Africa and elsewhere. The maximum sentence for killing a rhino in Namibia rose from R6,000 and/or six years in prison to R200,000 (about $45,000) and a possible 20 years behind bars.

Meanwhile, demand in Asia began to drop. Key to this was China's decision, in May 1993, to ban trade in rhino horn and its derivatives. China had been under considerable pressure from the CITES Standing Committee, the United Nations Environmental Programme (UNEP) and foreign NGOs to do something about the horn trade. The United States had just certified China and Taiwan under the Pelly Amendment to the United States *Fishermen's Protective Act* for undermining CITES by allowing trade in rhino horn (and tiger products) to continue. China responded by issuing an official circular strictly prohibiting import and export of horn. It forbade selling, purchasing, transporting, carrying or mailing rhino horn, and stated that anything marked as containing rhino horn would be treated as though it actually did (a necessary move when much of the medicines labeled as containing horn were sold as powders). All stocks of horn were to be registered, sealed and properly kept, and dealers were given six months to get rid of their stocks, including medicines. Rhino horn was removed from the official Chinese pharmacopeia, and the government announced that it would be encouraging research on substitutes.

In 1989 Lucy Vigne and Esmond Martin named Taiwan, a major entrepôt for rhino horn trade that, because of its political status, was unable to join CITES, as "the greatest threat to the survival of Africa's rhinos." Trade had been banned in 1992 but still flourished openly. A damning EIA report in 1993 named the island as the major eastern Asian importer of horn, causing a sensation in the local press after its release in Taipei. In response to the furor, Taiwan publicly burned 19 confiscated rhino horns and more than 700 kilograms of ivory in June 1993. In 1994, China followed suit, burning 450 kilograms of horn (from a one-tonne stockpile amassed by a Taiwanese syndicate and purchased by a government-owned pharmaceutical company in south China) before a high-level CITES delegation in Guangzhou.

Enforcement against the Taiwan trade was still poor despite the fire. In August 1994, Bill Clinton became the first (and so far only) president to impose sanctions under a Pelly certification: about $25 million worth, against Taiwanese exports of all CITES-listed specimens, including coral, mollusk-shell jewelry, and lizard- snake- and crocodile-skin shoes and other leather products. In the wake of Clinton's sanctions, Taiwanese officials instituted a three-year crackdown on the trade. Maximum fines and penalties for trading in rare wildlife were raised, and in response the United States lifted its sanctions in June 1995. South Korea and Vietnam enacted their own bans on domestic sale in 1993 and 1994 (following South Korean bans on imports in 1983 and 1986). Japan, which had officially removed rhinoceros horn from medicinal prescriptions in 1980, issued a ban on horn and easily identified horn products in 1995.

The bans did not entirely eradicate the underground market, but the results on the ground were tangible. Except during the early 1990s, poaching levels in Kaziranga fell from 29 animals per year between 1980 and 1997 to an annual average of only five between 1998 and 2004. Numbers of Greater One-horned Rhinos continued to climb in Nepal despite the Maoist insurgency of the late 1990s and early 2000s, which saw losses of perhaps 200 animals to poachers and the abandonment and destruction of most anti-poaching outposts in the country's rhino parks.

A 2007 report to CITES by IUCN and TRAFFIC showed that the overall population of Southern White Rhinoceros had risen steadily from 1991 to

2005, from just under 6,000 to 14,550, while Black Rhino numbers, after bottoming out at 2,410 in 1995, had climbed to 3,725 by the end of the same period. Poaching overall remained at low levels. An average of only 56 poached carcasses per year was reported between 2002 and 2005. The report concluded that, in both Africa and Asia, the greatest conservation successes had "occurred in stable political and economic situations where governments have demonstrated significant political will, providing sufficient resources to enable dedicated staff to undertake effective field conservation" (noting, of course, that "this all costs money").

The CITES ban, despite its naysayers, seemed to be having at least a contributory effect. As Tom Milliken and Jo Shaw reported for TRAFFIC in 2012, "CITES served as the global vehicle for focusing international action and systematically pushing major consuming countries in Asia and the Middle East to instigate and implement rhino horn trade bans ... by the mid-1990s, almost all major traditional consuming countries/territories in Asia, including China, Hong Kong, Japan, South Korea and Taiwan, had rhino horn trade bans in place." Yemen, after 15 years of attempts to persuade it to join CITES, had finally acceded to the Convention in 1997, and its role as one of the major markets for rhino horn had already begun to diminish (see p. 42).

There were, of course, still problems. The 2007 report concluded that "poaching for rhino horn remains the main threat to rhinos in Africa, and this has already led to the serious decline of Northern White Rhino in the Democratic Republic of the Congo and the feared extinction of the Western Black Rhino in Cameroon. Further, targeted rhino poaching, and loss of rhinos to collateral and targeted snare injuries is threatening rhino conservation efforts in Zimbabwe, and to a lesser extent in other range States." But, for many rhino populations, it had been far worse. At long last, in the early years of the new century, rhino conservationists began to breathe a cautious sigh of relief.

It was the eye of the storm.

PART TWO

WHAT WENT WRONG?

CHAPTER NINE

RE-OPENING THE TRADE

As recently as ten years ago, out of every ten African elephants that died, four fell at the hands of poachers. The figure today is eight. Officially, the CITES ivory ban is still in place. Most elephant populations remain on Appendix I, and even those countries whose populations have been transferred to Appendix II cannot sell ivory today. Many in these countries feel that the ban still constrains them and, by restricting their ability to sell ivory legally, hands the trade over to the black market and hobbles elephant conservation. They can point, with some justification, to Michael 't Sas-Rolfes's 1997 prediction that "The ivory trade ban is likely to prove unsustainable and even counterproductive in the longer term," and argue that the resurgence of elephant poaching since that time has proved him right.

Those of us who support the ban argue, however, that it was crippled in 1997 and dealt a fatal blow in 2008, and that we — and the elephants — have been paying the price for our mistake ever since. Here is what happened.

During the 1990s, poaching of African elephants was nowhere near the levels of the 1980s, when poachers in Kenya alone were killing at least two thousand elephants annually. By 1995, KWS director David Western was able to report to *The Times* that only 35 Kenyan elephants had been poached that year. In 2000, a study of ivory markets in Africa showed that ivory sales, and prices, had declined or even collapsed almost everywhere on the continent since the ban. Sales of ivory in South Africa had fallen by 80 percent, and the price of raw ivory in Zimbabwe (sold legally to local buyers by the Department of Parks and Wildlife) had dropped by 85 percent from

1989 levels. A 2003 follow-up study in Côte d'Ivoire, Senegal and Nigeria found even smaller amounts of ivory on local markets, except in Nigeria, one of the few places in which Martin and Stiles had recorded a price increase.

Nonetheless, the ivory ban — instead of being hailed as one of the conservation success stories of the century — became the victim of remarkably bad press. It was portrayed as an imposition by Western-dominated preservationists on Africans seeking control of their own resources. Despite the fact that far more African countries opposed re-opening the ivory trade than supported it, its opponents claimed repeatedly that the ban had been forced down the throats of unwilling Africans by Western animal-loving "bunnyhuggers."

Pro-ban countries, in particular Kenya, were portrayed as the tools, or dupes, of Western "animal rights" organizations. The best answer to this was made by Richard Leakey at the 1992 CITES meeting: "I would like to appeal to our colleagues from the proponent countries not to continue to believe that this initiative to keep elephants on Appendix I is a foreign initiative. It is an African concern, and we as Africans in the majority at this meeting truly and firmly believe that that course of action is the correct action. To say that we are being manipulated externally is an insult to our intelligence."

The five southern African countries that had taken reservations against the Appendix I listing for African elephants — Zimbabwe, Zambia, Malawi, Botswana and South Africa — were joined in 1990 by a sixth, Namibia, when it became independent and acceded to CITES. South Africa, still under its apartheid regime, pursued its own policies, but on June 20, 1991, Zimbabwe, Zambia, Botswana, Malawi and Namibia signed an agreement creating the Southern African Centre for Ivory Marketing (SACIM, later renamed the Southern African Convention on Wildlife Management). They thus became the only CITES Parties to set up a formal plan for marketing products the treaty had banned from international commercial trade. Any ivory the SACIM countries sold was to be marketed through a common floor in Gaborone, Botswana. The problem was finding a buyer.

Taking reservations meant that the SACIM countries did not have to observe the ban themselves. As long as the ban lasted, though, they could sell ivory only to countries that were not CITES Parties, or to other countries that had also taken reservations. By then there were very few such countries left. After 1991, the only other Parties with reservations were Malawi and South Africa, and under CITES rules no new reservations are possible except for countries joining for the first time. If the SACIM countries wanted to sell ivory to their most valuable former customers, like Japan or the United States, they had to overturn the ban, at least for their own populations.

In preparation for the 1992 CITES meeting in Kyoto, Japan, the SACIM countries drew up proposals to have their elephant populations transferred back to Appendix II — as did South Africa for its population. With the formal procedure under way, they launched a publicity campaign to convince the world that the ivory ban had been a mistake. They pointed out that elephant populations, in Zimbabwe and Botswana at least, were large and growing, and Zimbabwe claimed that it needed the money from ivory revenues to fund conservation and to benefit local people.

A few months before the meeting, the government of Kenneth Kaunda fell in Zambia, a country particularly identified as a center for illegal trade in ivory. In January 1992 the new government announced that Zambia would drop its reservation and withdraw from SACIM. Once a ban opponent, Zambia now became a leader in the fight to maintain it.

By the time the CITES Parties met in March 1992, evidence was beginning to mount that lifting the ban, even locally, would spur the return of large-scale poaching. There was an upsurge of poaching in Kenya for the first time since 1989. Dealers were reportedly scouting for new customers in Asia even before the meeting opened. A shipment of smuggled ivory was confiscated in Kobe, Japan, while the meeting was going on — prompting accusations that the ivory had been planted by pro-ban activists to derail the vote!

Despite complimentary statements from the Panel of Experts (see p. 62) about the health and management of elephant populations in SACIM countries, there were serious concerns about the crucial issue of controls against ivory smuggling. Norbert Mumba, head of the Zambia Species Protection Department, was particularly blunt. "Departments of Customs in all the states in the subregion are extremely important if trade has to be monitored effectively," he said during the debate. "Today, I can tell you, Mr. Chairman, that most of the customs officers don't even know the difference between an elephant tusk and a banana."

Not a single African country, other than the proponents, supported the downlisting proposals. Faced with this opposition (or, if you like, "entrenched protectionist provisions from influential industrialized nations"), the southern African countries withdrew.

At the 1994 CITES meeting, both South Africa and Sudan proposed downlisting their populations. The Sudanese proposal, seeking permission to sell its ivory stockpile, was poorly justified and failed to win support. The South African proposal, though restricted to sales of meat and hides, made it clear that ivory would be on the table at the next meeting. Once again there were minor upsurges of poaching, particularly in Zambia.

This time, though, there was no lengthy debate. South Africa met privately with other African delegations, who made it clear that they would not support any listing change for elephants. Instead, they agreed to support another South African proposal, for a limited downlisting of its population of White Rhinoceroses. With this quid pro quo established, South Africa withdrew its proposal.

The 1997 CITES meeting was held in Harare, Zimbabwe, in the heart of opposition to the ban. Botswana, Namibia and Zimbabwe lobbied heavily for retransfer of their populations to Appendix II. Trade was to be restricted to live animals and hunting trophies and to ivory, to be sold, in a one-time-only controlled sale from government stockpiles, directly to a country to be approved as a buyer by the CITES Standing Committee — in this case, obviously, Japan. Japan agreed that the ivory would not be re-exported, and the proponents promised to drop their reservations if they succeeded. Zimbabwe, in addition, asked to trade in elephant hides, valued for leather boots and similar products.

The stockpile issue was a serious one. Huge stockpiles of confiscated ivory lay in government warehouses throughout Africa. It was easy to understand the desire to realize a profit on them. Stockpiled ivory, though, posed the same threat as ivory from a freshly killed elephant: once it was on the market, distinguishing it from smuggled ivory would be impossible. Most African countries were very uneasy about permitting its sale.

The Panel of Experts reported that Zimbabwe's control of its local ivory trade was "grossly inadequate." Despite local laws restricting exports to personal effects, tonnes of stockpiled Zimbabwean ivory — including large commercial shipments of signature seals — had been sent to Japan, China, Thailand, Hong Kong, the Philippines, Indonesia, the United States and South Africa. According to *The Times* of November 29, 1996, "The findings effectively demolish Zimbabwe's hopes of winning a reversal of the ban."

Doubts were cast on Japan's ability to prevent smugglers from operating once legal ivory appeared on its markets. A major Japanese ivory dealer, who admitted to having dealt in illegal ivory in the past, sent a statement to the December 1996 meeting of the CITES Standing Committee stating that a new control system implemented in Japan would encourage smuggling. He pointed out that once ivory had entered Japan and had a registration sticker placed on it, there would be no way of distinguishing legal ivory from illegal.

The southern Africans, though, had compelling arguments of their own. Proponents of "sustainable use" argued that if wildlife was not given economic value, land-hungry people in poor countries would be unwilling to allow it to survive. Elephants were raiding crops, damaging farmers' fields and, in too many cases, killing people. A restored ivory trade, according to the SACIM countries, could provide benefits that would prevent a much more serious battle between humans and elephants.

Zimbabwe made much of a program called CAMPFIRE (Communal Areas Management Programme for Indigenous Resources). CAMPFIRE, established in the 1980s, was designed to give local communities a share in both the management of their wildlife and the profits that might be derived from it. Ninety percent came from big-game hunting safaris, with more than 60 percent contributed by elephant hunts. Zimbabwe now argued that ivory sales should be added to the mix (even though its pre-ban ivory revenues had gone not to earmarked conservation programs or local community organizations but directly into the central treasury, and in any case most of Zimbabwe's elephants did not live in CAMPFIRE districts).

There were stories that Zimbabwean president Robert Mugabe, who opened the meeting with a fiery speech, had personally called in favors from other African leaders to secure a pro-Zimbabwe vote. When the Tanzanian government ordered its delegation to switch its vote, Costa Mlay, Director General of the Serengeti Wildlife Institute and a long-time fierce opponent of the ivory trade, told me with tears in his eyes that he had been betrayed by his superiors. In the end the proposals passed. Rejoicing crowds danced and sang in the streets of Harare.

After further approval by the CITES Standing Committee and verification by the Secretariat, the one-time "experimental" sale, the first legal shipment of ivory to Japan in ten years, took place in 1999. Nearly 50 tonnes of ivory from Botswana, Namibia and Zimbabwe, marked, inspected and sealed, left Africa in July in return for nearly $4.7 million. What happened next is equivocal, and its interpretation rather depends on who is reporting it. A few vendors and ivory craftsmen in West and Central Africa told Esmond Martin and Daniel Stiles that they saw the sale as a sign that the CITES ban would soon be lifted and the market would revive, but their counterparts in South and Southeast

Asia, interviewed by the same investigators, never mentioned it. In general, ivory traders and dealers told Martin and Stiles that the sale had had no perceptible effect on their business. Japan continued to seize shipments of illegal ivory, and in 2002 Singapore intercepted a contraband shipment of more than six tonnes (see p. 93), the largest single seizure since the 1989 ban. In Taiwan, the retail market for ivory declined between 1997 and 2002.

Did the 1997 downlisting and the 1999 sale send a signal to the poachers and dealers of this world that the ivory ban was nearing its end? Did it legitimize the sale of illegal ivory in Japan, at least in buyers' eyes? Did it spur ivory smuggling to other destinations, including the country that was fast becoming the biggest market for contraband ivory, China? The arguments raged on both sides, but as it is always difficult to prove that one event caused another, there may be no final answer. The ban, though, had been broken, and from that point on the possibility of more legal ivory was very much on the table.

The next few CITES meetings featured calls for new sales from southern Africa, countered by concerns from other African countries that the downlisting and sale might have contributed to a new poaching initiative. South Africa submitted a new proposal to downlist its population in 2000, and Botswana, Namibia and Zimbabwe asked for further sales. Kenya and India countered with a move to return all elephant populations to Appendix I. The South African proposal was accepted only after an amendment setting a zero quota for ivory exports. The other proposals were withdrawn.

At the 2002 meeting in Chile, Zambia, now back in the pro-trade camp with most other members of the Southern African Development Community (SADC), asked unsuccessfully for its population to be transferred to Appendix II. A proposal for further ivory trade from Zimbabwe was defeated, and a repeat of the 2000 proposal from Kenya and India was withdrawn. However, the Parties did agree to allow a further one-off sale to Japan from Botswana, Namibia and South Africa, to be delayed until at least May 2004 to allow for a number of checks, including analysis of baseline data from MIKE (Monitoring the Illegal Killing of Elephants), a program established at the 1997 meeting (see p. 94).

At the 2004 meeting in Bangkok, Namibia asked not for a one-off sale but for an annual quota of 2,000 kilograms of raw ivory (accumulated from "natural management-related mortalities") and unlimited commercial exports of worked ivory. That idea was overwhelmingly rejected, but the Parties accepted an amendment that allowed Namibia to export *ekipas*, hand-carved buttons traditionally made by Namibia's Ukwanyama tribe, frequently from elephant ivory, and valued as tourist souvenirs and collectors' items. Ivory *ekipas* could be exported for non-commercial purposes as long as they were "individually marked and certified" and "incorporated in finished jewelry." Though the amended proposal succeeded, an investigation by the David Shepherd Wildlife Foundation revealed that Namibia's promised control system had not been implemented and that ivory from other countries had been smuggled into the country to take advantage of the *ekipa* market. The Namibian Ministry of Environment and Tourism placed a moratorium on *ekipa* sales in September 2008.

Meanwhile, the sale approved in 2002 had yet to take place. Although no specific importing country had been named in the 2002 proposals, the obvious customer was Japan, and its status as a buyer was approved in 2006. Activists continued to raise concerns about whether the Japanese ivory control system, which among other perceived weaknesses did not require private owners to register whole tusks, was tight enough to prevent smuggled ivory from being mixed with legally imported stock. Their concerns carried little weight with the CITES Standing Committee.

Now, however, as the 2007 meeting approached, China emerged as a potential buyer. Unlike Japan, China shared borders with many other countries and was a known destination for illegal wildlife products smuggled in through Vietnam, Myanmar and other neighboring states. Large amounts of illegal ivory had already been recorded entering the country, and the ivory market in China was burgeoning. The Environmental Investigation Agency (EIA) alleged that China had "the largest illegal ivory trade of any nation in the world." Whatever control problems existed in Japan, it seemed that the situation in China could be exponentially worse.

The 2007 CITES meeting nonetheless approved the biggest one-off sale yet. To the 50,000 kilograms in ivory exports already approved in 2002 (20,000 kilograms from Botswana, 10,000 kilograms from Namibia and 30,000 kilograms from South Africa) was added "government-owned ivory from Botswana, Namibia, South Africa and Zimbabwe registered by 31 January 2007 and verified by the Secretariat." As long as those countries registered in time, they could top up the sale with their entire government stockpiles of ivory. In return, in a deal hailed as a consensus-building compromise, the Parties agreed to a "moratorium" on any further requests to sell ivory from populations already on Appendix II, to run for nine years from the date the sale took place. In return for allowing southern Africa to clear out its stockpiles, the anti-trade countries in Africa assumed that they were buying a "resting peri-od" during which the effects of the sale could be assessed, and a break for both elephants and elephant-weary CITES delegates.

Unfortunately, though the African range countries agreed to this deal by consensus, some of them apparently failed to understand the fine print. The mor-atorium deal may not have been enforceable in the first place, as countries have a sovereign right to put forward any proposals they like. The words "from popula-tions already on Appendix II" left open the possibility that countries whose pop-ulations were still on Appendix I could propose transferring them to Appendix II before the nine years were up. That is, of course, exactly what happened.

At the 2010 meeting, despite cries that they were betraying the "spirit" of the moratorium, both Tanzania and Zambia put forward downlisting propos-als. A protest published in *Science* by 26 prominent elephant biologists and conservationists argued that most of Africa lacked adequate controls for the protection of elephants. The Environmental Investigation Agency alleged that illegal ivory was widely available in both countries, controls were minimal at best and government officials were reportedly implicated in poaching and il-legal trade. Both bids were rejected. Tanzania submitted a further proposal in October 2012 for consideration at the 2013 meeting, but withdrew it in December (see p. 146). The "resting period" was a phantom.

In July 2008, with the support of conservation organizations including WWF and TRAFFIC — but in the face of outraged objections from other environ-mentalists and organizations, including the Born Free Foundation, EIA and the International Fund for Animal Welfare (IFAW) — the Standing Committee approved China's status as a buyer and gave its approval to the combined sale. The United Kingdom tried to defer sales from Zimbabwe "until such time as a legitimate, democratically elected government based on the outcome of the elections on 29 March has replaced the current regime," but without success.

That November, 101,767 tonnes of ivory were sold at auction, 39,434 tonnes going to Japan and 62,333 tonnes to China, netting the four exporting countries $15,430,777 — far less than the ivory was probably worth, thanks to alleged price-fixing between the Japanese and Chinese buyers. The shipments reached their destinations in the spring of 2009. Once again there was (and there continues to be) considerable disagreement about the effect of this mas-sive sale. This time, though — whatever its cause — there could be no question about what was happening to the rate of poaching and illegal trade.

It was on its way up.

CHAPTER TEN

NEW MARKETS FOR HORN

In the early years of the new century, it would have been easy to assume that rhinoceros conservation was well in hand. Except for the very rarest subspecies, populations were rising. Anti-poaching measures were working well in a number of countries, and poaching in Africa seemed to be under control at last. The *jambiya* market in Yemen appeared to be dying out and the formidable demand for traditional medicine in China seemed to be receding.

South Africa's White Rhinoceros population was transferred to Appendix II in 1994, after unsuccessful proposals by South Africa (for White Rhinos only) and Zimbabwe (for both its species) in 1992. Trade in horn remained illegal, although South Africa sought, without success, to remove that restriction in 1997. In 2004, Swaziland's White Rhino population was downlisted, on the same basis as for South Africa (for hunting trophies and trade in live animals "to appropriate and acceptable destinations"). South Africa and Namibia each won permission to allow trophy hunts of five Black Rhinoceroses per year (allowable under CITES rules even though the species stayed on Appendix I).

Then the slaughter, unexpectedly, began again. In 2009, the SSC and TRAFFIC were still able to report growing population figures to CITES — 17,475 White Rhinos and 4,230 Blacks by 2007 (20,170 and 4,880 by December 2010). Of the countries with the largest populations, only Zimbabwe showed a decline in rhino numbers. The poaching story, though, had grown considerably grimmer. Poaching had "markedly escalated" in the previous two years, with the far rarer Black Rhino accounting for more than half of the 470 rhinos known to have been killed.

Ninety-five percent of the killings took place in Zimbabwe and South Africa — two countries that had become "the epicentre of an unrelenting poaching crisis in southern Africa." Zimbabwe's rhino custodianship scheme (see p. 71) had already been overwhelmed by land invasion and general lawlessness, and poaching levels were already high enough to threaten all the population gains achieved there since the mid-1990s. Its losses amounted to 26 percent of the entire living rhino population, and 89 per cent of all the Black Rhinos killed in Africa.

In South Africa, a country that had been rightfully applauded for its successes with both White and Black Rhinos, the wave of poaching came as a particular shock. Between 1990 and 2007, there had never been more than 36 rhinos poached in any one year. The number was often much lower than that: five in 1991, six in 1996 and 1997, nine in 2001 — only 234 in all. In 2008, the country lost 83 rhinos to poaching. After that, the totals spiked with alarming speed: 122 in 2009, 333 in 2010, 448 in 2011 and a horrifying 668 rhinos killed by poachers in 2012. Richard Emslie, Scientific Officer of the IUCN SSC African Rhino Specialist Group, predicted in 2012 that if the carnage continued to increase at that rate, coupled with the growing number killed by sport hunters, overall rhino numbers in South Africa could start to fall by 2018 if not earlier.

Nearly 60 percent of the animals poached in 2012 were killed in Kruger National Park — not surprisingly, as more than half of South Africa's rhinos live there and the park shares a long border with Mozambique and Zimbabwe. A skilled poacher from Mozambique can be hailed as a hero on his return from a successful rhino hunt in the Kruger. The government deployed security forces into the park to deal with the problem, including members of the South African National Defence Force. A ranger strike from February through April may have contributed to the high kill numbers in early 2012.

Poachers, local or foreign, are increasingly well trained. Snares and spears are being replaced by heavy-caliber weapons and, in Mozambique, South Africa and Zimbabwe, by quiet killing techniques that use veterinary immobilizing drugs, poison, crossbows and, increasingly, weapons fitted with silencers. As the authors of the 2009 report pointed out, "This points to a growing and cunning sophistication in the illicit procurement of rhino horns and the involvement of marksmen with specialized skills and equipment." In response, professional anti-poaching units, often staffed with ex-military personnel, now offer service packages to help private rhino owners protect their animals.

The South African crisis has apparently spawned a new breed of poacher: "khaki-collar criminals," renegades from the wildlife industry, primarily whites from the Afrikaans community. They include landowners, wildlife veterinarians and game-capture professionals, killing on private land with military-style crossbows and heavy-caliber rifles that can stop a rhino or an elephant in its tracks. Dawie Groenewald, accused of being a kingpin in the trade, operated a safari tour company. In 2010 twenty rhino carcasses, their horns missing, were found buried on his property. In 2011 charges were brought against eight men accused of supplying M99 (etorphine), a drug used to dart rhinos for dehorning operations — ironically, to protect them from poachers — to a rhino poaching syndicate. Charges against five of the men were withdrawn in April 2012, to the fury of South African animal activists, but the three that remained included Dr. Douw Grobler, a world-famous wildlife professional and former head of Kruger National Park's wildlife capturing and veterinary services unit. Grobler had been fired from the Kruger in 2003 for alleged illegal transactions.

The horns from the new poachers' kills pass through a tightly organized network of "runners" who coordinate with the poachers by cell phone. The runners transfer their goods through a series of hands to South African businessmen, who sell them to the criminal syndicates that transfer the horns to end markets in Asia. A horn can be available in Asia within 24 hours of the time the rhinoceros that bore it was killed or maimed in South Africa. In 2012, David Mabunda, Chief Executive of the South African national conservation agency SANParks, said that the fight against rhino poachers in his country could now "rightfully be called a low-intensity war."

This insidious and sophisticated criminal network has been made possible by soaring prices. Rhino horn is now regularly said to be worth more than gold, or on a par with cocaine. An entirely new, affluent and growing market for rhinoceros horn has arisen, not in China or Yemen (though there are rumors, denied by China's CITES authorities, that a substantial market for horn as a tangible investment asset exists in China) but across the Chinese border in Vietnam. This is the message of an extensive report, released in August 2012, written for TRAFFIC by Tom Milliken and Jo Shaw. Its title pulls no punches: *The South Africa–Viet Nam Rhino Horn Trade Nexus: A Deadly Combination of Institutional Lapses, Corrupt Wildlife Industry Professionals and Asian Crime Syndicates*. Its authors, fearing a "progressive poaching conflagration" that could threaten every rhino population on the planet, state unequivocally that "The emergent rhino horn trade between South Africa and Viet Nam stands as the most serious challenge to rhino conservation in Africa over the past 15 years and threatens to undermine decades of conservation achievement."

Once a war-ravaged backwater, Vietnam has become one of the new powerhouses of Asia. It has a population of over 90 million people and a per capita income that has more than quadrupled in the past decade and a half. It has a rising and increasingly affluent middle class eager for the very latest in luxury goods. One of the best ways for a Vietnamese to flaunt wealth and success is "face consumption": consuming, preferably where others of wealth and status can see you do so, something rare and expensive. For the young, rich and status-conscious in Vietnam, rhinoceros horn has become the party drug of choice, an ingredient in "the alcoholic drink of millionaires" according to a Vietnamese website. It is taken by local and visiting businessmen and members of so-called "rhino wine associations" to prevent or cure hangovers. Its popularity, of course, has nothing to do with whether it actually works. Its users either don't know about the environmental consequences of their favorite habit or, more likely, don't care. "In sum," Milliken and Shaw conclude, "young, affluent, habitual users of rhino horn are, generally speaking, the most superficial, one could argue mindless, consumers in Viet Nam, but probably account for the greatest volume of rhino horns consumed in the country today."

A step up (perhaps) from this devastating frivolity is the use of rhino horn as a special, expensive "gift of life," an ideal way to curry favor with business partners or political officials. In one well-publicized case in 2010, Nguyen Van Khoe, Chairman of the Hoc Mon District People's Committee, was sentenced to 26 years in prison for accepting a bribe that included, besides money, part of a rhinoceros horn valued at $10,000. The outcome is unusual — not, unfortunately, because the official had rhino horn in his possession, but because he was punished for it. Usually nothing is done.

Horn has even been used as a down payment on a new luxury car. Oddly enough, now that the traditional Western idea that Asians use rhino horn as an aphrodisiac has been thoroughly debunked, some Vietnamese men have started to buy it as a sexual stimulant and a cure for impotence. One Vietnamese Internet site has claimed that rhino horn is "more effective than Viagra allowing men to have sex for two to four hours." Has the Western myth returned to Vietnam in the guise of a marketing ploy?

For other Vietnamese, rhino horn has become something far more precious — a cure for cancer. The growing belief in rhino horn as a cancer cure was all the more unexpected because it had nothing to do with the age-old role of horn in Oriental medicine. Vietnamese medical tradition has long valued rhinoceros horn for many of the same reasons it has been used in China: to control high fevers and convulsions and as a purge for bodily toxins. Though it has been removed from the traditional pharmacopeia in China, practitioners still recommend rhinoceros horn in Vietnam for diseases ranging from epilepsy to measles. Middle-class young mothers may keep rhino horn on hand to treat their children. Its import, of course, is illegal, but that seems to have little effect on backdoor purchases, often arranged through personal connections.

The idea that rhino horn can cure cancer appears to have started as a modern Vietnamese urban myth, though it is increasingly believed elsewhere in eastern Asia. It is hyped by dealers selling their illicit goods at high prices to desperate customers. Rhino horn "touts," including hospital staff members, have been reported prowling the halls of cancer wards, flogging their goods to frightened and terminally ill people and their families. Stories have spread that important persons — politicians or celebrities — have been miraculously cured, or their cancers remitted, by taking rhinoceros horn. These beliefs have been debunked by a number of practitioners in Vietnam, but they have been endorsed, without supporting evidence, by some physicians and by officials of the highly influential Vietnam Oriental Traditional Medicine Association.

Today, after a surge of demand that began about a decade ago, Vietnam has become the number one end market in the world for rhino horn. Perhaps 80 to 90 percent of the "rhino horn" offered for sale in Vietnam, particularly in traditional medicine shops, is part of a widespread and brisk trade in fakes, usually cleverly carved horn from a Water Buffalo, a fact that makes it harder to track trade in the real thing but emphasizes how eager Vietnamese consumers are to get their hands on the stuff.

Vietnam is a Party to CITES, and trade in rhino horn is supposedly illegal under Vietnamese law. Nonetheless, Milliken and Shaw report that it is relatively easy to buy rhino horn (real and fake) in Vietnam, including over the Internet. Most of the genuine article comes from South African animals, and particularly from its growing population of Southern White Rhinos. It reaches Vietnam through a variety of transit countries, including Laos in Asia and Mozambique in Africa. Vietnamese Customs has seized horns coming into the country, but the seizures have not been followed by prosecutions or further investigations. Vietnam reported only 11 seizures between 2003 and September

2012, though there is considerable evidence that increasing amounts of horn were flowing from South Africa to Vietnam at the time.

Vietnamese nationals within South Africa appear to be "strongly implicated" in the trade. Milliken and Shaw cite specific cases of Vietnamese embassy personnel involved in smuggling. First Secretary Vu Moc Anh was filmed by the South African news program *50/50* in September 2008 passing rhino horns to a known smuggler outside the embassy in Pretoria. She was recalled, but the Vietnamese Foreign Affairs Ministry later claimed that she was only helping the dealer "review his papers."

Not all the smuggled horns have come from poached animals. Some, probably several hundred in all, have been stolen or removed from private and public stockpiles, often built up with horns deliberately removed by the animals' owners. In 2009, there was an attempted armed theft of horn stocks from a government store in Addo National Park. Until a national moratorium on internal trade in horn was declared in 2011, some horns from private stocks appear to have been sold by their owners to South African citizens, who then transferred them to foreign buyers. It has even been suggested that, by closing this semi-legal loophole, the moratorium may have directly contributed to poaching levels in South Africa.

Outside of South Africa, there have been thefts of rhino horns and horn artifacts from museums, galleries and private collections in a number of European countries (see p. 126). Still more were imported "legally" as a by-product of the deliberate misuse of South Africa's trophy-hunting program (see p. 103). The result is "massive illegal activity managed at local, national, regional and international levels by organized crime syndicates."

The Vietnamese government, perhaps not surprisingly, has dismissed the entire 176-page TRAFFIC report as "not objective and evidence-based," claiming instead that "rhino horn is not used in Vietnam but rather it arrives in transit to a third country." The CITES Standing Committee had put Vietnam on notice that it was to report on what progress it had made in dealing with illegal trade and the local black market in rhinoceros horn. Perhaps not coincidentally, the Committee's deadline coincided with the Vietnamese denial that it had a problem.

If not willing to admit actual complicity, Vietnam was at least willing, in the words of Nguyen Ba Ngai, Deputy Director General of Viet Nam's Administration of Forestry, Agriculture and Rural Development, to "join hands with global efforts" to combat illegal trade. It was already engaged — after heavy lobbying from activists — in negotiations with South Africa, aimed

at signing a memorandum of understanding (MoU) on biodiversity conservation and protection that would bind the two countries to cooperate in the fight
against poaching and illegal trade. The MoU hit a snag in October 2012, when
a signing ceremony scheduled at a meeting of the United Nations Convention
on Biological Diversity in Hyderabad, India, had to be called off because the
Vietnamese minister scheduled to sign the document failed to show up. The
signing eventually took place in Hanoi, on December 10, 2012. Since then,
Vietnam has issued a circular banning government officers (according to an
unofficial translation) from buying, selling, giving or receiving rhino products, and a Presidential Decision barring exports of African rhino and elephant products for commercial use. We can only hope that this is the start of
real change.

CHAPTER ELEVEN

BEHIND
THE SURGE

Today the global ivory trade is back with a vengeance. Perhaps the first unequivocal evidence that things were changing came in late June 2002, when a shipping container was seized in Singapore. In February 2002, authorities in Malawi had raided a carving factory that was supposedly using legal Malawian ivory for domestic sale. They discovered, along with far more ivory than the factory was supposed to have, records showing 19 shipments out of the country over the previous nine years. The latest shipment had yet to sail, and by June authorities had tracked it to Beira in Mozambique. From there, it was loaded onto a ship for Durban, South Africa, and transferred to another ship bound for Singapore. Singapore authorities had just four hours' notice to move in before the ship docked.

Concealed inside the container they found more than 6.5 tonnes of contraband ivory, including 532 tusks of various sizes, some marked "Yokohama" (indicating that they were bound for Japan), and 42,120 carved *hankos*. It was the largest seizure since the ban in 1989. DNA analyses led by Dr. Sam Wasser of the University of Washington, the leading authority on genetic tracking of ivory, traced the haul to Savanna Elephants probably killed in or near Zambia and smuggled into Malawi. Ivory dealers were not only back in business but were part of a well-organized, elaborate smuggling and marketing network with a growing list of customers.

More seizures followed. On July 3, 2006, customs officials in Taiwan noticed that documents for two shipping containers in the port of Kaohsiung, en route from Tanzania to the Philippines, claimed that they were carrying sisal fiber. Suspicious that anyone would ship sisal to the Philippines, one of the largest sisal producers in the world, they opened the containers. Inside were 1,094 African elephant tusks, weighing 5.2 tonnes in all. Five days later, Hong Kong authorities, responding to a fire alarm, found seven people cutting and packing another 2.6 tonnes of ivory.

On August 28, 2006, Japanese customs agents seized a further 2.8 tonnes. It was the largest ivory seizure ever reported in Japan: enough pieces to make 260 whole tusks, and 17,928 blank ivory *hankos*. Japan failed to report the seizure to the CITES Standing Committee, which was in the process of deciding whether to approve Japan as a legal buyer for the one-off sale approved in 2002. The story did not come out until it was broken by the *Asahi Shimbun* newspaper that October. One man was eventually convicted of smuggling, but he received only a suspended sentence and a fine amounting to less than one percent of the ivory's estimated street value.

Elephants, as Iain Douglas-Hamilton put it in 2009, were in for tough times ahead. Ivory prices on the black market were already rising rapidly. They doubled again between 2007 and 2009, reaching a reported $6,500 per kilogram in southern China by March 2008. In Kenya, ivory poaching in 2008 doubled 2007 levels. Black-market ivory prices around Samburu in northern Kenya, where Douglas-Hamilton has been studying the local population for over 15 years, doubled from 2007 to 2012. In Zakouma National Park in Chad, home to a multi-million-euro conservation project, elephant numbers dropped from 3,800 in 2006 to just over 600 in 2009 after repeated raids by mounted ivory poachers from Sudan. Both the Kenya Wildlife Service and the survey teams conducting the censuses in Chad, including well-known elephant biologist Michael Fay, blamed the CITES-approved sales in 2008 for the poaching resurgence. Douglas-Hamilton, as a veteran of the elephant wars of the 1970s and 1980s, warned that history might be repeating itself.

Ivory continued to pour out of Africa, in increasing quantities. Alarming figures emerged from a program set up by the CITES Parties in 2000. Monitoring the Illegal Killing of Elephants (MIKE) was designed to gather data on elephant mortality at selected sites in Africa and Asia (though the Asian, and some of the African, sites have been woefully underreported, and the program depends on often self-serving figures supplied by government authorities). MIKE relies on a measure called PIKE (proportion of illegally killed elephants), the ratio of deaths from illegal killing to overall elephant mortality. PIKE doesn't measure how many elephants are dying (which would require you to count all the living elephants as well, a much more difficult task), but it does show what proportion of all recorded deaths are at the hands of poachers (as well as a few killed illegally over conflicts with farmers or villagers). Even if MIKE's data is only a pale reflection of what is actually going on, PIKE provides, most of the time, an easy index of how bad things are.

After a period of stability between 2002 and 2006, overall PIKE levels in Africa increased sharply, reaching a peak in 2008, the year of the second one-off sale. Though the continent-wide rate declined in 2009, PIKE levels continued to rise in areas such as the Laikipia-Samburu MIKE site in Kenya monitored by Iain Douglas-Hamilton and his co-workers. In Tanzania's Selous National Park, where 50 elephants were reportedly being poached per month, PIKE figures rose from 18 percent in 2004 to 53 percent in 2009. Overall vulnerability and the degree of available protection made a big difference in how likely elephants were to be killed. PIKE figures reported in 2010 were particularly high in the vulnerable, strife-torn MIKE sites in the eastern Democratic Republic of Congo (DRC), reaching over 90 percent in the Okapi Faunal Reserve and Garamba National Park. On the other hand, they were very low in South Africa's Kruger National Park and zero in Etosha National Park in Namibia.

After the 2009 lull, PIKE figures shot upwards, reaching new peaks in 2010 and again in 2011. Perhaps more significantly, they rose in every region of Africa. Things were still grim in Central Africa, where in 2011 the PIKE level reached 100 percent at five of fifteen MIKE sites — meaning that every dead elephant counted had been killed. At a further four sites the level was 87 percent or higher. The killing fields were shifting to the rainforests of Central Africa, where poverty and war are destroying human life as they drive the poachers deeper into the forest. In southern Africa, Kruger levels remained extremely low and Etosha remained poacher-free, but in Namibia's northeastern Caprivi Strip, levels spiked from zero, or nearly so, to 33 percent in 2010 and 59 percent in 2011. 2011 PIKE levels at the two MIKE sites in Mozambique, a major outport for smuggled ivory, hit 83 and 89 percent.

Behind these dry, though alarming, statistics lies a growing environmental and human tragedy, measured best by the two local factors that correlate most strongly with high PIKE levels in Africa: poverty (measured by human infant mortality) and poor governance (a euphemism for the chaotic lawlessness in places like the eastern DRC). Ivory prices have now risen so high in Africa that poachers are willing to risk targeting even well monitored and well protected populations. Elephants may no longer be safe anywhere, and the rangers who try to protect them are at increasing risk of losing their own lives. All of the evidence points to what Douglas-Hamilton, in his testimony before the United States Senate Committee on Foreign Relations in May 2012, called "a massive poaching surge."

Fewer elephants may be dying than in the 1970s and 1980s, but they are being taken from a population less than half as large. The DRC, home to 377,000 elephants only 30 years ago, is estimated to have fewer than 20,000 left. Forest Elephants, which may have represented a relatively small proportion of the elephants being killed in Africa in the 1970s and 1980s, lost 62 percent of their numbers between 2002 and 2011 (see p. 21). Genetic analyses show that poaching is disrupting the social structures and sex ratios of the surviving herds. Now that bulls with large tusks are becoming rare, poachers are turning to females and younger animals, leaving growing numbers of orphans. Elephants in the savannas of West and Central Africa are increasingly isolated, fragmented and in decline. Elephants are being killed not just for their ivory but for their meat, sold through a network of bushmeat vendors and potentially worth as much, or more, to a local hunter than a pair of any but the largest tusks.

Within Africa, there has been a disturbing resurgence of domestic ivory markets. In Ethiopia, ivory from Kenya and Sudan had reappeared by 2008 in markets in Addis Ababa, once the fourth largest ivory market on the continent, despite a government crackdown in 2005 that led to the arrest of any shopkeepers found with ivory and the confiscation of their stocks. Large retail ivory markets operate with apparent impunity in Nigeria and the DRC.

The market in Japan, once the largest in the world, has declined significantly, both because of the complexity of dealing with Japan's ivory control regulations and because a long-term economic recession and a westernization of taste has made ivory less fashionable, or even distasteful, to younger purchasers. A shift from cash transactions to credit cards has meant that Western signatures are replacing the mark of a *hanko*. Lucy Vigne and Esmond Martin reported in 2010 that a growing number of Japanese ivory dealers had closed down or were considering a move into other businesses.

In 2008 the highest ivory prices in the world, as much as six times higher than in 2001, were reported in Vietnam. The highest prices were for tusk tips (see p. 33). Daniel Stiles, who surveyed the Vietnamese market, was told that the raw ivory he saw on sale was from Asian, not African, elephants. African ivory seemed to be going primarily to China. The market in Vietnam was actually fairly modest, and the high prices appeared to be a reflection of restricted local supply. The ivory originated mostly from Laos, with smaller amounts from Cambodia and Vietnam itself, where the local elephants are on the point of extinction. Of the population of 6,250 Asian Elephants in Vietnam, Laos and Cambodia in the late 1980s, only 1,510 remained in 2000. Stiles argued that the 1989 ban, even when it was working to depress the market and cut off supply for African ivory, may have made matters worse for Asian Elephants in Indochina as local traders looked about for substitutes. Most of the buyers were visitors from other countries, including Chinese and Vietnamese-Americans. East Asians in the United States had reportedly been smuggling "significant quantities" of ivory into the country, despite the lowered markets there, or buying it illegally from numerous selling sites on the Internet.

Prices also rose steeply in Thailand, a country identified in 2009 as having "one of the largest and most active ivory industries anywhere in the world." Much of the ivory sold in Thailand is in the form of tourist souvenirs, and a surprising amount makes its way to the West. Controls over trade and ivory processing in Thailand are weak, and WWF has accused the country of allowing in "massive quantities" of illegal ivory from Africa. Though Thailand is a member of CITES, its internal legislation does not currently allow for the confiscation of African elephant ivory once it is smuggled into the country. This is a loophole the Thai government has promised to plug by listing the African elephants as "protected species" under its *Wildlife Act*. In December 2012 it announced that all ivory traders and producers must be registered, and instructed dealers not to sell ivory to foreigners. Nonetheless, as sale of domestic Asian Elephant ivory is allowed, African ivory may need only a false label to appear on the market. WWF called on Thailand to ban all ivory trade as it prepared to host the next CITES meeting in 2013.

The Philippines, long known as only a transit point for smuggled ivory, has recently been recognized as an important end market. Ivory is particularly prized in the Philippines for *santos* — cherished religious images of the Virgin Mary, the Christ Child, saints and other Christian religious figures, either entirely of ivory or with ivory heads and hands mounted on a wooden base. The whiteness of ivory represents purity and goodness to religious Filipinos, and the elephant that bears it stands for power, wisdom and longevity. Ironically, some of the suppliers bringing ivory into the Philippines are Muslims, who buy ivory in the course of religious pilgrimages to the Middle East and sell it openly to dealers on their return. According to Esmond and Chryssee Martin, who surveyed retail outlets in Manila in December 2010 and January 2011, some of the ivory confiscated from shipments in transit between 2005 and 2009 was stolen by government officers for sale to local dealers.

Though the Martins found ivory on sale in Manila over the 2010 Christmas season and warned that there seemed to be little control of the trade by Philippine authorities, it was an October 2012 article in *National Geographic* that brought the Philippine ivory trade into the public eye. Bryan Christy, its author, named names, including Monsignor Cristobal Garcia, a Catholic priest on the island of Cebu, who gave him advice on smuggling ivory into the United States ("Wrap it in old, stinky underwear and pour ketchup on it") and directed him to ivory-carving shops in Manila.

Christy's article caused a furor in the Philippines. Church and government officials issued denials, pointing out that many *santos* are antiques (the oldest date back to the sixteenth century) and denying that there was a market for new ivory in the country. They accused Christy of anti-religious bias and even suggested he be declared *persona non grata*. Just after the story broke in September, Msgr. Garcia was (conveniently?) stripped of all his ministerial duties by the Vatican, pending investigation of a 27-year-old case of child abuse in the United States. He dropped from sight and was reported to be on sick leave. In a letter to *National Geographic* the director of the Vatican press office claimed that the Church "knows nothing about and has nothing to do with him," agreed that "the massacre of elephants is a very serious matter," and promised to undertake an information campaign.

The Philippines National Bureau of Investigation (NBI) and the Department of Environment and Natural Resources (DENR) have conducted a nationwide probe, including raids, into the illegal trade, but how effective it will be remains to be seen. Christy reported in his article that "Corruption is so bad in the Philippines that in 2006 the wildlife department sued senior customs officers for 'losing' several tonnes of seized ivory. Chastened, the customs office turned its next big ivory seizure over to the wildlife department, which soon discovered that its own storeroom had been raided. Piles of tusks had been replaced with exact duplicates made of plastic." In a related story, in late October Italian forestry officials seized ivory religious statuettes and other artifacts on sale in a private shop adjacent to the Vatican itself. Vatican City is not a Party to CITES.

China remains the largest importer of illegal ivory in the world. The rapid rise in demand for ivory from an increasingly affluent market in China is al-most certainly the chief factor that has driven price increases and intensified poaching in Africa from 2004, and especially from 2008, onward. The rise in household consumption in China tracks closely to the rise in PIKE levels in Africa, suggesting a direct link between Chinese buying power and African poaching. This does not explain, however, why the demand for ivory in China rises at the same rate as the rise in the general level of consumer spending. That is why it is so difficult to tell if the one-off legal sale to China in 2008 is linked with the increase in poaching. The correlation, if it exists, is masked by other factors.

China tried to reduce illegal sales in 2004, before being approved by CITES as a trading partner, by requiring that all raw ivory materials and worked ivory pieces be labeled and entered into a centralized database, that ivory be sold only in registered shops, and that all items sold must carry an official iden-tification card. For any piece over 50 grams in weight, there must be a pho-tograph of the item on the ID card. Nonetheless, Esmond Martin and Lucy Vigne found in January 2011 that 61 percent of the 6,437 items carved from elephant ivory they saw on sale in Guangzhou, an important ivory center, were being sold without ID cards. The number of items on sale in Guangzhou had risen by 50 percent since Martin's previous survey in 2004.

The Chinese government reported to the CITES Standing Committee in 2012 that "we don't think that the ivory illegally entered into the Chinese mar-ket is huge." Much of the ivory openly on sale today may originate from older stocks already in the country (though some new pieces are deliberately stained to look antique). For some of it, "older" is an understatement. There is a brisk and growing trade in the surprisingly vast amount of mammoth ivory that can be found buried beneath the Siberian tundra. Martin and Vigne found over 6,000 mammoth ivory carvings on sale in their 2011 survey of Guangzhou. Almost all of the Chinese mammoth ivory supply is imported from Russia. Of over 26,000 kilograms brought in from January to November 2010 alone, 83 percent was Russian. Far smaller amounts were imported from the United States and Germany.

Hong Kong is the city with probably the largest number of ivory items on sale anywhere in the world. At the end of 2010 the Martins found more mam-moth ivory pieces than elephant — 35,127 to 33,526. The number of mam-moth ivory carvings had more than tripled since 2004. Ivory craftsmen who had left the business after the 1989 ban were returning to take up mammoth ivory, which could be imported and traded without having to worry about CITES (mammoths being, after all, past saving, though there must surely have been a lot of them at one time).

Ivory in China, like rhino horn among the Vietnamese, is a symbol of status and riches — only it has been one for centuries, not just for a decade or so. What is new in China, as it is in Vietnam, is the unbelievably rapid rise of an enormous and affluent middle class, the *bao fa hu* or suddenly rich, eager to show off the symbols of their newfound wealth and power. The sheer size and wealth of this sector of the Chinese population, and the growing numbers of Chinese living in Africa and buying ivory, have created a demand that the regulatory systems in China are unable to control.

Dealers in Africa don't even have to transport their ivory out of the continent to find Chinese customers. China has invested vast amounts of money in Africa. Government officials, businessmen, engineers and many others repeatedly visit the continent in connection with Chinese-funded development projects, and some of them come home with ivory in their luggage. According to an article by Alex Shoumatoff published in *Vanity Fair* in 2011, "Ninety percent of the passengers who are being arrested for possession of ivory at Jomo Kenyatta [Nairobi's airport] are Chinese nationals, and half the poaching in Kenya is happening within 20 miles of one of the five massive Chinese road-building projects in various stages of completion. There had been almost no poaching around Amboseli for 30 years before a Chinese company got the contract to build a 70 mile long highway just above the park." Nonetheless Shifan Wu, a spokesman for the Chinese embassy in Kenya, claimed in February 2013 that "The number of Chinese nationals involved in ivory smuggling and illegal trade are very few."

Did the CITES-approved ivory sales in 1999 and 2008, and in particular the 2008 sale to China, make matters worse for elephants, or did they — as their supporters claim — have little or no effect? The one-off sale in 2008 certainly failed to lower street prices or undercut the black market. Both have soared. Part of the problem is that the government's China Arts and Crafts Association (CACA), instead of dumping its legal ivory onto the domestic market at rock-bottom prices — the one thing that might have robbed the criminals of some customers — decided to dole it out at 5 tonnes per year over a ten-year period and charge such high markups to buyers (one entrepreneur reportedly paid a 650 percent markup over the auction price) that legal ivory ended up costing considerably more than its assumed black-market value.

If the 2008 sale had not taken place and all ivory imports to China had remained illegal, would Chinese consumers feel differently about buying ivory than they apparently do now? Iain Douglas-Hamilton certainly believes that the influx of "good" ivory into the market promoted demand in China, and Tom Milliken of TRAFFIC admitted to the BBC in April 2012: "Did allowance of legal ivory to go into China exacerbate a situation? One could probably argue now, with hindsight, that indeed it did. It created perhaps an image in the minds of many potential Chinese consumers that it was okay to buy ivory." That image, as much as anything, may have turned control of the ivory trade into a war against some of the most vicious militias in Africa, and a battle against worldwide organized crime.

CHAPTER TWELVE

RHINOS AND PROSTITUTES

There is something surreal about the images: slightly built young Thai women, some holding enormous guns they seem barely able to lift, posing over the dead bodies of Southern White Rhinos. What on Earth are they doing there? The answer tells perhaps the oddest tale in this whole sorry saga.

Trophy hunting brings millions of dollars to South Africa every year and provides employment for some 70,000 people. In 2008, a peak hunting year, the industry brought almost $125 million into the South African economy. Hunters from overseas, mostly from the United States or Europe, pay high fees to stalk the "big five" — lion, leopard, buffalo, elephant and rhinoceros.

According to the South African hunting industry and many conservationists, trophy hunting has contributed immeasurably to the success of White Rhino conservation in South Africa. A private landowner who buys a number of rhinos at a South African government auction creates the nucleus of a new population that can breed and grow. In return, the landowner can earn a very good profit by allowing carefully selected animals, usually males past breeding age, to be shot by foreign hunters. The result is an increase in rhino range and numbers, a flow of overseas revenue into South Africa, and incentives for private landowners to help conserve rhinos — in short, a happy ending for everyone concerned (except, one presumes, the rhinos in question).

This chapter, however, is not about the value or otherwise of South Africa's hunting system when everything goes according to the official plan. As long as a rhino trophy sent overseas with a government permit ends up no farther than a hunter's game room, it has nothing to do with illegal trade in horn. As long as the market value of horn stayed below the cost of flying to South Africa, shooting a rhino and taking the trophy home, this was not likely to change. That, of course, is not what happened.

Starting in 2003, applications for hunting permits began to come in, not from the usual sources in North America (historically, two-thirds to three-quarters of rhino hunters came from the United States) and Europe, but from Vietnam. This seemed odd, because hunting for sport is not a common pursuit in Vietnam. It is difficult for a Vietnamese to get permission even to own a gun. As the decade continued, though, the number of Vietnamese applications continued to increase until they took up most of the hunting permits that were being issued. According to South African CITES statistics, 657 rhino trophies were exported from South Africa to Vietnam between 2003 and 2010. In 2010 alone, 171 permits were issued to Vietnamese hunters.

There was soon more than a suspicion that these "trophy hunts" were actually being used to get rhino horn out of South Africa legally so that it could be sold onto the market in Vietnam. Many of the so-called "hunters" had no idea how to shoot, showed no interest in having their "trophies" properly prepared, and were ready to pay above the market price for a hunt. The price of horn was now so high that even a "hunter" using a permit as a laundering device could still turn a tidy profit. As early as 2007, South African law enforcement officers had already identified at least five separate Vietnamese-run syndicates that "actively probed the country's sport hunting industry for opportunities to come into the possession of rhino horns."

This was clearly illegal under CITES, South African law and Vietnamese law. Under the current CITES listing, a South African rhino hunting trophy (except for an antique) can be exported only as a personal item and may not be sold commercially. Under Vietnamese law, trophies are to be declared on arrival, but only 170 of the 675 trophies recorded by South Africa were properly reported on the "hunter's" arrival home. In 2009, South Africa enacted a new set of rules designed to limit hunters to one White Rhino per year and to make sure that only genuine trophy hunters were using the system.

Though the easiest thing to do might be to allow hunters to take home only a replica of their trophy, that could have been bad for business. Albi Modise, a spokesman for South Africa's Environmental Affairs Department, told the press in April 2012 that "If a hunter comes into the country in order to hunt a rhino, they expect to go back home carrying an original trophy." Horns could, therefore, be exported, but only as part of a trophy, with appropriate domestic and CITES documentation. Hunts were to be "strictly controlled" through individual hunting permits. Horns were to be microchipped by a government official immediately after the hunt. Unfortunately, though some provinces increased their enforcement efforts, in a few, where syndicates found an easy way around them, and especially in North West Province, the new rules didn't work.

On July 9, 2011, police in Edenvale, South Africa, arrested a Thai national named Chumlong Lemtongthai, known as "Chai" to his associates, and charged him with a number of offenses including violations of the *Customs and Excise Act*. The story that emerged — told in detail in investigative journalist Julian Rademeyer's book *Killing for Profit* — was truly bizarre. Lemtongthai had come to South Africa as a lieutenant for a smuggling syndicate based in Laos, a known hotbed of wildlife crime. His original job was to source lion bones for the Asian medicinal trade. He soon realized, after reading a newspaper article about rhino hunting, that there was much bigger money to be made.

Lemtongthai asked his boss, a notorious figure in the Lao wildlife business named Vixay Keosavang, for permission to get into the rhino horn trade. All he needed to do was to find out a way to use the legal hunting system to collect enough horns per year to maximize his boss's profit. To do that, he would need partners willing to help him get around the system: a landowner to buy up rhinos and put them on his property to be shot, a South African professional hunter or two to kill the animals, local officials to issue permits without asking too many questions (hunting permits are issued at the provincial level in South Africa), and foreigners ready to play the hunter once the kill was made. Allegedly — to the disgrace of the provinces involved and unscrupulous exploiters of the South African hunting system — he found them all.

The landowner was a lion breeder named Marnus Steyl. Steyl and his brother offered "canned hunts" — your chance to shoot a lion that has been living in a cage until shortly before you arrive. They had expanded into selling the bones to people like Lemtongthai and his associate Punpitak Chunchom, another Thai. Steyl and Lemtongthai reportedly struck a deal. Steyl would buy rhinos at government auction or from private landowners and transport them to his newly acquired Aurora Private Nature Reserve in North West Province. Here the services of a professional hunter named Harry Claassens were available, and the local authorities could be relied on, or bribed, to hand out permits like candy. The rhinos were supposed to be acclimated to their new home before they could be hunted, but this was a technicality that could be ignored. He and Claassens would handle the actual killing. All they needed to make it "legal" was foreign "hunters" who could claim, as South African law required, that they had fired the first shot.

Arranging that was Punpitak Chunchom's job, and he had a solution. Why go to the expense of bringing people in from Asia when he had a ready source of Thai nationals in the brothels and strip clubs of Johannesburg? Punpitak trolled the city's fleshpots, offering young women $560 to go on a "holiday" in the bush. All he needed was a copy of their passport to show the authorities. With the copies in hand, Steyl had no problem getting the necessary permits. The first hunts were ready to go in November 2010, and by mid-month Steyl was able to invoice Lemtongthai and his boss Keovasang, through their company Xaysavang Trading Export-Import in Laos, for approximately $27,600 for 4.1 kilograms of rhino horn.

Over the next eight months, Xayvasang allegedly supplied Steyl with at least 30 "hunters." All the women had to do was fire a low-caliber rifle to get some powder on their hands (in case anyone should check) and pose for a photo op with the downed rhino. North West Province nature conservation officers attended the hunt to snap the photos, fill out forms, microchip the horns, and reportedly get paid off with gifts of cash or cell phones. This might have gone on for years if one of the gang, a former police informant, hadn't tipped off a private investigator named Paul O'Sullivan. O'Sullivan lured in Lemtongthai with a photo, delivered through one of the women, of a massive pile of ivory and rhino horn that was supposedly for sale. The authorities were ready for him.

Lemtongthai's arrest was only the first. Punpitak Chunchom was arrested on November 4, 2011, and four days later Marnus Steyl turned himself in to the police. Another Thai, Tool Sriton, was arrested the following March, and Harry Claassens was picked up at his farm on May 17.

The sure-fire combination of rhinos and prostitutes made the ensuing court case a media sensation. When Lemtongthai pleaded guilty to 59 charges in a Johannesburg court in November 2012, he received an unprecedented 40-year prison sentence. Any rejoicings in the conservation community were cut short, however, when the prosecution suddenly dropped all charges against Steyl, Claassens and the remaining Thais. The case, which would have allowed in extensive evidence about the phony hunting scheme, was over almost before it started.

Lemtongthai claimed at his sentencing that his fellow accused were innocent dupes, with no idea that he was attempting something illegal. The evidence, including video footage that aired on the South African television program *3rd Degree* after the trial, seems to suggest otherwise. The video, filmed in January 2011, clearly shows a hunter, identified as Claassens, stalking a rhino, accompanied by an Asian "hunter" — male this time, named as Nimit Wongprajan, a Thai — who isn't even carrying a gun. The footage is taken from a GoPro brand camera strapped to the head of another gunman, who finally brings down the screaming animal with a barrage of shots. Nimit does nothing but watch. The shooter, when he takes off the camera, is identified as Steyl. If you have the stomach, you can watch the whole thing on YouTube.

The release of Steyl, Claassens and the others was greeted with outrage. It was widely assumed that Lemtongthai had taken the fall to protect the white hunters and, more broadly, the South African hunting establishment. There were stories of a probe into the conduct of local North West officials. Questions were asked in the South African Parliament, but the Minister for Justice and Constitutional Development, J.T. Radebe, was able to reply that new arrest warrants against Lemtongthai and Steyl were in the works. Punpitak had fled to Thailand after the verdict. Steyl appeared in Vryburg Regional Court on December 5, facing charges that included 23 counts of fraud, five of illegally hunting White Rhinos, and several counts of money-laundering. He was released on R100,000 bail, still insisting that he had no idea anything illegal was going on. His trial was postponed until March 25, 2013.

The Lemtongthai-Steyl case is only the most lurid example of what has been called "pseudo-hunting." Despite its questionable outcome, by the time the verdict was handed down, South Africa had already acted, with some success, to make sure that this sort of practice wouldn't happen again. On March 29, 2012, the government announced that it would no longer issue permits to foreign nationals from countries without appropriate legislation to monitor whether the trophy was used for the purpose reflected on the permits — in other words, to make sure it stayed a trophy.

Hunters now had to demonstrate that they were the real thing, including proving that they were members of a recognized hunting association in their home country. Any permits issued by the provinces had to be checked by the Department of Environmental Affairs (DEA) to be sure that the one-rhino-per-year rule was observed country-wide. A law enforcement official was required to attend every hunt and to take DNA samples from each downed rhino. The DEA recommended that Provincial Conservation Authorities refuse all applications for White Rhinoceros hunting by Vietnamese hunters until

Vietnam has confirmed, in writing, that all rhino trophies exported since 2010 are still in the possession of the original hunters.

That's something that Vietnam is unlikely to be able to do. It has conducted random checks on only forty of the suspected sham trophies. Seven had been lost or given away, and eleven could not be examined because their owners "were not at home." There has already been one well-publicized (and confusing) case of a horn, supposedly brought in as a trophy, that was stolen from a wealthy banker in Ho Chi Minh City named Tram Be on September 27, 2012. Be's name was not on Vietnam's list of legal importers, but the stuffed rhino from which the horn came was allegedly a gift from a Vietnamese hunter named Ngo Thanh Nhan, who shot it in 2006. Nhan is, apparently, on the official list. The case remains unsolved.

The new rules came into force on April 10, 2012. Applications from Vietnam, Thailand and China stopped at once. This, in turn, led to the rise of so-called "proxy hunters" — more or less genuine hunters from, at first, the Czech Republic, home to a large number of Vietnamese immigrants, and later from Poland. Proxy hunters presumably shot the rhinos themselves, but the real reason they were there was to get a trophy to transship to Asia once they brought it home. In one case, a senior Czech official told the Japanese newspaper *Asahi Shimbun* that authorities had seized ten rhino horns at Prague's international airport in March 2012. They questioned five Czech nationals, who told them they had received the hunts as a "gift" from a Vietnamese man and a Czech woman who had paid all their expenses. The original application form had read "Vietnam," but this was scratched out and changed to read "Czech Republic." The European Union had supposedly squelched this sort of thing with a ban on the re-export of rhino hunting trophies, adopted in 2011.

Requests for rhino hunting permits have fallen by 50 percent. Even Czech and Polish applications dropped off after an initial surge. However, there has been a rise in hunting applications from Russia and, particularly, the United States. American applications to hunt a rhino in South Africa tripled in 2012 as compared to 2010. Is this a coincidence, or are the syndicates looking for proxy hunters shifting their search from country to country? It is too early to tell. Just in case, Kenya submitted a proposal to the March 2013 CITES meeting that would impose a zero quota on exports of any Southern White Rhino trophies from South Africa and, for good measure, Swaziland (where pseudo-hunting was not a problem). Kenya's move would have ended legal exports of rhino horn trophies whether the hunters were legitimate or not. The proposal found little support.

The pseudo-hunting story may be having some impact in Vietnam. In January 2013 Vietnam announced a new directive banning trade in all rhinoceros and elephant specimens unless they "serve diplomatic or scientific research purposes; are to be used for biodiversity conservation, to be displayed at a zoo, or exchanged amongst CITES authorities and its national members." Non-profit specimens, presumably including hunting trophies, qualify for import only in accordance with a cooperative agreement between the CITES authorities in Vietnam and those in the exporting country (the unofficial translation says "importing," but that may be an error). This language presumably refers to the new biodiversity MoU that Vietnam signed with South Africa (see p. 91).

Pseudo-hunting may prove to be a temporary sideshow in the rhino poaching story, but it demonstrates the lengths to which criminal gangs will go to get their hands on rhinoceros horn. Even so, pseudo-hunting has never been responsible for more than a small proportion of the number of rhinos killed in South Africa every year. Pseudo-hunting may be on the decline, but the poaching wave continues. In January 2013, while floods in Kruger National Park hampered anti-poaching operations, a wave of poachers swept in from Mozambique armed with heavy hunting rifles and ammunition. Eighteen were arrested. While Chumlong Lemtongthai sat in jail, 82 Southern White Rhinos were killed in South Africa between January 1 and February 6. Sixty-one rhinos died in Kruger Park alone.

That's almost two a day.

CHAPTER THIRTEEN

WAR ON ELEPHANTS

The modern ivory trade has been built on war. The poaching wave of the 1970s and 1980s was made possible by the flood of weapons sold into Africa during the 1960s. South Africa surreptitiously traded weapons for ivory in the 1980s with Jonas Savimbi's UNITA guerillas in Angola (see p. 47). Armed bandits from Somalia invaded northern Kenya for ivory, reportedly on direct orders from then-president Mohamed Siad Barre. Though Barre, a Marxist, was not much interested in personal wealth, his family became deeply involved in the ivory trade. A letter dated March 19, 1987, published in *New African Magazine*, apparently signed by Siad Barre, authorized "Comrades Omar Hassan Khayare and Hussein Barre Hassan to bring elephant tusks from Kenya to Somalia." The Somali embassy denied it, but the magazine's editor insisted that the letter was genuine and had been leaked from the president's office. Siad Barre may be gone, but Somali raiders from Al-Shabaab recently invaded northern Kenya to kill elephants in the Arawale National Reserve.

War is not too strong a word to describe what happened in Cameroon's Bouba N'Djida National Park during the first three months of 2012. It was a near-perfect example of the way that seemingly unquenchable demand, insufficient trade controls, massive firepower in the hands of the wrong people, a remote and unguarded elephant population, and an ineffective (at best) central government can combine to create a conservation disaster.

Bouba N'Djida, at 850 square miles (220,000 ha), is the largest national park in the country. It protected, or was supposed to protect, somewhere between 400 and 1,000 elephants. The reality, unfortunately, is that much of this vast tract of dry savanna was hardly protected at all. A survey in 2004 reported that "the southern sector, covering roughly two-thirds of the park, is relatively well protected, but the northern sector is infested with poachers, cattle and migrant fisherfolk." The park had already lost its rhinos — probably the last Western Black Rhinoceroses in the world (see p. 120). Bouba N'Djida was suffering from a general lack of money for wildlife protection. According to Cameroonian journalist Julie Owono, "Cameroon's Ministry of Forests and Wildlife, the government agency in charge of the country's anti-poaching policy, saw its budget slashed from \$43 million in 2011 to just \$33 million in 2012. The money dedicated specifically to anti-poaching action was only \$2 million in 2011 — an amount clearly insufficient for tackling the problem."

Despite a 2011 letter from 12 foreign ambassadors warning the prime minister of Cameroon about the high level of insecurity in the country's parks, only five guards were assigned to patrol the whole of Bouba N'Djida (at a salary of \$160 per month). The official guards never went on patrol, leaving the anti-poaching work to be done by 25 community guards. Two of them had been killed by Sudanese poachers in 2009.

Small-scale poaching was an annual event in Bouba N'Djida, especially when the dry season drove elephants out of the park in search of food. The first inklings that something new was afoot came in December 2011, near the beginning of the 2011–2012 dry season, when Paul Bour, manager of a safari lodge within Bouba N'Djida, notified the Ministry of Forests and Wildlife that large-scale poaching was going on in the park. For two months Bour waited, in vain, for a reply.

Villagers living near the park reported encountering mounted gangs of armed men. The central government did nothing, though the local military tried unsuccessfully to intervene. According to Céline Sissler-Bienvenu of the International Fund for Animal Welfare (IFAW), warnings that armed poachers had invaded the area in early January "were simply ignored." According to the villagers, the poachers were quite open about what they were doing. They were there, they said, for a three-month stay. They intended to kill as many elephants and to collect as much ivory as they possibly could. Kill they did, with AK-47 assault rifles, RPG-7 rocket-propelled grenade launchers, M80 explosives and enough ammunition for a long siege.

By late February, when an IFAW team arrived on the scene, the park was littered with corpses. The poachers had apparently slaughtered every elephant they could find, regardless of sex, age or whether the animals had visible tusks.

According to Sharon Redrobe, the veterinarian on the IFAW team, they probably didn't even wait until the animals were dead before they hacked out their ivory with axes. As Sissler-Bienvenu reported, "In some groups the state of decomposition was different, suggesting that poachers waited until surviving elephants came back to 'mourn' their dead before shooting them as well."

We still don't know how many elephants the poachers killed. Media stories and government statements have given figures ranging anywhere from 200 to 650 (the latter being the number that the poachers themselves boasted of having killed to local villagers). Some 200 more may have crossed the border into Chad after the poaching raids. In February, park conservationist Mathieu Fomepa told Agence France-Presse that at least 480 animals had been killed, but it later emerged that he had rarely visited the area and had probably invented the figure to impress his superiors. He was fired, along with the governor of the North Province and the regional director of the Ministry of Forests and Wildlife. Paul Bour, who photographed carcasses and established their GPS coordinates, had located 380 by the end of April. He is convinced that there were more, particularly in hunting concessions surrounding the park, whose managers sometimes hid killings to avoid scaring off customers.

Ivory runs across the Sahel have probably been going on for centuries; the difference this time was weaponry and demand. Previous raiding expeditions had already slaughtered most of the elephants in the northern Central African Republic and in neighboring Chad, where the poachers probably had their base camp (and may have recently killed six Chadian soldiers who tried to intercept them). Some of the same poachers were now looking for easy pickings in Cameroon.

The raiders, estimated to number between 50 and one 100, were obviously experienced men. They operated with military precision (some, indeed, wore military khaki), dividing their troops into hunting squads and ivory collectors. They were not bandits or cattle raiders. Though there is a report that they kidnapped one villager and forced him to act as one of their trackers, they also relied on local poachers for help. They bought fodder, cornmeal, tea and sugar from locals and spent the occasional night in a local village. They even told their hosts where they could find elephant carcasses and invited them to collect the meat. Local villagers, many of whom had seen their crops destroyed by elephants from the park, were only too happy to tolerate the poachers' presence and to profit from it (though it is hard to see what they could have done about it if they had objected). Large chunks of elephant meat were soon being offered for sale along access roads into the area.

According to village informants, the poachers spoke Arabic. They rode horses, apparently animals in poor health, and carried away the ivory on the backs of camels. Some may have been Chadians, but most had probably ridden across more than 600 miles (1,000 km) of desert from Sudan. The IFAW team reported that the poachers took trophies from the ears of the dead elephants — a common practice in Sudan, "where fragments of elephant ears are worn on necklaces," but rare elsewhere.

Some news stories suggested that the invaders were linked to the Janjaweed militia or to Al-Shabaab (Harakat al-Shabaab al-Mujahideen), a Somali Islamist group with ties to Al-Qaeda. Though there is no direct proof of this, Jeffrey Gettleman wrote in the *New York Times* that "international law enforcement officials" now believed that Janjaweed were involved. Sissler-Bienvenu reported evidence that at least some of the Sudanese poachers could be Rizeigat, members of a large Bedouin tribe from Darfur in western Sudan. The money they would earn from their ivory raid would go to buy weapons to increase their clan's political might.

The massacre remained a closely guarded secret, known to only a few individuals within the Ministry of Forests and Wildlife, until the *Cameroon Tribune* published a story on the killings in mid-February. At some career risk to himself, Paul Bour decided to tell people outside the Ministry about what was going on. Shortly after he broke his silence, news of the Cameroon massacre hit the international media. Wildlife conservationists, foreign governments and the European Union implored Cameroon to take action. The government was at a loss at first, but (perhaps waking to the fact that lawlessness on this scale was doing the country's tourism industry no good) finally authorized military action at a high-level meeting between the Ministries of Defence and Forests and Wildlife on February 29, 2012.

A "rapid intervention battalion" of 600 Cameroonian soldiers entered the park on the same night, backed by a helicopter and two airplanes. At least one soldier died fighting the invaders. The IFAW team recorded hearing at least 63 gunshots exchanged between troops and poachers on March 5. The battalion's forces, for all their efforts and training, were not used to dealing with this sort of enemy. At least 20 more elephants were killed in the next two weeks. The general in charge of the military operation lost his job. The poachers, in the end, got away, sometime after their last raid in mid-March. In August 2012,

60 new (but reportedly poorly trained and equipped) Ecoguards were hastily posted to the park, and plans were announced to recruit 2,500 rangers and to establish a new national park authority.

Cameroon now arrests and prosecutes at least some of its poachers and illegal dealers, thanks to the efforts of NGOs in the country, including WWF and, particularly, the tiny but indomitable Last Great Ape Organization (LAGA). Only seven months after LAGA was founded by an expatriate Israeli, Ofir Drory, who first arrived in the country in 2003, Cameroon launched, entirely due to Drory's unique combination of exposure and encouragement, its first-ever prosecution for wildlife crime (though the laws had been on the books for years).

The international attention surrounding the Bouba N'Djida massacre may have forced Cameroon to turn its attention to another, quite different, population of elephants within its borders: the 4,000 or so Forest Elephants living in the rainforests of its southeast. In late March 2012, Cameroonian authorities arrested 12 suspected poachers near the adjoining national parks of Boumba-Bek and Nki. In April, after prosecution lawyers provided by WWF and LAGA argued for meaningful sentences from the court, four of the suspects were sentenced to unprecedented 18-month jail terms and fines of over $58,000.

In Chad's Zakouma National Park, mounted raiders reportedly linked to the Janjaweed militia and the military actions in Darfur wiped out 70 percent of its 3,900 elephants between 2005 and 2009 (see p. 94). The slaughters in Chad slowed after the near-elimination of the Zakouma herds, but in 2012 they flared up again. Stephanie Vergniault, founder of SOS Elephants, was staying in her camp in the Chari Beguimi area of southwestern Chad when armed horsemen with "war weapons" invaded the area in the early hours of July 24, killing 29 elephants. This time, the poachers appeared to be part of a local Chadian "ivory mafia" with alleged connections to government officials and Chinese labor at a nearby oil refinery.

Vergniault fears that "not a single elephant will be alive in Chad in three years time." SOS Elephants is working closely to prevent such an outcome with Chad's head of state, Idriss Déby Itno. President Déby is reportedly "passionate about the survival and future of elephants in Chad" and has deployed state soldiers to man most of the anti-poaching teams in his country. After the July 2012 raid he sent 200 soldiers to the Chari Beguimi area in two helicopters and 15 pickup trucks. Nonetheless, on July 27 the poachers killed four or five more elephants before melting away into the bush.

In Zakouma, a large security presence has been established near a swamp where the park's few remaining elephants, almost all females, congregate in the wet season. On August 12, the security team raided a poachers' camp. The poachers escaped, and on September 3 they took their revenge. Five rangers — Zakaria Ibrahim, Brahim Khamis, Daoud Aldjouma, Djibrine Adoum Goudja and Idriss Adoum — were gunned down during dawn prayers. A sixth, Hassan Djibrine, was missing. The attack was reported by the camp cook, who walked for two days to reach the nearest village, despite a gunshot wound.

The infamous Lord's Resistance Army and its leader, Joseph Kony, may be depending on the ivory trade to maintain their troops. "That's how they get their weapons," a Sudanese ivory trader told Jeffrey Gettleman. According to Gettleman, "Several recent escapees from the LRA said that Mr. Kony had ordered his fighters to kill as many elephants as possible and send him the tusks." Perhaps even more troubling is the evidence that military units from Uganda, South Sudan and the DRC — forces supposedly trying to bring Kony to justice, trained and supported with millions of dollars from the United States — are getting in on the action themselves. Soldiers in the DRC have been arrested for ivory poaching, and Gettleman reports that "South Sudanese forces frequently battle wildlife rangers."

In Garamba National Park in the DRC, where improved protection efforts and greater security had seen a reduction of poaching in recent years (see p. 121), a raid by a marksman in a foreign helicopter on March 15, 2012, killed 22 elephants "with a single shot to the top of the head" and carried off ivory valued at more than $1 million. Iain Douglas-Hamilton told a United States Senate Committee that "While the actual slaughter was not witnessed, a Russian manufactured Mi-17 troop-carrying helicopter was photographed in the vicinity at the same time." According to Gettleman, park officials, scientists and the DRC authorities now believe that the helicopter belonged to the Ugandan military. INTERPOL is currently trying to match samples taken from the carcasses with ivory recently seized at a Ugandan airport.

Anti-poaching operations in Garamba are a war in all but name. "We don't negotiate, we don't give any warning, we shoot first," the park's ex-Kenyan chief ranger, Mr. Onyango, told Gettleman. Its 140 rangers carry assault weapons, machine guns and rocket-propelled grenades, but they are still outgunned by LRA poachers, who have no compunction about using their weapons against people. "These guys were shooting like they were in Iraq," Onyango said of a June 2012 battle fought over the carcasses of several slaughtered elephants.

The story in Garamba can be told for much of the eastern DRC, where, according to Trip Jennings and Kyle Dickman of Sam Wasser's Elephant Ivory Project (see p. 138), "Stability means a calm between warring bandits and rebel groups." Over the past 15 years more than 183 rangers have lost their lives in Virunga National Park and nearby reserves, home to Mountain Gorillas (*Gorilla b. beringel*) as well as elephants. M23 military rebels, FDLR (Democratic Forces for the Liberation of Rwanda) and the Maï-Maï (an armed indigenous group) work together in the Virungas to poach ivory and extract minerals. They even organize visits for unsuspecting tourists who presumably don't realize that their hosts regularly fire on park guards.

The Okapi Faunal Reserve in the northeastern DRC was the site of Rene Beyers' 2011 study of the impact of poaching and civil war on elephants (see p. 49). It is also the hunting ground of a notorious elephant poacher and Maï-Maï gang leader named Morgan. Park guards had arrested Morgan three times, but the local courts set him free. Now he wanted to send a message that he was not to be interfered with. Terese Hart, who has worked on wildlife conservation in the DRC for many years, posted the story:

> At 5 o'clock Sunday morning, the 24th of June, at least 50 men, mostly naked and draped in leaves entered Epulu, the headquarters of the Okapi Faunal Reserve ... They came out of the forest from the south, about four kilometers east of Epulu and were led by the elephant poacher called Morgan. They were armed with AK 47s and at least two PKM machine guns. For an entire day scenes of horror and panic ripped through Epulu. Many people fled into the forest, others were taken hostage to carry the loot of the attackers. Women were raped. Seven people were killed. Among the dead are two park guards and the wife of another ... Others seemed shot almost at random: Two people on a truck passing through Epulu, two other Epulu residents. The administrative buildings of the Reserve were looted, then burned. Houses and stores in the village were pillaged.

The attackers also shot 14 captive Okapi (*Okapia johnstoni*), a rare forest relative of giraffes, and left them dead in their pens. Army troops did not arrive until after Morgan and his men left, and they made no attempt to pursue them. Over the next few weeks Morgan's gang carried out other attacks in the area, hijacking trucks and taking hostages. The military made no attempt to stop them, claiming that they lacked the communication equipment to enter the forest.

These tales of the ivory wars in central Africa are more than just horror stories, though for any thinking, feeling person they ought to be enough to mark "blood ivory" with the same moral stain as "blood diamonds." Even more so, because the guns bought with blood diamonds don't first have to be used to slaughter sensitive, intelligent animals before they are turned on human beings. The ivory wars of central Africa are more evidence that the system that links the poacher in Africa or Asia with an ultimate buyer is not just the mark of a criminal organization but the perpetuator of a great evil, one that we may have little power to stop unless the system itself can be weakened or broken.

CHAPTER FOURTEEN

THE LAST RHINOS

For two rhinoceros subspecies, and possibly more, our best conservation efforts are already too late. The story of the Vietnamese Rhinoceros (*Rhinoceros sondaicus annamiticus*), a subspecies of the Javan Rhinoceros, is a sad — if not disgusting — tale of lost, found, and lost again. For many years, it was assumed that the only Javan Rhinos left in the world were the ones in Ujung Kulon in Indonesia. The populations that once roamed commonly throughout much of Southeast Asia were thought to be, irremediably, extinct. The vanished subspecies *inermis* of northeastern India, Bangladesh and Myanmar was last recorded in the early 1900s. Then, in 1988 — to everyone's astonishment — a tiny population of *annamiticus*, perhaps 10 to 15 animals at most, was discovered in an area of southern Vietnam, a country so ravaged by war that it was thought that no creature as large as a rhinoceros could have survived. It later proved that some 39 more rhinos had been killed in Vietnam between 1957 and 1991. The last of them may have evaded notice for so long because they had shifted to a largely nocturnal way of life, perhaps in a futile effort to hide from poachers.

The area where they lived was proclaimed in 1992 as the Cat Loc Rhinoceros Reserve, incorporated in 1998 into nearby Cat Tien National Park. Despite the proclamation, human settlement flooded the reserve, converting much of the best rhinoceros habitat to rice paddies and cashew plantations. Motorbike tracks split the forest, and settlers left few places where the rhinos could reach vital water supplies in the dry season. Though Cat Loc covered an area of 135 square miles (35,000 ha), the rhinos were restricted to a mere 25 square miles

(6,500 ha). By 2005, when a rhino conservation project was established as a successor to a seven-year effort funded by the government of the Netherlands, it was already too late. The project relocated almost 1,400 people living within the boundaries of the park and mobilized guards for regular, though poorly managed and largely unsupervised, rhino patrols, but political support for conserving the rhinos was largely absent. By that time there were probably only five or six animals left.

The remaining handful included males and females, but the last evidence of breeding was in January 1999. Camera traps told a tale of slowly dwindling numbers as the last continental Javan Rhinos died — or, most likely, were killed — one by one. A survey team from WWF and Cat Tien searched the area from October 2009 to April 2010, but the 22 dung samples they collected all proved to come from a single female. Shortly after the survey ended, in April 29, 2010, her dead and partially decomposed body was found in the park. She had been shot through the leg, probably in late January or early February, and her horn had been hacked off. On the mainland of Asia, the Javan Rhinoceros was extinct — this time for real. A WWF report called the extinction of Vietnam's rhinoceros "a direct result of ... inadequate protection and protected area management from all parties involved in its conservation."

The Western Black Rhinoceros (*Diceros bicornis longipes*) was already on the verge of extinction in the 1930s. French colonial authorities tried to protect it, with some success: by 1980 there were probably about 100 of the animals in northern Cameroon. The tide turned from then on. Rhinos were last seen in the Central African Republic in the 1980s and in Chad in the late 1980s or early 1990s. By 1997 only ten to eighteen rhinos still roamed northern Cameroon, its last stronghold, and by 2001 only five to possibly eight were left. In 2000 IUCN's African Rhino Specialist Group recommended that the few remaining animals be transferred to a well-protected fenced sanctuary, but noted that support for this depended on substantial funding and on whether "the Cameroon authorities will demonstrate a significant political will to conserve the few remaining rhinos." Failing this, they suggested moving the rhinos out of Cameroon altogether, to a fenced sanctuary elsewhere. Neither happened.

The last animals probably fell to poachers in 2003 or shortly thereafter, but their demise was not confirmed until 2006. A 2004 survey led by an NGO, Symbiose, claimed to have found evidence of some 31 animals, but its team was misled by its own trackers. Fearful that they would lose their jobs if they failed to find signs of rhinos, the trackers placed and led the investigators to tracks they had faked with wood and stones. The 2006 survey (in which Symbiose also participated), despite multiple patrols covering over 1,550 miles (2,500 km) of bush, failed to find any trace of the animals. The survey's 2007 report declared the Western Black Rhinoceros "probably extinct." IUCN removed the "probably" in November 2011, only a few weeks after confirming the extinction of the Vietnamese Rhinoceros.

The Northern White Rhinoceros is not, technically, extinct. There are still a few surviving animals in captivity: two in the San Diego Wild Animal Park and, until 2009, six in the Dvur Kralove Zoo in the Czech Republic. The wild populations are gone. Concerns about the slaughter of the Northern White Rhinoceros had been expressed as far back as 1924, although just over 60 years ago there were still 2,250 of them distributed across five countries: Sudan, with over 1,000 animals, Uganda, the DRC, the Central African Republic (CAR) and Chad. In 1960, the Northern White Rhinoceros actually outnumbered its southern cousin.

By 1971 there were only 650 left. By 1984 they were gone from Uganda, the CAR and Chad. For many years their last stronghold was Garamba National Park in the DRC, a reserve created for them in 1938. Only 15 were known to survive there. From this nadir, their numbers slowly began to grow again. By 1997 there were 25 animals in Garamba, even after a year of civil war in which Sudanese poaching gangs were able to move freely through the area and 90 percent of the park's equipment for law enforcement activities was lost or destroyed. Rhinos were not the only victims. Half of the park's nearly 12,000 elephants were killed during the 1997 war. During a second war in the area in 1999–2000, Ugandan-backed rebel forces occupied the park, but guards were allowed to continue their anti-poaching efforts. The elephants, which appear to be a unique genetic mixture of Savanna and Forest Elephants, recovered slightly, and a survey in August 2000 found 30 Northern White Rhinos.

Over the next few years, mounted poachers invading Garamba from the Sudan inexorably destroyed the last surviving animals. By 2004 their numbers had dropped to perhaps 15. Their horns may have gone to feed the greatly diminished, but still active, horn trade in Yemen (see p. 41). Despite attempts by local conservationists and stakeholders to develop an emergency plan to save the subspecies, the last sighting of a Northern White Rhino in Garamba was in 2006. Though spoor was sighted in 2007, extensive searches since then have failed to turn up a single animal. There were rumors in 2009, but no proof, that three rhinos might have survived in what is now South Sudan.

Of the seven surviving captive animals — an eighth at Dvur Kralove died of old age in 2011 — only four appear capable of breeding. In 2009, the four were moved from the Czech Republic to the Ol Pejeta Conservancy in Kenya in the hope of encouraging them to breed. Unfortunately, they are related to each other, so inbreeding is a potential problem. One proposed solution has been to mate them to Southern White Rhinoceroses in the hope of preserving at least some of their genes. In 2011, after months of effort by their keepers to acclimatize the animals to their new surroundings, two of the Northern Whites started to mate with each other and a third began mating with a Southern White.

Colin Groves and his colleagues have argued that there are enough physical and genetic differences between Northern and Southern White Rhinos to treat them as separate species. The Northern White Rhinoceros, as *Ceratotherium cottoni*, would immediately acquire the dubious distinction of being the rarest rhinoceros species in the world — and, in all probability, the first one to disappear in modern times. Groves's views, though, have not been widely accepted.

The Sumatran Rhinoceros may be next. Only a few wild individuals remain: perhaps 140–210 in all, with 120–180 in Sumatra and 20–30 in Borneo. In Sumatra it survives in numbers in only three national parks: Bukit Barisan Selatan (about 50), Gunung Leuser (possibly as many as 80) and Way Kambas (25–35). It was hoped until recently that a few survived in Peninsular Malaysia, their last mainland stronghold, but there have been no confirmed sightings there for many years, and surveys since 2011 have found no trace of them. Their forest habitat is under increasing threat, and their numbers are so small and scattered that the biggest threat to their survival may be their sheer inability to find one another. Even during the 1980s and 1990s, when their numbers were half again as large, at least half of all the females caught in Sumatra, Peninsular Malaysia and Sabah appeared never to have been pregnant.

Sumatran Rhinos are still being poached, though the opportunities to do so must be increasingly rare. Eight subpopulations in Sumatra disappeared between 1997 and 2007, and poachers killed some 30 animals in Peninsular Malaysia between 1975 and 2005. Some of their horns may have passed through the hands of notorious Malaysian animal dealer Anson Wong, who offered to obtain Sumatran Rhino horns for United States Fish and Wildlife Service special agent George Morrison during the sting operation that nabbed him in the mid-1990s. The International Rhino Foundation (IRF) and its Indonesian partner, the Rhino Foundation of Indonesia (Yayasan Badak

Indonesia, or YABI), operate trained Rhino Protection Units in Bukit Barisan Selatan and Way Kambas. There has now been no poaching in these two parks for seven years, and IRF and YABI are helping to train similar anti-poaching units in Gunung Leuser.

The subspecies *Dicerorhinus sumatrensis harrissoni* of Borneo may be on a final track to extinction. The only wild population, in the Malaysian state of Sabah, was considered "doomed" at the 2012 meeting of the IUCN Asian Rhinoceros Specialist Group. There are three animals in captivity in Sabah, including two intended for a planned Borneo Rhino Sanctuary in the Tabin Wildlife Reserve. Unfortunately only one, a male, is considered capable of re-producing. As a last-ditch measure, his sperm is being collected and stored. The Sabah Wildlife Department believes that if cross-breeding with the other subspecies, *Dicerorhinus sumatrensis sumatrensis*, will help save the species it should not be ruled out, as the two subspecies are genetically very similar and time is not on our side. The IUCN Asian Rhino Specialist Group and the Global Propagation and Management Board that oversees the captive popula-tion have taken the same view.

Despite the failures of the 1990s, there is some hope that the species, or at least the subspecies *Dicerorhinus sumatrensis sumatrensis*, may survive in captiv-ity. That does not mean in a zoo — that lesson appears to have been learned (see p. 28) — but in a fenced enclosure in their native forest where the animals can be kept under close watch. The 247-acre (100 ha) Sumatran Rhino Sanctuary in Sumatra's Way Kambas National Park, founded in 1998, has four adult rhi-nos and a dedicated local staff that feeds and washes them daily. They include Andalas, born at the Cincinnati Zoo in 2001 and transferred to the sanctuary in 2007. It is fitting that the first of only three calves to have been born as a result of the captive breeding efforts of the 1990s, and the first born in captivity in 112 years, should now be back in its native habitat, if not in the wild.

Andalas is now the only adult male at the sanctuary after another male, Torgamba, died in 2011. He was mated in 2009 to a female named Ratu, who was brought to the sanctuary after wandering into a village just outside the park. In June 2012, after two miscarriages and a 15-month pregnancy, Ratu gave birth to Andatu, a healthy male calf. Rhinos, though, are slow breeders. In the wild, Sumatran Rhinos may give birth only once every two to three years, assuming pairs find each other in the right sort of habitat. This may mean that even the largest subpopulations may add no more than one new baby a year. Still, there is at least some hope that the smallest of all rhinos may escape what once seemed its inevitable fate. A Sumatran Rhino crisis summit, planned to be held in Singapore from March 31 to April 4, 2013, will attempt to consolidate, review and build on efforts to save it from extinction, and to begin raising the 30 million euros that we may need to get the job done.

CHAPTER FIFTEEN

CORRUPTION, THEFT AND ORGANIZED CRIME

The illicit trade in ivory and rhinoceros horn is kept alive by poachers who will risk anything, criminal syndicates that can, it seems, do anything, and customers who will pay anything to get what they want. In the end, as we have seen, it all comes down to price.

Gram for gram, ounce for ounce, ivory and especially rhino horn are the most valuable wildlife products in the world. In 2012 the United Nations Office on Drugs and Crime's Regional Office for Southern Africa put the street value of rhinoceros horn at $65,000 per kilogram. No poacher, of course, ever sees that kind of money, but in the desperately poor economies where many of them live, even a tenth of that may be the equivalent of months or years of regular work. With anti-poaching squads in Kenya, Zimbabwe and the DRC prepared to shoot to kill, the money is enough to risk dying for — or killing for. Six Kenya Wildlife Service rangers were killed by poachers in 2012, and KWS rangers shot three poachers dead in January 2013.

The real money is made further down the supply chain. The stakes are so high that the kingpins in the business can afford to be big spenders when it comes to getting their goods to market. In the 1980s, the top ivory-trade bosses could even afford to set up carving factories in Dubai whose sole purpose was to do a bit of surface whittling on smuggled-in whole tusks, in order to get around a restriction that barred raw (that is, uncarved) ivory from entering Hong Kong. Once the slightly modified tusks got through Hong Kong Customs, the master carvers would do the genuine work.

That particular subterfuge would be useless today. Although CITES does differentiate between raw and worked ivory in some circumstances, imports of partially carved whole tusks into Hong Kong are no longer permitted. Ivory and rhino horn smuggling on any sort of commercial scale, though, is still an expensive proposition. Getting that much contraband across oceans and through a raft of border checkpoints requires compliant customs officers and corrupt government officials, and they may not come cheap. Rhino horn is so valuable that it is worth paying huge fees for a hunting permit in South Africa or co-opting professionals in the wildlife industry to commit "khaki-collar crime" (see p. 87).

A somewhat surprising indicator of the amount dealers are willing to pay to get their hands on rhinoceros horn has been the enormous bids for old trophies or horn artifacts at European, Chinese and North American auction houses. In one 2011 auction held by Lolli Bros. Livestock Market in Moberly, Missouri, a pair of White Rhino horns went to a telephone bidder for $125,000. In Britain, where old rhino horn trophies once sold for a few hundred pounds, Tennant's summer sale in July 2010 netted prices in the tens of thousands. One set of White Rhino horns collected in 1930 sold for £106,000.

China's auction houses recorded an enormous spike in the sale of rhino horn "collectibles" in 2011. In all, 2,750 pieces, an increase of 90.77 percent over the number sold in 2010, were auctioned at an average price of $117,582 per item for a total of $179,000,000. After IFAW alerted authorities about a pending auction of 400 bottles of tiger-bone wine and a few pieces of ivory and rhino horn, the Chinese State Forestry Administration issued a circular to auction houses in January 2012 reminding them of its 1993 ban on the sale of tiger bone and rhino horn and asking them not to sell ivory, tiger bone or rhino horn products.

On March 12, 2012, the European Union issued a ban (valid until the end of the year, but subsequently renewed) on the export or re-export of any "worked items of rhino horn, except in cases where it is amply clear that the permit will be used for legitimate purposes." The UK, though it still allows the sale of works of art carved from rhino horn, now refuses any application to export horn objects to mainland China, "regardless of merit." Auction prices in Britain have fallen since the ban.

If you can't buy horns you can always steal them. According to the European Union's criminal intelligence agency Europol, in the past few years there have been over 50 thefts of rhino horns from museums, private collections and auction houses in Europe alone. There have been similar thefts in South Africa and the United States. Museum curators have been forced to take extraordinary measures to protect their rhinoceros horns. Horns on exhibit have been replaced with replicas, some dyed green to convince the robbers that there is nothing to steal. Sometimes the replicas are stolen anyway — evidence, perhaps, to show the bosses behind the raids that the thieves have done their work.

The thefts can be particularly brazen. Thieves at the Museum of Natural History in Gothenburg, Sweden, in July 2011 smashed open a glass case and sawed the horns off a mounted rhino during regular visiting hours. That December, two people made off with a rhino horn from the Museum of Hunting and Nature in Paris after overpowering the guards with some sort of paralyzing gas. Four thieves invaded the Offenburg Museum in Germany in broad daylight on March 2012, and while two of them distracted the guards, the others removed a Black Rhinoceros head mounted 13 feet (4 m) above the floor and broke off its horn with a sledgehammer.

Europol has identified the gang behind many of the thefts as the Rathkeale Rovers, a violent Irish traveller crime network also involved in "drug trafficking, organized robbery, distribution of counterfeit products, tarmac fraud and money laundering." The Rovers have operations in Europe, the Americas, South Africa, China and Australia. They invest much of their money in Irish real estate. In January 2013 a police sweep across eight European countries arrested 30 suspects. At least nine Rover members were served with tax demands totaling nine million euros.

United States law enforcement got wind of Rover activities when "two Irish men, Richard O'Brien and Michael Hegarty, from Rathkeale, Co Limerick ... were arrested after paying undercover agents in Colorado some $17,000 for four black rhino horns." They served six months in prison. In February 2012, the United States Fish and Wildlife Service (USFWS), Homeland Security and the Internal Revenue Service set up a massive crackdown on rhino horn smuggling in the United States. They called it Operation Crash, as in a "crash of rhinos" — oddly enough, also the name of a British indie rock band.

The investigation covered more than 25 states. It resulted in the arrest of a motley band of offenders, including a Vietnamese father-and-son team, an ex-professional rodeo cowboy and a New York antiques expert. A Chinese national, Jin Zhao Feng, arrested soon after the operation's launch, coordinated the horn shipments to Asia. The cowboy, Wade Steffens, was arrested with

"$337,000 in cash, some of it stuffed in a diaper bag. In later searches, USFWS and ICE officials discovered 17 packages with 37 rhino horns, $1 million in gold ingots, diamonds, Rolex watches, and another $1 million in cash." When USFWS Law Enforcement chief William C. Woody was asked why all this was happening, he had a simple answer: price, the "sole driving force" behind the American lust for horn.

Vast stores of ivory and smaller, but still extraordinarily valuable, piles of rhinoceros horn sit in government stockpiles throughout Africa and in some end-market and transit countries — the product of confiscations, natural mortality and control of problem animals. Though some countries, including Kenya and Gabon, have torched theirs as a deliberate declaration that their contents are not for sale, others, including the owners of growing private stocks of rhinoceros horn in South Africa, see them as a priceless source of future revenue (see p. 148). Meanwhile, they remain a potential target for robberies, including inside jobs.

In February 2012, thieves stole 266 elephant tusk pieces stored in a National Directorate of Lands and Forests warehouse in Mozambique. The ivory was supposedly under 24-hour surveillance from cameras operated by a private security firm. There was no evidence of the thieves, and the police "investigating" the incident reportedly did not bother to question the guards on duty or view the camera tapes.

In April or May 2012, thieves broke into a Department of Wildlife warehouse in the border town of Kasane, Botswana, and made off with about 26 tusks. A suspect was arrested in Zambia with ivory marked "BWK," for Botswana Wildlife Kasane. According to a spokesperson for the Botswanan Ministry of Environment, Wildlife and Tourism, "The security where the ivory was kept is very tight therefore we do not know how the tusks were eventually stolen but the police will probe the matter."

In June 2012, three tonnes of tusks vanished from a vault in the headquarters of the Zambia Wildlife Authority (ZAWA) only three weeks after they were confiscated. Two game scouts were quickly arrested but the ivory could not be found. The antigovernment *Zambian Watchdog* claimed that the ivory was actually sold to Chinese businessmen to raise money for political campaigns.

There have been no successful thefts from government rhino horn stockpiles in South Africa. All the same, stockpiles are a security nightmare and, at least in some cases, are easy pickings for a syndicate or, perhaps more often, a corrupt official planning an inside job.

With the exception of a few named groups like the Rathkeale Rovers and the odd alleged kingpin such as Laotian wildlife crime boss Vixay Keovasang (see p. 105), the spiders at the center of the web remain largely unnamed and, in some countries, untouchable. Keovasang, described by Thai investigators as "Mr. Big in Laos," is said to have close ties to Laotian military and government officials. Supposedly he even accompanied the deputy prime minister on an official visit to Vietnam. People like Keovasang, though, probably do not represent the highest echelons of the trade, the ones capable of shipping ivory by the hundreds of tonnes. They remain in the shadows.

The fingerprint of organized crime is most easily seen in the sheer scale, complexity of operation and flexibility of planning that make the system work. Ivory shipments are increasingly likely to be very large. In October 2012 authorities in Hong Kong made one of the largest illegal ivory seizures in history, and the largest ever recorded in Hong Kong: 1,209 tusks, weighing in total almost two tonnes, the equivalent of more than 600 dead elephants. Seven people were arrested.

Every time that a really big shipment turns up, one of 800 kilograms or more, it is a sure sign that larger criminal elements are at work. In 2011, the Elephant Trade Information System (ETIS), a database of ivory seizures established under CITES in 2002, recorded 13 large shipments amounting to over 23 tonnes of ivory. In 2010 there had been only six. It was the first time in 23 years that the number reached double digits. Even these figures represent only shipments that were discovered, confiscated and reported to ETIS. More — much more — must be getting through.

Trade routes are much more fluid now than they were in the 1980s, when most of the smuggled ivory in the world ended up in Hong Kong, in the hands of a few well-known families that were clearly in charge of the racket. Smuggling syndicates are able to shift their shipping routes when customs officials in previously favored ports start to get tough. As Singapore cracked down on ivory shipments, nearby Peninsular Malaysia became an increasingly popular transit point. When ETIS reported this to CITES in 2010, the Malaysian government took umbrage at the suggestion. In the succeeding months, though, TRAFFIC Southeast Asia was able to raise awareness of the problem with Malaysian authorities, culminating in a Wildlife Trade Awareness Programme for customs officers in February 2011.

In August 2011, a Malaysia-bound container with 1,041 tusks concealed in a shipment of, of all things, anchovies was seized in Zanzibar, Tanzania, before it could leave port. Perhaps the smugglers thought the smell would prevent customs officials from being too diligent. Three days later, Hong Kong officials confiscated 794 ivory pieces from a ship that had just left Malaysia. Finally, in Malaysia itself that same month, authorities in Penang seized a shipment of 664 tusks weighing 1,586 kilograms. Barely two weeks later, Malaysian authorities in Port Klang found another shipment, of 695 tusks weighing about 2,000 kilograms, concealed in a container supposedly filled with recycled plastic. Both shipments had originated in Tanzania, and the ivory in them was bound for China. Other seizures followed. In December 2012, authorities at Port Klang found 2,341 African elephant tusks and tusk pieces, weighing 6,034.3 kilograms, bound for China from the West African country of Togo. The ivory was concealed beneath some mahogany planks in two shipping containers labeled "wooden floor tiles."

Singapore may be back on the smugglers' route. In late January 2013, Singapore customs officials uncovered a shipment of 65 sacks containing 1,099 ivory tusk pieces from Africa, weighing 1.8 tonnes and valued at $2.5 million. The consignment was labeled as waste paper. It was the biggest ivory haul in the island nation since the seminal seizure in 2002.

Ivory and rhinoceros horn are only the jewels in the crown of the professional wildlife criminal. The hand of organized crime is being detected in wildlife trafficking of almost every kind, from illegal logging and fishing to the massive poaching of almost every reptile or amphibian that hunters in places like Indonesia or Madagascar can smuggle into the Chinese medical market or the European pet trade. From the criminal's point of view, it's the best racket in the world. The profits are immense, and as long as you're a middleman or kingpin and not a poacher in a shooting war with rangers, the risk is minute.

One of the reasons that the sentence handed down to Chumlong Lemtongthai (see p. 105) created such a stir is that serious consequences are rare in the world of wildlife crime. Sentences, when they are handed down at all, often cost far less than the profit from the offense. In January 2013, four Chinese citizens were arrested at Jomo Kenyatta Airport in Nairobi with 21 pounds of raw ivory and several carved pieces, valued at $24,000 in total. They were let off with fines of $340 each. The presiding magistrate regretted that the defendants' crime "is still considered as a petty offence" and called for Kenya's *Wildlife Act* to be amended. Things may be changing. Uganda has proposed amendments to its *Wildlife Act* that would impose mandatory fines of over $75,000, plus prison terms of 10 years, for poaching and smuggling of "blood ivory." Even

$75,000 may represent only a tiny tax on the profits of international syndicates dealing in ivory or rhino horn.

The involvement of organized crime in the wildlife trade has finally reached the desks of world leaders. In November 2012, then United States Secretary of State Hillary Rodham Clinton hosted an international partnership meeting on wildlife trafficking at the State Department. To those who might have wondered why the subject had become a State Department issue, she explained, specifically referring to ivory and rhinoceros horn, that "wildlife trafficking has become more organized, more lucrative, more widespread, and more dangerous than ever before," that protecting wildlife is "a national security issue, a public health issue and an economic security issue that is critical to each and every country represented here," and that trafficking presents "a global challenge that spans continents and crosses oceans, and we need to address it with partnerships that are as robust and far-reaching as the criminal networks we seek to dismantle." Senator John Kerry, Clinton's successor as Secretary of State, has already called ivory trafficking "a multi-million dollar criminal enterprise" and the poaching that supports it "a menace to developing economies ... [that] thrives where governance is weakest." In South Africa, rhino crimes have drawn the attention of Natjoints, the top security committee in the country, and have become the subject of committee hearings in the South African parliament.

On September 25, 2012, for the first time, poaching and wildlife trafficking were raised on the floor of the United Nations General Assembly. Strong statements by the United States, France and Gabon affirmed that wildlife crime is a threat not just to the environment but to the rule of law. The next day a UN Committee adopted a draft resolution aimed at strengthening the United Nation's Commission on Crime Prevention and Criminal Justice. In the course of recognizing the role of transnational organized crime in such evils as the traffic in human beings, narcotic drugs, cultural treasures, and firearms and ammunition, the committee expressed "deep concern about environmental crimes, including trafficking in endangered and, where applicable, protected species of wild fauna and flora, and emphasiz[ed] the need to combat such crimes by strengthening international cooperation, capacity-building, criminal justice responses and law enforcement efforts."

"Deep concern" may not be much of a substitute for tough action, but it's a start.

PART THREE

WHAT CAN BE DONE?

CHAPTER SIXTEEN

COMING TO GRIPS WITH POACHING

The headline in *The Times* for February 1, 2013, was blunt: "It's war, and in Africa's killing fields the poachers are winning." Jerome Starkey concluded his article on poaching, local corruption and collusion in Kenya with a despairing comment on poachers from a Kenyan farmer and conservationist: "They are killing so many elephants that, at this rate, they will all be gone. I don't want to have to explain to my son what an elephant looks like."

That doesn't mean that there is nothing we can do. Not so very long ago, in the 1990s, we beat back enormous waves of poaching and illegal trade. With the proper focus and the requisite will, we can do it again.

In his testimony before the United States Senate Committee on Foreign Relations, Iain Douglas-Hamilton set out the three main challenges for elephant conservation: "elephant poaching in the field, illegal trade both national and international, and excessive demand for ivory at the consuming end that drives the whole process." Substitute *horn* for *ivory* and the same can be said for rhinos.

Effective anti-poaching operations, with proper support at local, national and international levels, can make a great deal of difference. In 1989 Tanzania launched Operation Uhai, a 21-month initiative against poachers combining 1,000 men each from the army and police with 200 Wildlife Department and National Parks officers in the Selous region. The operation, which cost $5.2 million, netted 11,411 firearms, 3,044 elephant tusks and 2,607 poachers, dealers and traders. It effectively brought poaching to a standstill country-wide. Improvements in enforcement and governance in Ghana, including both anti-poaching efforts and raids on shops selling ivory, dramatically reduced the number of elephants being killed by poachers after their introduction in 2004. Reduced poaching levels for Greater One-horned Rhinoceroses have been directly related to the effectiveness of anti-poaching operations in India and Nepal (see p. 69). No rhinos at all were poached in Nepal in 2011, a first in 29 years and a tribute to its enforcement efforts.

Douglas-Hamilton's testimony described recent anti-poaching success stories in Kenya, Chad and Central Africa, including the drop in poaching levels in Chad's Zakouma National Park from an average of 800 elephants killed per year to only seven in 2011. Successes may be temporary, and things have gotten worse in Zakouma in recent months (see p. 115). That doesn't mean that anti-poaching efforts are futile, only that they need continuous commitment and support. Douglas-Hamilton assured the Committee that the fight "is not impossible to win, and good enforcement on the ground can work."

In Kenya today, both Savanna Elephant and Black Rhino numbers are growing despite local pockets of poaching (rhinos on private ranches in the Laikipia district have been particularly hard hit). Though some KWS rangers have colluded with poachers or even become poachers themselves — in April 2012 KWS director Julius Kipng'etich admitted that a ranger in Tsavo had been dismissed, and was to be prosecuted, for his role in killing an eight-year-old rhino — others have fought bravely with poaching gangs. Five KWS rangers were killed on duty in 2011, and in early 2012 two unarmed officers, a man and a pregnant woman, were gunned down by a gang of six poachers on a private ranch in Taita.

Anti-poaching efforts can make a difference even in the desperate ivory battlegrounds of Central Africa. For the first time in many years, the Dzanga Sangha Protected Areas (APDS) in the northern border region of the Central African Republic did not lose a single elephant during the winter of 2011–2012. Douglas-Hamilton ascribed the success to

> … Strong protection efforts that have been developed over several years by conservation NGOs, such as World Wildlife Fund, and governmental and non-governmental partners, including USAID through its Central African Regional Program for the Environment (CARPE). Another major factor helping to secure the park has been the cross-border cooperation that has been developed between park guards of the three bordering countries — CAR, Cameroon and

Republic of Congo — each of which contain a portion of the Sangha River Tri-national landscape (Dzanga Sangha is the CAR portion). Park guards engage in regular communication, joint patrols and joint law enforcement, so that information is rapidly shared and potential poachers can be pursued across international borders.

Poachers can and do move from country to country, and the cross-border cooperation Douglas-Hamilton describes can be crucial in their pursuit. In 1994, six African countries signed the Lusaka Agreement on Cooperative Enforcement Operations Directed at Illegal Trade in Wild Fauna and Flora, designed to coordinate anti-poaching and wildlife crime enforcement activities across a broad swathe of the continent. Currently the Lusaka Agreement has seven Parties, Congo, Kenya, Liberia, Tanzania, Uganda, Zambia and Lesotho, and three signatories, South Africa, Ethiopia and Swaziland. Its heart is the Lusaka Agreement Task Force (LATF), a permanent group of seconded enforcement officers and local support staff that carries out investigations, promotes awareness and shares information on illegal trade. LATF continues to be involved in seizures and arrests. In April 2012 it carried out a successful sting operation against two ivory-poaching kingpins in cooperation with the Zambian Wildlife Authority (ZAWA).

In 2012 ministers from eight member countries of the Central African Forest Commission (COMIFAC) attending an Extraordinary Meeting in N'Djamena, the capital of Chad, signed a five-year action plan to strengthen law enforcement and combat poaching (Plan d'Action sous-régional 2012–2017 des pays de l'espace COMIFAC pour le renforcement de l'Application des Législations Nationales sur la Faune sauvage, or PAPECALF). One of its aims is to carry out regular high-profile raids against domestic ivory markets. All ten COMIFAC countries — Burundi, Cameroon, Central African Republic, Chad, Democratic Republic of the Congo, Republic of the Congo, Equatorial Guinea, Gabon, Rwanda and São Tomé and Principe — have now signed on, and a high-level conference scheduled for 2013 will include government leaders, UN representatives and funding agencies such as the Africa Development Bank.

Investigations and seizures require their own set of skills. Kenya and India deploy sniffer dogs to nose out smuggled ivory. Kenya's canine unit, on 24-hour duty at its international airports in Nairobi and Mombasa, has uncovered more than eight tonnes of ivory since 2009. Smugglers sometimes try to derail the dogs' talents by spraying their cargo with tobacco and pepper. One dog named Tracey helped forest officials in Jharkand, India, uncover 32 kilograms of buried ivory in early 2012. Sniffer dogs are now being introduced in China and are being used to track poachers in the DRC.

If poachers are caught with ivory or rhinoceros horn, there is little question of who was doing the killing and where they were doing it. If the confiscating is done by customs officers at a distant market or transit point, tracking the haul to its source (and doing something about it) becomes much trickier. That is where the comparatively new science of wildlife forensics comes in. Sam Wasser and his team at the University of Washington's Center for Conservation Biology have been pioneers in extracting and analyzing the DNA in elephant ivory, using techniques borrowed from dental forensics.

Once you know the DNA fingerprint of an ivory sample, the next step is to link it to a local population somewhere in Africa. Tying down its origin, says Wasser, "allows authorities to direct law enforcement to poaching hot spots, potentially stops trade before the wildlife is actually killed, prevents countries from denying their poaching problems at home, and thwarts trade before it enters into an increasingly complex web of international criminal activity."

Wasser and his colleagues set out to build a continent-wide reference map of African elephant DNA. They established as many data points as they could using information from elephant dung samples, then linked the points together with a computer algorithm bearing the appropriate acronym SCAT (smoothed continuous assignment technique). We have already seen (see p. 93) how Wasser's technique traced the huge ivory shipment seized in Singapore in 2002 to killing fields in Zambia. Wasser's results, though they represent a forensic breakthrough of enormous value, have not always been welcomed by governments. The truth, apparently, makes some people quite uncomfortable.

Forensic techniques nonetheless continue to improve. Male elephants leave their family groups upon maturity while females do not, and a 2013 study showed that mitochondrial DNA (mtDNA), which is inherited from females only, tracks differently across migratory elephant populations from the nuclear DNA found in both sexes. Using both types of DNA allows us to triangulate the origins of confiscated ivory even more precisely than tracking methods based on nuclear or mtDNA alone. A team of Chinese scientists has recently developed liquid chromatography "fingerprints" that can be used to distinguish traditional medicines containing rhinoceros powder from those made with substitutes such as Water Buffalo horn.

The only full-time dedicated wildlife crime laboratory in the world is the United States Fish and Wildlife Service Forensic Laboratory (USFWS-FL) in Ashland, Oregon. Today, however, more and more countries are acquiring the capacity to do forensics on their own. The member countries of the Association of Southeast Asian Nations Wildlife Enforcement Network (ASEAN-WEN), a project begun in 2005 with funding from the UK government, have been working together since 2009 to improve their forensic capabilities. In June 2012 the Global Environment Facility (GEF) approved in principle a $2.8 million project to improve South Africa's ability to use wildlife forensics in its fight against wildlife crime, including rhino poaching. South Africa is currently preparing the proposal it needs to secure the funding. It hopes to use the money to, among other things, boost the capacity of its RhODIS laboratory at the University of Pretoria, home to a rhino DNA database used to investigate and prosecute rhino-related offenses. In its first three years RhODIS has already received close to 16,000 samples from 6,500 individual rhinos. If South Africa succeeds, it will be one of the few times GEF money will have been used to fight wildlife crime.

A number of CITES Resolutions have asked its Parties to take action to control the trade in ivory and rhino horn. Of those still in force, Res. Conf. 9.14 (Rev. CoP 15), *Conservation of and Trade in African and Asian Rhinoceroses*, urges relevant Parties, among other things, to identify, mark, register and secure any government stockpiles of rhinoceros horn, to cooperate with each other, "to be vigilant in their law enforcement efforts" and "to develop and implement strategies for reducing the use and consumption of rhinoceros parts and derivatives." Yet since Resolutions are not fully binding, to "urge" is often all they can do. If range countries do not have a budgeted conservation and management plan for rhinoceroses, they are urged to "develop and implement one as expeditiously as possible."

Res. Conf. 10.10 (Rev. CoP 15), *Trade in Elephant Specimens*, is a much more comprehensive document dealing with marking of stockpiled ivory, control of domestic ivory trade and authorizing the MIKE and ETIS monitoring systems (see pp. 82 and 129, respectively). It agrees that "Parties [should] assist range States to improve their capacity to manage and conserve their elephant populations through improved law enforcement, surveys and monitoring of wild populations" and establishes a quota system, now unused, for trade in raw ivory. It has been revised several times and is up for further revision at the March 2013 CITES meeting (CoP16) in Bangkok.

CITES Resolutions are of use only if the Parties follow through. A 2012 WWF report by Kristin Nowell names China, India, Laos, Malaysia, Nigeria, Russia, South Africa and Zimbabwe as countries that have improved their compliance, mostly by passing legislation and imposing stricter penalties. Indonesia's anti-poaching efforts have improved (see p. 122) — a good thing, given that it is home to the only surviving Javan and most of the surviving Sumatran Rhinos in the world. China scored surprisingly high for its control of the rhino horn trade. After major enforcement actions in April and June 2012, the availability of rhino horn via Internet sites in China dropped by over 70 percent.

Enacting laws and penalties is not the same thing as using them. The report comments that "major prosecutions for wildlife crime are still rare, and overall the scoring shows that enforcement has lagged behind compliance." Nowell cites a "serious lack of progress" in many key range countries, transit points and end-market countries. She hands Vietnam a red score for its poor compliance on rhinos, but Vietnam's recent directives (see p. 91) may represent a step forward. Laos, Myanmar and Thailand receive red scores for failure to deal with the ivory trade. China's legal mechanisms in place for ivory appear to comply with CITES, but Nowell comments that in practice the country "has failed to effectively police the system and track the sale of legally-imported ivory, although authorities are intercepting a growing number of illegal trade cases."

Both Cameroon and the CAR support domestic ivory markets, and Cameroon permits ivory to be carved and stored without a license. Not surprisingly, Cameroon, the CAR and the DRC received failing grades for compliance. So did Egypt, one of the largest illegal ivory markets on the continent. It is illegal to offer ivory for sale in Egypt, but Esmond Martin and Lucy Vigne found over 9,000 pieces openly on sale in an April 2011 market survey of Cairo and Luxor. The authorities hadn't confiscated a single piece of ivory from a retail store since 2003. Most of the ivory apparently enters the country from Sudan and ends up being sold to foreign tourists, over half of them (according to the vendors) Chinese.

Even our best efforts to combat poachers and deal with wildlife crime are susceptible to poor governance, corruption, lack of resources and the failure of political will. What does it tell us, for example, when the highly praised ASEAN-WEN is based in a country, Thailand, that has been named as one of the three countries most heavily implicated in the trafficking in illegal ivory?

Weak (or, as in Egypt, practically non-existent) enforcement and protection systems are still the rule in many countries. They may be based on outmoded legislation, depend on overworked staff and rely on limited sources of information. We need high-level, systemic, across-the-board international and national commitments to fight wildlife crime, and ivory and rhino horn smuggling in particular. As Elizabeth Bennett warned in her 2010 paper, "Another Inconvenient Truth: The Failure of Enforcement Systems to Save Charismatic Species," "we have to start taking wildlife enforcement seriously."

Perhaps that is beginning to happen. Bennett herself noted the creation in November 2010 of the International Consortium on Combating Wildlife Crime (ICCWC, pronounced "eye-quick"). ICCWC is a combined effort of the CITES Secretariat, INTERPOL, the United Nations Office on Drugs and Crime (UNODC), the World Bank and the World Customs Organization (WCO). The CITES Secretariat chairs the alliance. With these forces and resources behind it, ICCWC could accomplish a good deal. In 2012 it released a Wildlife and Forest Crime Analytical Toolkit that should help law enforcement, and it will assist the GEF-funded rhino enforcement project in South Africa. It may be too early, however, to call ICCWC more than (as Bennett did in 2010) "potentially" powerful.

In March and April 2012 INTERPOL carried out the most wide-ranging operation in its history against ivory poachers and traffickers. Dubbed Operation Worthy, it involved judiciary, customs, police, wildlife and revenue services in 14 African states. Operation Worthy led to 214 arrests and netted hauls of almost two tonnes of ivory, 20 kilograms of rhino horn and more than 30 military-grade weapons, including AK-47s, G-3s and M16s. Intelligence from the operation passed down the supply chain to the market end, providing leads that allowed China to uncover and prosecute more than 700 cases of illegal trade in wildlife. Operation Worthy was part of a wider INTERPOL initiative, Project Wisdom, designed to help governments improve their intelligence-gathering and enforcement techniques as they deal with elephant and rhino poaching.

In January 2013, wildlife enforcement professionals from 11 national and international wildlife agencies, including LATF, ASEAN-WEN and the governments of China, Nepal, South Africa, India, Indonesia, Vietnam, Thailand and the United States, met in Bangkok to carry out a month-long information-sharing exercise chaired by China. It ended in a massive crackdown aimed at tracking and dismantling wildlife crime networks across 22 African and Asian countries. According to China's Xinhua News Agency, Operation Cobra sent out some 100,000 law enforcement agents to crack down on more than 200 wildlife trafficking cases and arrest over 100 suspects. Among the confiscated booty were 6.5 tonnes of ivory and ivory products and 22 rhino horns. In the words of Deputy Chief Edward Grace of the United States Fish and Wildlife Service Office of Law Enforcement, Operation Cobra sent a message to poachers and smugglers that "The world's endangered wildlife and plant resources are not theirs for the taking."

These proudly trumpeted figures, however, may be misleading. Some of the arrests claimed by Operation Cobra may have been carried out before it began (this sort of credit-grabbing is apparently not uncommon). Authorities in Gabon asked Luc Mathot of the NGO Conservation Justice to report some of its anti-poaching actions as part of Operation Cobra, but Mathot refused to do so. Besides, confiscations and arrests are one thing; prosecutions and convictions — and truly meaningful sentences — are something else altogether. Often only a small number of such cases — less than 10 percent of tiger poaching cases in Thailand since 2010, for example — actually reach court. As we have seen in the Chumlong Lemtongthai case (see p. 106), even in a highly publicized trial some of the allegedly biggest fish may get away. The achievements of Operation Cobra will have to be won, or lost, in the courts before we can truly judge if they represent genuine progress, a good but ineffective try, or face-saving window dressing.

There is more to anti-poaching efforts than hunting, arresting or shooting down poachers, and more to successful enforcement than arresting and prosecuting smugglers or bringing sophisticated forensics to bear on their booty. Most governments cannot stop a major poaching incursion by brute strength alone. We need to understand what actually works on the ground. Studies of elephant poaching in the Luangwa Valley of Zambia, for example, suggest that increasing fines in proportion to the number of trophies in a poacher's hands has a deterrent effect, but increasing the severity of punishment works less well than devoting more effort to tracking down and prosecuting poachers in the field.

To succeed in the long term, even the most dedicated and efficient anti-poaching operations must be part of a general effort to improve people's lives. It is easy for us to recoil from poachers' atrocities, but we would do well to remember that things may look very different to the people who have to live with elephants or rhinoceroses. To a poor farmer in Africa or Asia, elephants are not "charismatic megafauna" but powerful, hungry monsters that can destroy their livelihoods or, more frequently than we might think, kill them. Rampant elephants can influence a villager's psychological state and can even affect rural education if the risk of encountering them keeps children off the road to school. Rhinos, too, can fall afoul of local farmers, particularly in the more densely populated croplands of Asia. Javan Rhinos, when there were enough of them to matter, were once shot by planters when they invaded tea plantations.

Human–animal conflict, especially involving elephants, is a huge and important subject beyond the scope of this book. It should not surprise us, though, that villagers in Cameroon or Kenya have been as likely to help poachers as to report them to the authorities. It doesn't have to be this way. As Winnie Kiiru has written, "Many African communities appreciate the intrinsic value of wildlife conservation. Building on this ethic by creating an enabling environment for elephant conservation while minimizing conflict is the way forward." Those who deal with the poaching crisis have to consider the very real conflict between humans and the animals we are trying to save, and they must try to do something about it. That can be as simple as treating a crop fence with an irritating concoction of chili and engine oil, or installing beehives full of stinging insects around farmers' fields. Not every solution is high-tech.

A herd of African Savanna Elephants crosses the plains of Tsavo East National Park, Kenya, on May 18, 2011. If the present wave of elephant poaching continues, scenes like this may soon exist only in photographs.

African Forest Elephants in the Mbeli River, Nouabalé–Ndoki National Park, Congo. The Forest Elephant, only recently recognized as a distinct species, has more rounded ears and thinner tusks than the better-known Savanna Elephant.

A Bornean Pygmy Elephant, smallest of
the Asian Elephants, photographed by the
author along the Kinabatangan River in
Sabah, Malaysian Borneo, in May 2010.

An elephant calf and her keeper inside her stall at the Daphne Sheldrick Elephant Orphanage in Nairobi, Kenya, July 21, 2011. Like thousands of other elephant calves, this one was orphaned when her mother was killed for her tusks.

PHOTO: BRENT STIRTON / REPORTAGE BY GETTY IMAGES

A Thai customs official displays smuggled elephant tusks during a press conference at Bangkok Airport, Thailand, July 17, 2012. Thai Customs had seized a shipment from Kenya containing 158 pieces African elephant tusks, weighing 456.12 kilograms with an estimated value of 22.80 million Thai baht (722,000 US dollars or 588,000 euro).

A customs officer stands next to stacks of seized ivory at a Hong Kong Government Customs and Excise facility in Tsing Yi, Hong Kong, China, in January 2013. Hong Kong customs officers seized a total of 779 elephant tusks weighing 1,300 kilograms and worth roughly 1,000,000 Euros. The tusks were hidden in a container of "architectural stones" arriving from Kenya.

Kenyan President Mwai Kibaki (right) sets ablaze a pile of elephant tusks in Tsavo West National Park in July 2011 as a part of the celebrations during the first-ever African Elephant Law Enforcement Day. The ivory had been confiscated in Singapore in June 2002, as part of the largest seizure of illegal ivory in years. This was Kenya's third burning since July 1989, four months before the passage of the CITES ivory ban, when President Daniel Arap Moi set fire to 12 tonnes of ivory in Nairobi National Park.

Undercover Kenya Wildlife Services Rangers
remove the tusks from a bull elephant killed
by a spear in the Amboseli ecosystem in the
shadow of Amboseli, Kenya, May 2011. It is
unknown whether the killing was a poaching
attempt, or in retaliation after the animal
invaded the crops of local Maasai.

Remains of some of the victims of the largest mass killing of elephants in recent history, photographed on April 6, 2012. The slaughter took place between January and March 2012, in and around Bouba N'Djida National Park in northern Cameroon. The ivory poachers themselves told local villagers they had killed over 650 elephants in the almost 2,000 square mile (500,000 ha) region.

Luang Poo Bru Ba Dhammamunee, head
abbot of Wat Suan Paa Phutthasatharn
Supraditme thee Temple, walks through the
elephant graveyard in Surin Elephant Village
in Surin, Thailand. The monk buys his ivory
carvings of Bhuddist icons for resale purposes
to his followers. Despite a public relations
campaign as a carer of elephants in Thailand,
he has commented openly on the presence
in Thailand of illegally imported African ivory
and advised on how to get it into Thailand
past customs authorities.

African Savanna Elephant females and their
young in Etosha National Park, Namibia.

A Javan Rhinoceros wades through a brook in Ujung Kulon National Park, Indonesia, the species' last stronghold.

A Greater One-horned Rhinoceros in Royal Bardia National Park, Nepal.

A three-week old Black Rhino calf born at
the Victoria Falls Private Game Reserve,
Zimbabwe, April, 2011.

A female Southern White Rhinoceros with an unusually long front horn. This animal was photographed outside its natural range in Kenya, where a number of South African White Rhinos have been translocated in recent years.

PHOTO: NIGEL PRAVITT / JAI / CORBIS

Portrait of a Black Rhinoceros in Tanzania.

PHOTO: BIOSPHOTO / MICHEL & CHRISTINE DENIS-HUOT

Kenya Wildlife Service game wardens prepare to relocate a captured Southern White Rhino from Lake Nakuru National Park in the Rift Valley to Meru National Park in Kenya's north.

PHOTO: BIOSPHOTO / CYRIL RUOSO

ABOVE: A female Sumatran Rhinoceros being fed by hand at Way Kambas National Park, Indonesia.

OPPOSITE: Members of the Camel Corps, an anti-poaching force, transport a tranquilized White Rhino to a safe location. Meru National Park, Kenya.

Park wardens hold up a confiscated rhinoceros
skull in Garamba National Park, Democratic
Republic of Congo. Garamba was the last refuge
of the Northern White Rhinoceros, now extinct
in the wild.

The carcass of a Southern White Rhinoceros, killed for its horn.

"Rambo," a 9-month old Southern White Rhino orphan, is being raised by hand on a game farm outside of Klerksdorp, South Africa, after being abandoned by his mother at 5 days old. When he was found, jackals had already begun eating his tail.

A traditional medicine specialist pours grindings of rhino horn mixed with water into a cup for drinking in Saigon, Vietnam, in October, 2011. His client has been told that drinking Rhino horn can cure her breast cancer, though there is no medical evidence that this is true.

A Southern White Rhinoceros in Zimbabwe has its horns cut off with a chainsaw to deter poachers.

PHOTO: BIOSPHOTO / MICHEL GUNTHER

A White Rhino cow is dehorned as an anti-poaching measure on a game farm outside of Klerksdorp, South Africa in March 2011. The veterinarian's assistant holds the horns for an identity picture while the vet does a final check on the animal. On average a de-horning takes an experienced vet no more than 25 minutes from start to finish.

PHOTO: BRENT STIRTON / REPORTAGE BY GETTY IMAGES

One of the young women allegedly recruited to pose as a "hunter" in the Chumlong Lemtongthai case.

PHOTO: JULIAN RADEMEYER / *KILLING FOR PROFIT*

Members of the Sumatran Rhinoceros Protection Unit at a mud wallow in Way Kambas National Park, Indonesia. The unit collects data and looks for tracks to measure rhino attendance at wallows.

PHOTO: BIOSPHOTO / CYRIL RUOSO

A four man anti-poaching team keeps one of only seven surviving Northern White Rhinoceroses (*Ceratotherium simum cottoni*) under permanent guard. Photographed at Ol Pejeta Conservancy in Kenya, 13 July 2011.

SHOULD TRADE BE LEGALIZED?

The argument for eliminating all trade in ivory assumes that illegal stock will always be mixed with legal, and that illegal stock will be offered as legitimate to unsuspecting buyers as long as a legal supply exists. The ivory crisis of the 1980s proved that legal trade can provide laundering opportunities for smugglers. The rise in demand following the 2008 one-off ivory sale to China suggests that the presence of legal ivory on the market may legitimize its use among purchasers. This seemingly inextricable linkage means that legal ivory trade should never be allowed while poaching remains out of control. If poaching is out of control because legal trade has been allowed to happen, then legal trade should remain off the shelf forever.

China, which continues to sell within its borders the legal ivory it imported in 2008, still maintains that it has sound mechanisms for ensuring that legal ivory stays out of its registered shops. In February 2013 Hong Lei, a foreign ministry spokesman, rejected accusations that Chinese demand for ivory has led to increased poaching. China's legislative and enforcement actions, he said, "have helped crack down on ivory smuggling and effectively curbed it." The *China Daily* claimed that China's ivory control measures — including a maximum life sentence for smuggling — were stricter than CITES requires. It noted that every finished ivory product had to carry an ID card linked to an online database, and blamed "lack of expertise and experience" for survey reports claiming that illegal ivory was available in Chinese markets.

Brendan Moyle, a New Zealand economist who has long been a critic of CITES, echoed China's arguments after a recent tour (sponsored by the

International Fund for Elephant Conservation, which was sat up by the quasi-governmental China Wildlife Conservation Association) of five Chinese cities. Moyle claimed that "The legal market caters to a clientele of informed, repeat customers after quality pieces, which distinguishes it from the illegal market where we saw generally cruder and smaller carvings which could be pumped out by less skilled carvers." He concluded that "The legal market is insulated from the illegal market at several levels. Blaming the legal trade for elephant poaching is simplistic, wrong and a threat to the conservation gains the industry has yielded." Moyle's article did not specify what these "conservation gains" were.

China's critics, however, say that though the government may well be trying its best to rein in its smuggling problem, there is little real evidence of success. Why, for example, did Esmond Martin and Lucy Vigne find in 2011 that over 60 percent of the ivory items in retail outlets, including registered markets, in Guangzhou lacked the required government certificates (see p. 99)? Was this simply inadvertence or carelessness on the shopkeepers' part? Or are we to assume that Martin, an expert on the trade with decades of experience in Asian and African markets, did not know elephant ivory when he saw it?

Until December 2012, it seemed that the March 2013 CITES meeting in Bangkok, Thailand, would see another battle over legalized trade. For the second time, Tanzania had asked CITES to transfer its elephant population to Appendix II. It planned to sell off 101,005.25 kilograms of ivory, the entire sellable content of its government stockpile. The chief result of the proposal, though, was to highlight the extent of the poaching crisis within Tanzania. A Tanzanian MP informed the National Assembly in August 2012 that the country was losing 80 elephants to poachers every day. A few months later the country's Minister of Natural Resources and Tourism confirmed that a haul of 1,330 kilograms of ivory seized in Hong Kong, representing the slaughter of some 150 elephants, had originated in Tanzania. Allegations followed that senior government officials were implicated in the trade.

Facing intense criticism from conservationists, opposition members and other elephant-range countries, the Tanzanian government withdrew its proposal in December. Its Director of Wildlife, Alexander Songorwa, admitted that the country could not meet the conditions for downlisting. Under CITES rules a withdrawn proposal cannot be reintroduced, and so the bruising debate that would certainly have ensued at the meeting in Bangkok will not take place.

Elephants will not be entirely off the CITES table in Bangkok. Kenya and Burkina Faso want to redraft the nine-year "moratorium" (see p. 83) so that it actually does what the anti-trading range countries intended — namely prevent any country, no matter what CITES Appendix its elephants are on, from asking for an ivory sale for as long as the moratorium has left to run. Resolution Conf. 10.10, *Trade in Elephant Specimens*, was up for revision again (see p. 139), and there is a proposed amendment to Resolution Conf. 10.9 calling for the Panel of Experts (see p. 62) to be made permanent.

More crucial for the future may be the further progress of a plan to solve the ivory trade impasse once and for all. The "solution," in wording adopted by the Parties in 2007, is to develop "a decision-making mechanism for a process of trade in ivory under the auspices of the Conference of the Parties" (DMM). The idea, as explained by the CITES Secretariat, was "to establish a basis for agreeing upon how to make the decision, under CITES, on whether or not there should be international trade in elephant ivory, under what circumstances such trade could take place, and what would be the related institutional and financial arrangements."

The southern African countries that have participated in the previous one-off sales can complain, quite legitimately, that the auction prices they received were well below what they might have gained on the open market, and those countries would far prefer to see ongoing regular trade. Most CITES Parties, and particularly most of the elephant-range countries of West, Central and East Africa, are not about to approve a free and open ivory market, especially under current conditions. An acceptable DMM would have to be based on criteria tough enough to satisfy countries now opposed to any legal trade but not impossible for countries aspiring to trade to satisfy. Requiring the DMM to be "under the auspices of CITES" should allow approved trade to be modified or stopped if the situation gets out of control.

The wording the Parties adopted, unfortunately, is particularly obtuse. A first stab at what a DMM should look like resulted in a commissioned study that was not at all what most Parties had in mind. Its chief author, Rowan Martin, fielded an idea he had first proposed almost 20 years earlier: a sellers' cartel, based on the system De Beers has used to sell diamonds. Martin's proposal left no role for range countries not trading in ivory and largely eliminated any supervisory role for CITES. It was heavily criticized, and the Parties in Bangkok plan to make another try at setting up a workable process to develop an acceptable DMM over the next few years. Whether a legal ivory trade will follow its (presumed) adoption, though, is anybody's guess.

Meanwhile, calls have come from within South Africa for a legal trade in rhino horn, something that has not existed since 1977. In December 2011, veteran South African conservationist Ian Player called for activists to unite behind legalization, dismissing objectors as "those screaming against legal trading," the bulk of whom come "from countries that no longer possess a single rhino." In February 2012 South African environmental economist Michael 't Sas-Rolfes, an advocate of privatizing conservation and legalizing the horn trade, supported legal sales with a thought-provoking analysis of the economics of the horn market.

In March 2012, the South African Hunters and Game Conservation Association (SAHGCA) announced that it would ask the South African government to petition CITES for permission to open the trade (technically, this would require an amendment to the annotation that currently restricts trade to live specimens and hunting trophies). This was a fairly mild follow-up to a submission from SAHGCA to a Parliamentary Committee in January calling for South Africa to "demand the down-listing of South Africa's white rhino from Appendix II to Appendix III of CITES" (impossible under CITES rules) and "to seriously contemplate the relevance of South Africa remaining a member country of an imperialistically orientated CITES."

Legal trade would be in line with South Africa's philosophy of sustainable use, but the government was reluctant to oblige the hunters, the Private Rhino Owners Association (an owners' coalition founded in October 2009 in response to the rise in poaching) or Ezemvelo KZN Wildlife, the provincial conservation authority for the state of Kwazulu-Natal. Water and Environmental Affairs minister Edna Molewa cited "legal obstacles" with both China and Vietnam, the two countries that would likely need to be approved as partners if CITES were to agree to open trade. All privately held stockpiles of rhino horn would have to be registered with the government, marked and verified before any legalization plans could go ahead.

Supporters of legal trade were furious. David Cook, a former Natal Parks Board senior officer, wrote that "A supreme opportunity was missed to declare to the international conservation bureaucracies of the Western world that 35 years of a ban on trade in rhino horn had done absolutely nothing to save the species. It had, in fact, played directly into the hands of the black-market trade in rhino horn and reduced South Africa, which holds 75% of the world's rhino population, to the role of a spectator at an extinction event."

The government's refusal was not good enough for Ezemvolo and the other supporters of trade. Ezemvelo presented details of its sales proposal to the International Wildlife Management Congress in Durban in July 2012, with support from Ian Player. Its plan called for a tightly controlled selling

organization, marketing only horn from naturally deceased animals direct-
ly to approved Chinese pharmaceutical companies. Ezemvelo's CEO, Bandile
Mkhize, announced plans to consult Nicky Oppenheimer, Chairman of De
Beers, for advice on how to set up a sellers' cartel for rhino horn. Roger Porter,
Ezemvelo's conservation planning chief, urged the conservation community to
"try it out for five years."

In the end, the South African government decided not to take Porter's
advice. On October 4, 2012, the deadline for proposals for the 2013 meeting,
it announced that it was not going ahead. Noting that a report by rhino-issue
manager Mavuso Msimang was not due until the end of the month, a government spokesman said that it would, instead, prepare a case for the next CITES
meeting in 2016.

The arguments for legalization have not gone away. Supporters have used
an analogous case to argue the benefits of legalized sales. The Vicuña (*Vicuna
vicugna*) is a small South American member of the camel family that bears
wool so fine and valuable that it was once reserved, on pain of death, for Inca
nobility. After the Spanish conquest, intense hunting reduced its numbers
from perhaps two million to as few as 10,000 animals by 1960. The Vicuña was
placed on Appendix I of CITES in 1975. It was saved, however, by coordinated
efforts among its four range countries (Argentina, Bolivia, Chile and Peru),
which signed a treaty for its protection in 1979.

By the early 1990s Vicuña populations had grown to over 66,000 in Peru
alone. As populations recovered, Peru, and later the other range countries, instituted a program that allowed local communities to shear and release the animals and weave the wool into garments for sale. Since 1994, CITES has agreed
to transfer a number of Vicuña populations to Appendix II, with restrictions
allowing sale of wool from local community industries. By 2010, Vicuña numbers had reached some 421,500 across their range.

Is this a model for rhinos? Trade supporters point to parallels: intense poaching and a trade ban, followed by the development of a local industry based on
collecting a valuable product without killing the animal, the removal of the
ban, recovery of the species and a growing source of income for local people.
However, the Vicuña program, though a commendable success in many ways,
has not solved the biggest problem facing rhinos: how to drive the poachers out
of the market. On the contrary, the Vicuña program's success depends on keeping poachers under control through other means. Poaching is once again on the
rise. It is already serious in some areas, and one study in Peru has warned that if

poaching is not controlled the gains of the program, both to Vicuñas and to local people, could be lost. A 2009 story reported slaughters of thousands of animals by armed poaching gangs in some regions of Peru — a parallel to the rhino situation that the supporters of legalization have not, understandably, chosen to mention.

No one advocating a legal trade in horn suggests killing rhinos, as poachers do, to get it. Yet is it not unethical to legalize a source of medicinal fraud? The question is debatable (and open to accusations of cultural insensitivity). Nonetheless, even if some beliefs about the medical value of rhinoceros horn are deeply held and backed by thousands of years of tradition, the notion that horn cures cancer is not. The most fervent supporter of trade-for-conservation might balk at the idea of supplying the "cancer touts" who prey on helpless victims in Vietnamese hospitals. Or does an ethical argument that, if pursued, might lead to the extinction of a species have ethical problems of its own?

WWF International's Wildlife Trade Policy Analyst, Colman O Criodain, said in August 2012 that there were sound, practical reasons for not supporting trade in rhino horn at this time. Chief CITES Enforcement Officer John Sellar had pointed out in 2011 that, since all the Asian consuming countries, including Vietnam, have banned the sale of horns, the only available customers are criminals, and CITES would hardly agree to that. Rhino horn, unlike ivory, can regrow once removed and is, at least to some extent, a "renewable resource." Expecting, however, that a legal trade could undermine poachers and deprive them of their customers may be hopelessly unrealistic. African traders might find themselves competing not only with poachers but with proposed rhino farming operations in China. A Breeding Center for the Artificial Propagation of Rhinoceros has been established in Sanya City, Hainan Province. It has already acquired Southern White Rhinoceroses, and its apparent intent is to breed them as "endangered medicinal-use animals." A company called Longhui Phamaceutical apparently also intends to breed rhinos for their horn, which it described as having "detoxification and anti-cancer" properties. The Chinese government has yet to approve officially any commercial farming operations for rhino horn.

Michael 't Sas-Rolfes argues that the demand may not be as great as critics fear. Rather than a vast market, there may be only a few determined, wealthy purchasers who want rhino horn no matter what its source and will pay any price to get it. Eric Dinerstein has pointed out that rhinoceros horn is so valuable, and is used in such tiny quantities by traditional medical practitioners, that a very small amount — perhaps as little as one horn per consumer country per year — might satisfy whatever real medicinal demand exists. He argues that the effect on the rhino horn trade of the demand for traditional medicine may have more to do with the expectations of poachers and traders than with the market itself. However, Dinerstein is no fan of legalization. In *The Return of the Unicorns* (2003) he agrees that the bans on trade have been both useful and necessary: "Given the efficacy of the bans, the availability of substitute medicines, and the risks of stimulating illegal trade posed by limited legal trade, most parties agree that the use of rhinoceros horn as medicine should remain a thing of the past."

Even if 't Sas-Rolfes is right, it does not mean that a legal trade would satisfy, or even appeal to, putative customers. The biggest purchasers today are not buying from traditional pharmaceutical outlets supplied by the "accredited buyers," as envisioned by Ezemvelo. To get horn to, say, impress a superior (or bribe an official), they may still have to resort to illegal sources.

The assertion that legal trade in rhinoceros horn, even if operated by a central organization with the power to set prices, would depress the market and reduce poaching remains unproven. For its supporters, though, the most compelling reason to legalize the sale of horn is the financial situation of private rhinoceros owners within South Africa.

Keeping rhinos has been an attractive proposition for game farm owners, who see the animals as a source of income from hunting and game viewing. Over 20 percent of South Africa's White Rhinos are in private hands (in 2010, 4,531 out of 18,780 were privately owned). The Private Rhino Owners Association has some 400 members, and some individual ranchers own hundreds of animals. A hotel magnate named John Hume, who claims to be the world's biggest private owner, owns more than 800 rhinos and reportedly has a registered private stockpile of over 500 kilograms of horn.

Rhino poaching in South Africa, however, is turning privately owned rhinos into liabilities. Many wildlife ranchers are dehorning their animals in the hope of deterring poachers, an expensive process that must be repeated at least once a year. Hume dehorns all of his rhinos annually. Since poachers sometimes kill the dehorned rhinos anyway, owners have been forced to hire full-time security guards. Hume hired 40 new guards in 2012. Frustrated rhino owners find themselves put to greater and greater expense to protect their animals, while at the same time amassing growing stockpiles of horn that they cannot sell.

A legal trade would solve their problems. If it succeeded in once more making rhinos attractive propositions for wildlife ranching, owners claim, not only would they benefit but so would rhino conservation in general. In late September 2012 South African big-cat conservationist John Varty publicly urged Hume to gather together 100 or so rhino owners to defy the government by staging a joint horn auction as an international event. The government couldn't, he suggested, arrest them all.

Despite the undoubted conservation importance of private rhino stocks, even in South Africa most rhinos are not in private hands. The biggest numbers are in the Kruger. Is a legal trade that benefits only private rhino owners in South Africa a viable option for the global conservation of rhinos? Even if the Kruger itself got into the business of selling horn from natural mortalities, as has been suggested by some, what might a legal horn trade out of South Africa do to rhino populations elsewhere? Horn from the Asian rhinoceroses has traditionally fetched higher prices than African horn. Any upsurge of demand that might follow a "legitimized" trade could place greater pressure on the Asian species. Keshav Varma, program director of the Global Tiger Initiative, warned in May 2012 that support for legal trade from South Africa could cause a surge in demand for horns from India.

The two biggest arguments made for legalization — undercutting the poachers and earning revenue for private owners, conservation departments or local communities — are mutually contradictory. You can't undercut prices and make big profits at the same time. Would legal sellers be prepared to keep the price low enough to draw customers from the smugglers, especially when they can argue that they need the money to justify conserving elephants and rhinos in their own countries? One would think that if the aim was to gut the poachers' earnings and not just to make money, the best move (and it has actually been suggested) would be to give the stuff away for free. Of course, some bright entrepreneur would probably snap it up to sell for high prices later.

One of the most frequent arguments from supporters of legal trade in rhinoceros horn is that nothing else has worked. As we have seen in earlier chapters, this narrow view is simply incorrect — rhino success stories in countries like Nepal stand as proof. Demand has declined in the past in Japan, South Korea and Taiwan, but it did so under the CITES ban on commercial trade. Legalization might help — or it might create a set of truly insurmountable problems on top of the current crisis. Tom Milliken and Jo Shaw have written that "There is still much uncertainty as to how illegal markets would be affected by legal trade in terms of supply–demand dynamics. More research into the poorly-understood Asian end-use markets is required to increase understanding of these issues and advise the best solution going forward." In other words, we have no idea what the effects of a legal trade might be. Until we do, I don't believe that we should risk a decision that could make matters worse.

CHAPTER EIGHTEEN

DEALING WITH DEMAND

As long as consumers are prepared to pay enormous prices for ivory and rhinoceros horn, criminal syndicates will control the trade route while gangs and militias will control the poaching. Disarming and eliminating the gangs or breaking up the criminal syndicates might make for a good action movie, but is probably beyond the competence or political will of most governments. Toss corruption into the mix, add a few untouchable kingpins safe in countries beyond the rule of international law, and the situation becomes very nearly impossible.

If, however, the prices come down substantially — below the level at which it would be profitable for the syndicates to operate — the scale of operations of the criminal enterprises dealing in ivory and rhinoceros horn will be forced to diminish. That doesn't mean that illegal trade will stop. There is a vast trade in lower-cost wildlife for the pet trade the meat market, and for traditional medicine. But since elephants and rhinoceroses are in much shorter supply than many of the other species in the wildlife business, and the job of getting tusks and horns to market is considerably more difficult, a price drop could bring things down to controllable levels. That is what happened to the ivory trade in the early 1990s.

So how do we lower the prices? If the laws of supply and demand apply to ivory and rhino horn, is it better to control supply (and try to control prices in so doing) or to reduce demand (and hope that the prices will fall on their own)?

Advocates of legalized trade tend to concentrate on controlling supply. The advantages of that approach, if it could be made to work, are admittedly considerable. If its proponents are right, controlled sales could turn stockpiles of ivory and rhinoceros horn from a security millstone around government necks to a source of valuable and much needed conservation revenue, while they reduce or eliminate the illegal market. The question, of course, is whether this approach can work. Restricting supply to control price may be more likely to drive prices up. The aftermath of the 2008 ivory sale suggests that the risks of trying it may be considerable indeed.

Even without the risks, is a legal trade at lowered prices a viable option for countries with small elephant populations, or for any country with rhinos besides South Africa? It is unlikely that more than a few countries in Africa are capable of producing a sustainable supply of legal ivory, especially if no elephants are to be killed to get it. Rowan Martin's idea that you could support a sustainable trade on the basis of natural-mortality ivory (see p. 34) may seem promising if you look only at elephant demographics, but his idea assumes both that each country in question has a large national population to start with and that rangers can successfully locate a reasonable proportion of elephant carcasses in time to remove their tusks before they weather and crack. These requirements are difficult enough (and, probably, expensive enough) to meet in the open savanna, but in the dense rainforests where the Forest Elephant lives it may be all but impossible. For countries with depleted elephant populations clinging on in remote areas, the idea of a profitable legal ivory trade seems an impractical fantasy.

Rhino horn sales face the same problem, even allowing for the fact that horns, unlike tusks, grow back. Other than South Africa, which Richard Emslie told me could potentially supply 3.5–4 tonnes a year from dehorning operations, natural mortality and other sources without touching its stockpiles, few countries have enough rhinos to benefit from the supply of horn that could be available for legal sales, unless, of course, the price remains sky-high. If it does we are back where we started, in an expensive battle with poaching syndicates. Even if trade encouraged other countries to bolster their rhino populations by importing stock from South Africa, how many decades would it take to build up a herd worth harvesting from? And how would a legal trade affect the other rhino species, including the Asian rhinos?

The other approach is to focus on demand. We cannot eliminate demand altogether, but we can try to make ivory or rhinoceros horn so undesirable to most potential buyers that they will no longer be good investments for a criminal syndicate. Kristin Nowell's report on CITES implementation for WWF (see p. 140) recommends a demand-centered approach, for tigers as well as for rhinos and elephants:

> International wildlife crime is demand-driven, and it is recommended that China and Viet Nam, in particular, prioritize the development and implementation of well-researched demand reduction campaigns. Targeted strategies should be developed to influence consumer behavior around tiger parts, rhino horn, and ivory of illegal origin. Such strategies should include working closely with user groups, including the traditional medicine community ... Egypt, Thailand and China need to increase their efforts to educate consumers about the rules regarding ivory purchases ... China, Thailand and Viet Nam should increase efforts to educate their citizens traveling abroad about the illegality of returning with tiger, rhino and elephant products. The [CITES] CoP15 ETIS analysis found that (since 1989) Chinese nationals have been arrested within or coming from Africa in at least 134 ivory seizure cases, totaling more than 16 tonnes of ivory, and another 487 cases representing almost 25 tonnes of ivory originating from Africa was seized en route to China (CoP15 Doc. 44.1 Annex).

Renowned elephant biologist Cynthia Moss agrees that the best solution is to curb demand in China. "We've been through this once before, in the 1970s and 1980s," she told Jerome Starkey of *The Times* in 2013. "Back then ivory was being carved in Asia and China but ending up in Europe and the US. We were able to stop demand with huge public awareness campaigns. People stopped buying ivory. We need to do that again."

But can we? It has often been said that it is impossible to eliminate or even reduce, demand for ivory or rhinoceros horn in the Far East because it is too deeply entrenched. Even if you eliminated 99 percent of the demand for ivory in a huge country like China, or for rhino horn in a country as populous as Vietnam, there might still be millions of people who want the stuff (though note the opinions of Eric Dinerstein and Michael 't Sas-Rolfes in the previous chapter, who argue that the real demand for rhino horn may be considerably smaller than we have assumed). The use of rhinoceros horn in medicine is already prohibited almost everywhere that Chinese-based traditional medicine is practiced. At least some traditional practitioners are aware of the reasons for not using it. The modern translator of the *Shen Nong Ben Cao Jing* (see p. 39), while listing a large number of conditions that rhinoceros horn can treat, notes that "because this medicinal is from a severely endangered species, it should no longer be used. Instead, one can substitute Cornu Bubali (Shui Niu Jiao, water buffalo horn) in larger doses."

Reducing demand will require a massive public education and awareness campaign. It must be designed primarily for (and culturally sensitive to) the markets in eastern Asia, but aim, as well, at tourists worldwide who are tempted to buy ivory products in countries like Thailand. Because the bulk of the market is in Asia it would obviously be ideal if the impetus and direction for such a campaign came from Asia as well. The Chinese government says that it is already conducting public education and awareness campaigns to discourage its nationals from purchasing ivory either within China or abroad. China has reportedly cracked down on Internet sales. According to Yan Xun, an official with the State Forestry Administration, the government has been warning Chinese visiting or working in Africa not to bring ivory home. Chinese ambassador to Kenya Liu Guangyuan told reporters in February 2013 that a group of 600 Chinese tourists had received text messages asking them to keep off ivory products during their visit to Kenya.

It is hard to judge, especially from the West, how successful steps like these are likely to be. Certainly China should be encouraged to step up its awareness campaigns as much as possible. However, critics might ask how strong a message against buying ivory can be when it is sent out by a government that is, at the same time, the largest retailer of legal ivory in the world. China does not want its ivory carving industry to die, or the industry's customers to stop buying. The message it is putting out is not "don't buy ivory," but "don't buy illegal ivory."

Is that too mixed a message to get across? It might not be if China were as successful as it claims to be in prosecuting smugglers, handing down stiff sentences and keeping illegal ivory out of legitimate shops. China would, however, have to be better at enforcement than either Japan or the West managed to be in the 1980s. Before the first ivory ban, Western buyers were not actively seeking illegal ivory, but they ended up buying it anyway because the smuggling syndicates were able to launder their supply onto the legal market. It would be an incredible achievement if China were able to prevent this from happening in its much larger and looser market — perhaps, even with the best of intentions, too incredible.

Even if China succeeds, there is still the problem of the value that both ivory and rhinoceros horn carry as symbols of status, wealth and power. In the West, buyer revulsion against ivory did not gain real momentum until the campaign that led towards the 1989 ban. "Don't buy smuggled ivory, but legal ivory is a beautiful and valuable substance you should be proud to own" was not half as successful a public message as "Don't buy any ivory, because the cost in suffering and death is too great and you can't be sure that the ivory you are buying is legal." Even ivory dealers responded to that message. A few months before the 1989 CITES meeting, Henry Birks and Sons, a major Canadian jewelry chain, began promoting a sale of ivory jewelry. I wrote them a single (polite!) letter, on behalf of the International Wildlife Coalition, providing information on the poaching crisis at the time. Birks responded by canceling its promotion and recalling and writing off its entire stock of ivory merchandise, valued at over $80,000. The company's vice-president, Thomas Birks, joined me on national television to urge people to stop buying ivory.

That suggests that the most promising way to reduce demand for ivory and rhinoceros horn is to convince buyers to stay away from all of it, not just to avoid the black-market supply (assuming they can tell the difference). For that conviction to get across, a total trade ban, without exceptions, may be essential. That is why there is so vehement a debate between the supply and demand sides of the issue: a supply solution requires us to allow legal sales, while a demand solution almost certainly requires us to ban them. It is also why ivory bonfires lit by a number of countries, including Kenya and Gabon, to demonstrate that an ivory stockpile is, to them, a burden rather than a resource, have been scorned by others as wanton destruction of their country's wealth.

If we aim to reduce demand by raising awareness, what should our message be? Attitudes towards wild animals and the threat to endangered species may have difficulty crossing cultural or economic lines. Not everyone thinks the way animal advocates or wildlife conservationists do. This difference in attitude is not necessarily because we are (whatever we may think of ourselves) more knowledgeable or better educated than those who do not see things our way.

Is it enough to argue that, no matter how beautiful, luxurious or socially desirable it may be, the only place for ivory is on an elephant's face, and the only place for rhinoceros horn is on a rhino's nose? Do we spell out the human and environmental cost of the ivory and horn trades, and the waves of crime and violence that follow in their path? Can we meet the conviction that rhinoceros horn cures cancer with medical facts and exposure of the "rhino touts" who lie to desperately ill people?

There will be buyers who will not change their habits no matter how valid the reasons. For the rich and status-conscious in Vietnam who see rhino horn as a status symbol, a social facilitator or — and this still boggles the mind (see p. 38) — an aphrodisiac, medical facts won't make a difference (well, they might for the aphrodisiac users, but that seems somehow unlikely). What, though, of the people who buy ivory in China or rhinoceros horn in Vietnam, in the belief that elephants are not killed for their ivory or that there are plenty of rhinos left? Once they learn otherwise, they may change. This is already happening for shark fin soup, long considered a delicacy that Asians would never abandon. If the right approach can be found there is no reason to suppose that the same thing cannot happen for ivory and rhinoceros horn as well.

Rhino poaching is not out of control because of centuries-old beliefs held by millions, but in response to a new fad among a relatively small number of affluent people. Fads change. An object of desire may lose its allure when it is no longer seen as a symbol of status or proof of wealth. If, for example, celebrities and other trendsetters disown the use of ivory or rhino horn — for whatever reason, or even for no reason at all — their followers may do the same.

It may be that the nature of the message will prove to be less important than the person who carries it. The celebrated Chinese basketball player Yao Ming, who has taken up the cause of elephants and rhinoceroses, accuses poachers and smugglers of "sabotaging African economies and stealing from us all ... As the vast majority, we need to let them know that this is not acceptable and is damaging China's relations with our friends and trading partners in Africa. We would be outraged if people were killing our pandas, we should be just as upset with what's happening to rhinos and elephants in Africa." If Yao Ming's legions of admirers hear him, he may prove a better ambassador for these great beasts than any conservationist, scientist or environmental advocate could ever hope to be.

CHAPTER NINETEEN

THE
FUTURE

February 27–March 2, 2013

My flight for Bangkok leaves in a few hours. Soon I will be mingling with experts, advocates, traders, conservationists, trophy hunters, bureaucrats and journalists as the 2013 CITES meeting tries to find its way forward for elephants, rhinos and a host of other species.

As the delegates assemble, the slaughter continues. Poachers have killed 102 of South Africa's White Rhinos in the two months since the year began, 92 of them in Kruger National Park alone. In India's Kaziranga National Park, 50 Greater One-horned Rhinos have been lost to poachers and natural disasters in the past 13 months. WWF has estimated that 25,000 African elephants were killed for their ivory in 2011, and expects that the numbers for 2012 will be even higher when all the figures are in. WWF has called for tough sanctions against Nigeria, the DRC and Thailand — our host for the upcoming meeting — for their failure to control illegal trade in ivory.

The market continues to flourish. Ivory dealers in China report that business is booming. Buyers unwilling to visit a real marketplace can find a virtual one. A recently released study by Erika Ceballos finds ivory for sale on Internet sites in Algeria, Morocco, South Africa, the United Arab Emirates, Saudi Arabia, India, Japan and the Philippines (China could not be included).

In the run-up to Bangkok, the war on elephants and rhinos gives way to a war of words. Press releases and op-ed pieces fly in all directions. Bryan Christy, in *National Geographic's* blog *A Voice for Elephants*, excoriates CITES for its "glaring error" in agreeing to the 2008 sale to China and refusing to recognize its dire consequences. In the *New York Times* Dan Levin calls the 2008 sale a "colossal failure." He reports on a burgeoning demand for ivory that China, with its mixed message as a proponent of legal ivory sales, is unable to control. A trafficker named Xing tells Levin that he regularly smuggles ivory over the Vietnamese frontier, while compliant border guards look the other way, and transfers it deep into China in vehicles belonging to the People's Liberation Army. China, meanwhile, denies any claims of corruption and continues to insist that it has already dealt with its smuggling problem. Thailand scurries to avoid being highlighted yet again as one of the worst offenders in the ivory black market, claiming that it is improving its legislation as activists call for a total ban on its domestic ivory trade.

South Africa's Water and Environmental Affairs minister Edna Molewa releases a media statement before the CITES meeting. She questions suggestions that all of the country's rhinos should be dehorned, noting "various challenges and concerns relating to costs, risks to the rhino, potential biological and social impact, logistics to undertake an extensive dehorning exercise, and considering that the horn grows back, the impact (financial and biological) of repeat dehorning." She cites a dehorning study that concluded "dehorning is only a deterrent and only a viable option for small populations where other security interventions are in place." Legal trade remains an option, she says, but it "can only be done if the current international prohibitions are removed through agreement of CITES Parties, a potential trade partner has been identified and discussions have been initiated to determine the viability, especially considering that consumer states have trade prohibitions in place that will have to be repealed."

Trade advocates nonetheless continue to press for legal trade in ivory and rhinoceros horn. A paper in the eminent journal *Science*, co-authored by Rowan Martin, calls legal sales "the only remaining option" and proposes, again, a De Beers–type central selling organization.

It's a good time to sum up.

CITES, effective as it has been in the past, cannot be the sole cure for the lawlessness, corruption, crime and greed that have brought rhinos and elephants to their present state. At its best, though, it can catalyze the sort of cooperative actions we must have if real solutions are to be found and implemented. CITES has been the vehicle that has brought African countries together (not always, I admit, amicably) at a number of elephant range State

Dialogue Meetings. The Lusaka Agreement Task Force (see p. 137) might not have existed without the 1989 CITES ivory ban.

In February 2008, representatives of 19 African CITES Parties met in Bamako, Mali, for the first meeting of the newly formed African Elephant Coalition (AEC). In a joint declaration, they pledged to "strive to have a viable and healthy elephant population free of threats from International ivory trade" and to "develop an elephant action plan that will encompass national and regional elephant strategies that promote non consumptive use of elephants through development of ecotourism for the benefit of local communities." At their 2012 meeting in Ouagadougou, Burkina Faso, the AEC member countries "agreed that reducing the seemingly insatiable demand for illegal ivory in countries such as China is essential. China is the single largest market for illicit ivory in the world. The African Elephant Coalition believes that it has become imperative to reduce the demand for ivory in China and for China to send a clear message to consumers, saying that it will not tolerate the ivory trade."

The AEC now includes most African elephant range countries: Benin, Burkina Faso, Central African Republic, Republic of Congo, Democratic Republic of Congo, Côte d'Ivoire, Guinea, Guinea-Bissau, Equatorial Guinea, Ethiopia, Eritrea, Ghana, Kenya, Liberia, Mali, Niger, Nigeria, Rwanda, Senegal, Sierra Leone, South Sudan, Chad and Togo. Two African countries without elephants, Comoros and Mauritania, have also joined the coalition.

Though not every elephant range country in Africa agrees with the aims of the AEC, every one of them has endorsed a far-reaching action plan adopted by the CITES Parties at their 2010 meeting in Qatar. The African Elephant Action Plan (AEAP) is a particularly African blueprint for the future of elephant conservation. It sets out its purpose in the broadest terms:

> Development of this document has been owned and managed by the African elephant range States, and as such represents and seeks to address the real 'situation on the ground' in terms of what actions must be taken in order to effectively conserve elephants in Africa across their range. It is not intended to be an exhaustive analysis of the status of elephant populations and their conservation across Africa, but rather a concise and clear statement of those activities which MUST be implemented and most urgently require funding if Africa's elephants throughout their range are to be protected from the multiple and serious threats they face.

The AEAP's eight objectives address illegal killing and illegal trade, elephant habitats, human–elephant conflict, public awareness, elephant management, cooperation and understanding among range countries, and cooperation with local communities. Its aims include responsibility (with the CITES Secretariat) for the "Action Plan for the Control of Trade in Elephant Ivory," designed to "eradicate illegal exports of ivory from the African continent and the unregulated domestic markets that contribute to illicit trade."

It's an ambitious undertaking, and like many other grand initiatives its chief stumbling block is money. The total amount that would be needed to put the AEAP in place is roughly $100 million — a piddling sum by international standards. The amount that has actually been pledged so far to the plan's financial arm, the African Elephant Fund (AEF), since its launch in August 2011 is $700,000, of which $200,000 comes from the Government of China.

Much of the donor money aimed at conserving elephants in Africa — some $20 million so far, most of it from the European Union — has gone not to the AEF but into MIKE, the CITES data-collecting program that monitors illegal killing (see p. 94). Even MIKE is a long way from achieving the level of coverage it needs, and scientists who have analyzed its results have commented that "the flow of data through the MIKE process has been patchy and sometimes painfully slow." The long-term future of elephants in Africa still lies in donors' pockets.

An Asian Elephant conservation strategy is in the works. There is nothing for rhinos of similar scope to MIKE or the AEAP, nor is there indication that the funding such a plan would require would be forthcoming. South Africa launched its own "Biodiversity Management Plan for the Black Rhinoceros" in 2011, a successor to two earlier plans, with a goal of building up its national population to over 3,000 animals by 2020. It plans to improve its 2010 "National Strategy for the Safety and Security of Rhinoceros Populations in South Africa." Other countries have their own rhinoceros action plans, including Indonesia, Malaysia (Sabah) and Nepal (Nepal's plan ended in 2011). The African Wildlife Foundation convened a Rhino Summit in Nairobi in April 2011 that developed its own action plan, "Toward a Comprehensive Response to the Rhino Poaching Crisis," which calls for increased security, demand reduction, stiffer penalties for rhino crime and increased funding and collaboration.

The closest thing CITES has come up with was a one-time Ivory and Rhinoceros Enforcement Task Force that included a number of countries,

INTERPOL and the Lusaka Agreement Task Force. It met in 2011 with funding provided by the EU. A possibly surprising attendee was the World Bank
(a member of ICCWC), which offered its expertise on anti–money laundering tactics and asset recovery — potentially valuable weapons against criminal
syndicates (after all, they got Al Capone on tax evasion).

All of this sounds encouraging. Action plans, though, are not the same
thing as action. Nor is enacting tougher regulations and setting stiffer penalties the same thing as actually enforcing them, both in the field and in court.
Even in the throes of the international politicking that goes on at a CITES
meeting, we should not mistake words for deeds.

My NGO colleagues are not waiting for governments to act. Several are
stepping up campaigns to reduce demand for ivory and rhino horn in Vietnam
and China. In Vietnam WildAid is working on rhinos with martial arts star
Johnny Nguyen and Vietnamese-American actress Maggie Q. In China,
WildAid and Save the Elephants are working with sports superstar Yao Ming
(see p. 182), whose face now looks out from billboards in Beijing to remind
passers-by that "When the buying stops, the killing can too."

The fight against wildlife crime, and against the catastrophic slaughter of
elephants and rhinoceroses in particular, demands the attention of the world.
It should get it. The world has to lose patience with pariah states, like Laos,
that refuse to touch the kingpins of wildlife crime. Vietnam and, particularly,
China need to abandon their policy of denial in the face of overwhelming evidence of the illegal ivory and horn trade in their midst. Vietnam must take serious steps to counter the craze for horn that has made it the prime destination
for rhino contraband. China needs to re-examine its attachment to its legal
trade in ivory, and consider whether the money it earns is worth the growing
cost of dealing with the escalating crime it almost certainly feeds.

Mike Knight, Chairman of the IUCN African Rhino Specialist Group,
wrote in 2012: "the conservation of rhinos still depends upon good-old fash-
ioned protection, monitoring, biological management of free-ranging rhinos,
adequate application of controls of illegal trade in consumer countries, with
sufficient incentives and funding to successfully protect and grow rhino numbers and range into the future. Let us get these right, for the sake of rhinos."
Much the same could be said for elephants.

We know who the villains are: Joseph Kony and warlords like him, corrupt officials, smuggling gangs, phony rhino hunters with their stable of prostitutes, and cancer touts peddling useless wares to the helpless and dying in

Vietnamese hospitals. Banning legal trade and reducing demand on the one hand, or allowing the trade and controlling supply on the other, are nothing more than competing strategies for putting these villains out of business. Nobody in this highly politicized debate is opposed to achieving that.

We can't stop every last smuggled shipment of ivory and rhinoceros horn, any more than we can stop the flow of any other kind of contraband. Trade bans aren't really expected to do that. Their purpose is to assist law enforcement, to help reduce demand (as the ivory ban did in 1989) and to eliminate opportunities to launder illegal goods onto a legal market. A clear-cut ban robs the illegal trade of one of its best advertisements.

I come down firmly on the side of those who believe that, particularly under the current dreadful circumstances, legal trade — or even talk of legal trade — is a very bad idea. It is made so by the nature of the trade, and by the unstable, weak or corrupt governance under which it flourishes. Certainly it should be impossible for anyone to believe that this paradigm, in which some of the biggest profits from the ivory and horn trade today go to buy weapons for some of the most ruthless and violent militias on the planet, is in any way tolerable.

We are joined in a battle against greed, poverty, corruption and war. We are fighting for living elephants, not carvings or jewelry (however beautiful), and living rhinoceroses, not medicines or cures (however fraudulent). We are fighting, in the end, for human dignity. Have we grown so callous and avaricious that rhinoceroses and elephants, and the other wild species we exploit around the world, matter less to us than the luxury goods they provide? I hope that we are better than that. I hope that our answer, in the end, will be "no," and that our actions will prove it.

We are fighting, too, for people. Over the past ten years more than 700 rangers have been killed by poachers in Africa and Asia. The civilian victims of the Lord's Resistance Army, Janjaweed, Al-Shabaab and their ilk may never be counted. As long as organized criminal gangs and vicious, power-hungry militias are able to feed off the profits of the trade in elephant ivory and rhinoceros horn, people, as well as animals, will suffer and die, caught in the crossfire of an undeclared war. The title of this book is *Ivory, Horn and Blood*. Let us never forget, as we think of the magnificent animals that are the victims of this evil trade, that much of that blood is human.

POSTSCRIPT
THE 2013 CITES MEETING

Yingluck Shinawatra, the Prime Minister of Thailand, was being careful with her words. As she opened the 16th Meeting of the Conference of the Parties to CITES (CoP16 for short), at the Queen Sirikit Conference Centre in Bangkok on March 3, 2013, she insisted, "no one cares more about elephants than the Thai people." She stopped short though, of proclaiming a full ban on domestic sales of ivory. Instead, government stockpiles would be limited to domestic ivory, and Thailand would "work toward" amending national legislation "with the goal of putting an end of ivory trade and to be in line with international norms."

As "international norms," in a CITES context, refer only to cross-border trade, where did that leave ivory sales from Thai domestic elephants, reportedly used to cover up large-scale dealings in smuggled ivory from Africa? The Prime Minister didn't say, though her government did issue a warning to tourists that they risked arrest if they tried to carry ivory products out of the country. A few days later, Buddhist leaders gathered at Wat That Thong in downtown Bangkok for a merit-making ceremony, to pray for the thousands of elephants poached every year.

CoP16 proved, on the fortieth anniversary of the Convention's signing, far more positive than the previous meeting in Doha, Qatar, in 2010. The Doha gathering was, for many conservationists, an embarrassing debacle featuring the highly political defeat of proposals to protect declining sharks. This time proposals for some of the same sharks were adopted by a narrow, but sufficient, margin. Parties also voted to increase protection for turtles, tropical timber trees and the West African Manatee (*Trichechus senegalensis*), an aquatic elephant cousin.

Thanks to the withdrawal of Tanzania's proposal to sell off its stockpile (see p. 170), for the first time since 1989 the Parties did not have to debate proposals for elephant downlistings or ivory sales. This robbed the proceedings of some of their usual excitement (probably for the best). Rhino horn, too, was off the table, though in a series of side events a large South African delegation presented details of its rhino conservation strategy and set out arguments for a future legal trade in horn. Water and Environmental Affairs Minister Edna

Molewa stayed through the entire first week (most unusual for a politician at her level). She insisted that she was open-minded on the subject and was there in a learning capacity. Will we face a rhino trade proposal when South Africa hosts the 17th CITES CoP in 2016? Molewa stated before the CoP that trade "can only be done if the current international prohibitions are removed through agreement of CITES Parties, a potential trade partner has been identified and discussions have been initiated to determine the viability, especially considering that consumer states have trade prohibitions in place that will have to be repealed." If the trade partner proves to be China, as Molewa has suggested, will China repeal its 1993 sales ban (which covers not only rhinos, but tigers)?

CITES CoPs divide their business between two Committees, one to handle (mostly) species proposals and the other for administrative matters. In Committee I, Burkina Faso and Kenya withdrew their proposal to redraft the language of the 2007 ivory moratorium (see p. 171). After discussions with South Africa, Kenya dropped its proposal for a temporary zero export quota on White Rhino trophies from South Africa and Swaziland (see p. 108). Instead the Parties decided that "the export [and re-export] of rhino horn and elephant ivory contained in hunting trophies does not qualify for the personal and household effects exemption," thereby closing a loophole that had allowed some trophies to be exported without CITES permits. They urged each other to "consider introducing stricter domestic measures [that is, tougher than CITES requires] to regulate the re-export of rhinoceros horn products from any source." If countries do that, proxy hunting (see p. 108) should be all but impossible.

Other rhino and elephant discussions, usually thrashed out in the more dramatic atmosphere of Committee I, ended up in Committee II. From here, draft papers were massaged into mutually agreeable form in Working Groups before tweaking, adoption and final confirmation in the plenary sessions. For rhinos the final result was a series of Decisions, calling for action in the short term. Parties seizing smuggled horn are to inform other countries along the trade route. If they don't know where the horn came from, they are to contact the CITES Secretariat for help. Parties fighting wildlife crime are to draw on a broad range of forensic and investigative techniques, passing laws to do so if they don't already exist. These include controlled delivery (letting a shipment proceed, under close watch, to its destination in the hope of trapping the kingpins at the other end), anti-money laundering regulations, prosecutions and genuinely deterrent sentences. If possible they are to control internal trade in rhinoceros products, and to consult with importing countries to ensure that any exports are being sent for a proper purpose.

Countries implicated in illegal trade in horn are to undertake demand reduction and community awareness programs. Vietnam in particular is to improve its legislation on horn trafficking, establish a database to track hunting trophies, and report to the Secretariat, with an update on arrests, seizures, prosecutions and penalties, by 31 January 2014. Mozambique, the source of many of the rhino poachers invading the Kruger, is to improve its laws, including beefing up its penalties against wildlife crime. It, too, must report by the 2014 deadline. The Secretariat is given a number of tasks, and must convene "a CITES Rhinoceros Enforcement Task Force consisting of representatives from Parties affected by rhinoceros poaching and illegal trade in rhinoceros horn, the International Consortium on Combating Wildlife Crime partner organizations, EUROPOL and, as appropriate, other Parties and experts."

For elephants, a crucial new provision requires Parties to submit samples from seizures of ivory greater than 500 kilograms in total weight to "an appropriate forensic analysis facility" within 90 days, and, if possible, to send samples from "all large seizures from within the past 24 months to … a facility capable of reliably determining the origin of such ivory samples with the aim of addressing the entire crime chain." Sam Wasser, who has been fighting for such a requirement for years, offered Parties the forensic services of the Center for Conservation Biology at the University of Washington. Some Parties, including Thailand, nonetheless complained that the provisions were too onerous, and insisted that they would do any DNA analyses themselves.

A few elephant items were kicked to the Standing Committee or the next CoP. Côte d'Ivoire's proposal to make the Panel of Experts permanent and to make Parties seeking downlisting of their elephant populations pay for its services (see p. 171), after meeting with resistance from Botswana and South Africa, was folded into a vague agreement to review the relevant resolution. The controversial Decision-Making Mechanism (see p. 171) was handed to the Standing Committee, which struck a Working Group in its closing session that is supposed to come up with something appropriate by CoP17. The Group must consult with all African and Asian elephant-range countries as it does so. It has a daunting task (especially as some of the Parties think that even considering the issue while the current crisis rages is a bad idea).

A new Resolution urges the Secretariat, Parties, international bodies such as UNEP and others to support the African Elephant Action Plan and help to build up the African Elephant Fund. Resolution Conf. 10.10, *Trade in Elephant Specimens,* was thoroughly revised, adding new provisions that (among other things) call on countries with large ivory stockpiles to maintain inventories of their contents and to report each year to the Secretariat, require the Secretariat to report on countries whose stockpiles are "not well secured," and recommend that all Parties "prohibit the unregulated domestic sale of raw or worked ivory" — the last, be it noted, was not intended to affect China, whose domestic ivory trade is, according to its government, regulated. A further new provision addressed, for the first time, illegal trade in live elephants, a particular problem in Thailand.

The Secretariat was directed, subject to funding, to convene an Ivory Enforcement Task Force. Eight of the nine countries named as members — China, Kenya, Malaysia, the Philippines, Thailand, Uganda, Tanzania and Vietnam (but not South Africa) — had already been named by ETIS "as being involved in substantial illegal ivory trade as a source, transit, or destination country" and had been required to submit reports on their ivory trade controls before the CoP. All eight missed the deadline, but by the end of the meeting six had developed draft national ivory action plans. The remaining two, China and Tanzania, promised to do so as soon as possible.

The media, rather undiplomatically, dubbed the offending countries the "Gang of Eight." Several expressed their annoyance at the post-CoP session of the Standing Committee. Malaysia defended its enforcement record. China accused TRAFFIC of bias in preparing the ETIS reports. Patrick Omondi of Kenya objected to his country — which, he argued, is doing all it can to control the trade — being compared to a country like China, which can devote infinitely greater resources to reduce demand and beef up enforcement: "If you give me screens to screen tonnes of containers we'll screen all containers passing through Mombasa airport. If you give me 50 more sniffer dogs, we'll be sniffing every animal part that passes through."

While we debated, the slaughters continued. Even as the meeting progressed, the carcass of a female Asian Elephant, apparently killed to steal her calves, was discovered only a few hours away in Thailand's Kaeng Krachan National Park. News trickled in of more rhino killings in Kaziranga and the Kruger, and of the deaths of 28 Forest Elephants in the Nki and Lobeke National Parks in southeast Cameroon. On March 14 and 15, as delegates headed for home, a gang of mounted poachers in southern Chad near its border with Cameroon — apparently the same group responsible for the Bouba

N'Djida massacre last year — shot at least 86 elephants, including 33 pregnant females and 15 calves.

Will our work in Bangkok do anything to make such horrors a thing of the past? It is just possible that they might, though some NGOs criticized the CoP for sending out "mixed messages" that "confuse consumers and encourage criminals, putting elephants, rhinos, tigers and the people who protect them in grave danger." I hope, nonetheless, that our presence in Bangkok will at least persuade Prime Minister Yingluck to follow up her speeches with genuine action. I hope, too, that China will stop denying that much of the problem lies within its borders. It was depressing to hear Chinese delegates claiming that the only reason China came up so often was faulty or biased data analysis, and insisting that China's name be struck from documents on ivory.

During the first week of the meeting, Tom Milliken of TRAFFIC presented an ETIS report to the Parties on ivory seizures. China figured large in his comments, and its delegation took to the floor to complain that it was being blamed unfairly for the ivory crisis. I made the following reply. I meant it as a plea to China, and to the other countries named as end markets (legal or illegal) in the rhino and elephant trade:

> Mr. Chairman, we welcome the ETIS report, and would like to observe that what it presents is data. It is not an accusation or blame — it is information. It should be welcomed and acted upon. We agree with China that dealing with what we have all said is a global crisis is not just their task — the world has to pitch in seriously with financial contributions, as China has done. Mr. Chairman, $700,000 for the African Elephant Fund, for example, does not begin to be enough. Nonetheless, we appeal particularly to those countries that have been identified as having the greatest role in the end market, because they also have the greatest opportunity to deal with that market and reduce demand. They are the countries that can lead the world in the fight against illegal ivory trade. We believe that, in addition to what they are already doing, if these countries decided to set aside their domestic trade — however steeped that trade is in tradition, culture or history — they could take that leadership role. If they do that, Mr. Chairman, they would earn the gratitude of the world.

SOURCES

Chapter 1: The Living Elephants

Alfred, R., L. Ambu, S.K.S.S. Nathan and B. Goossens. (2011). "Current Status of Asian Elephants in Borneo." *Gajah* 35: 29–35.

Amranand, P., and W. Warren. (1998). *The Elephant in Thai Life and Legend*. Bangkok: Monsoon Editions.

Associated Press. (2013). "3 Borneo Pygmy Elephants Found Dead in Malaysia, Total Now 13." January 30. http://www.ctvnews.ca/sci-tech/3-borneo-pygmy-elephants-found-dead-in-malaysia-total-now-13-1.1135517.

Bibi, F., B. Kraatz, N. Craig et al. (2012). "Early Evidence for Complex Social Structure in Proboscidea from a Late Miocene Trackway Site in the United Arab Emirates." *Biology Letters* 8(4): 670–73.

Bist, S.S., J.V. Cheeran, S. Choudhury et al. (2002). "The Domesticated Asian Elephant in India." In *Giants on Our Hands: Proceedings of the International Workshop on the Domesticated Asian Elephant*, 129–48. RAP Publication 2002/30. Bangkok: Food and Agriculture Organization.

Blake, S., S. Strindberg, P. Boudjan et al. (2007). "Forest Elephant Crisis in the Congo Basin." *PLoS Biology* 5(4): e111.

CITES. (2012a). *Control of Trade in Ivory in China*. SC62 Inf. 8.

———. (2012b). *Elephant Conservation, Illegal Killing and Ivory Trade*. SC62 Doc. 46.1 (Rev. 1).

Cranbrook, Earl of, J. Payne and C.M.U. Leh. (2008). "Origin of the Elephants *Elephas maximus* L. of Borneo." *Sarawak Museum Journal* 63(84): 95–125.

de Silva, S., and G. Wittemyer. (2012). "A Comparison of Social Organization in Asian Elephants and African Savannah Elephants." *International Journal of Primatology* 33(5): 1125–41.

Douglas-Hamilton, I. (1975). "The Elephants' Sense of Death." *Africana* 5(8): 20–25.

Douglas-Hamilton, I., S. Bhalla, G. Wittemyer and F. Vollrath. (2006). "Behavioural Reactions of Elephants Towards a Dying and Deceased Matriarch." *Applied Animal Behaviour Science* 100(1/2): 87–102.

Fernando, P., and J. Pastorini. (2011). "Range-Wide Status of Asian Elephants." *Gajah* 35: 15–20.

Food and Agriculture Organization [FAO]. (1997). *Gone Astray: The Care and Management of the Asian Elephant in Domesticity*. RAP Publication 1997/16. Bangkok: FAO.

Grubb, P., C.P. Groves, J.P. Dudley and J. Shoshani. (2000). "Living African Elephants Belong to Two Species: *Loxodonta africana* (Blumenbach, 1797) and *Loxodonta cyclotis* (Matschie, 1900)." *Elephant* 2: 1–4.

Hance, J. (2011a). "Africa Gains New Elephant Species." *Mongabay.com*, January 19.

———. (2011b). "Busted: 1,835 Elephant Tusks Confiscated in Two Seizures Connected by Malaysia." *Mongabay.com*, August 31.

Haynes, G. (2012). "Elephants (and Extinct Relatives) as Earth-Movers and Ecosystem Engineers." *Geomorphology* 157/158: 99–107.

Herbst, C.T., A.S. Stoeger, R. Frey et al. (2012). "How Low Can You Go? Physical Production Mechanism of Elephant Infrasonic Vocalizations." *Science* 337(6094): 595–99.

Ishida, Y., T.K. Oleksyk, N.J. Georgiadis et al. (2011). "Reconciling Apparent Conflicts between Mitochondrial and Nuclear Phylogenies in African Elephants." *PLoS ONE* 6(6): e20642.

Lee, P.C., and C.J. Moss. (2012). "Wild Female African Elephants (*Loxodonta africana*) Exhibit Personality Traits of Leadership and Social Integration." *Journal of Comparative Psychology* 126(3): 224–32.

Li, J., Y. Hou, Y. Li and J. Zhang. (2012). "The Latest Straight-Tusked Elephants (*Palaeoloxodon*)? 'Wild Elephants' Lived 3000 Years Ago in North China." *Quaternary International* 281: 84–88.

Lundberg, J., and D.A. McFarlane. (2006). "Speleogenesis of the Mount Elgon Elephant Caves, Kenya." In R.S. Harmon and C. Wicks, eds., *Perspectives on Karst Geomorphology, Hydrology and Geochemistry: A Tribute Volume to Derek C. Ford and William B. White*. Geological Society of America Special Paper 404, 51–63.

Lundquist, C.F., and W.W.J. Varnedoe. (2005). "Salt Ingestion Caves." *International Journal of Speleology* 35(1): 13–18.

Maisels, F., S. Strindberg, S. Blake et al. (2013). "Devastating Decline of Forest Elephants in Central Africa." *PLoS ONE* 8(3): e59469.

McComb, K., L. Baker and C. Moss. (2006). "African Elephants Show High Levels of Interest in the Skulls and Ivory of Their Own Species." *Biology Letters* 2(1): 26–28.

McComb, K., G. Shannon, S.M. Durant et al. (2011). "Leadership in Elephants: The Adaptive Value of Age." *Proceedings of the Royal Society B: Biological Sciences* 278(1722): 3270–76.

McNeely, J.A. "Elephants in Folklore, Religion and Art." In J. Shoshani, ed., *Elephants*, 158–65. New York: Checkmark Books.

Mongabay.com. (2012). "Elephant Numbers Halved in Central Africa in 5 Years." June 8.

Nyström, V., L. Dalén, S. Vartanyan et al. (2010). "Temporal Genetic Change in the Last Remaining Population of Woolly Mammoth." *Proceedings of the Royal Society B: Biological Sciences* 277(1692): 2331–37.

O'Connell-Rodwell, C.E., J.D. Wood, M. Wyman et al. (2012). "Antiphonal Vocal Bouts Associated with Departures in Free-Ranging African Elephant Family

Groups (*Loxodonta africana*)." *Bioacoustics* 21(3): 215–24.

Redmond, I. (1982). "Salt Mining Elephants of Mount Elgon." *Swara* 5: 28–31.

Rohland, N., D. Reich, S. Mallick et al. (2010). "Genomic DNA Sequences from Mastodon and Woolly Mammoth Reveal Deep Speciation of Forest and Savanna Elephants." *PLoS Biology* 8(12): e1000564.

Schuttler, S.G., S. Blake and L.S. Eggert. (2012). "Movement Patterns and Spatial Relationships among African Forest Elephants." *Biotropica* 44(4): 445–48.

Smith, K.H. (2000). "The Elephant Domestication Centre of Africa." In J. Shoshani, ed., *Elephants*, 152–54. New York: Checkmark Books.

Stiles, D. (2012). Review of *The Ivory Dynasty: A Report on the Soaring Demand for Elephant and Mammoth Ivory in Southern China*, by Esmond Martin and Lucy Vigne, and *Making a Killing: A 2011 Survey of Ivory Markets in China*, by Grace G. Gabriel, Ning Hua and Juan Wang. *Pachyderm* 51: 94–96.

Stiles, D., E.B. Martin and L. Vigne. (2011). "Exaggerated Ivory Prices Can Be Harmful to Elephants." *Swara* 34(4): 18–22.

Sukumar, R. (2003). *The Living Elephants: Evolutionary Ecology, Behavior and Conservation*. New York: Oxford University Press.

Switek, B. (2012). "Bronze Art Sparks Debate over the Extinction of the Straight-Tusked Elephant." http://phenomena.nationalgeographic.com/2012/12/27/bronze-art-sparks-debate-over-the-extinction-of-the-straight-tusked-elephant/.

Turkalo, A.K., and J.M. Fay. (1995). "Studying Forest Elephants by Direct Observation: Preliminary Results from the Dzanga Clearing, Central African Republic." *Pachyderm* 20: 45–54.

———. (2001). "Forest Elephant Behavior and Ecology: Observations from the Dzanga Saline." In W. Webber, L.J.T. White, A. Vedder and L. Naughton-Treves, eds., *African Rain Forest Ecology and Conservation*. New Haven, CT: Yale University Press.

Wittemyer, G. (2011). "Family Elephantidae (Elephants)." In D.E. Wilson and R.A. Mittermeier, eds., *Handbook of the Mammals of the World*. Vol. 2, *Hoofed Mammals*, 50–81. Barcelona: Lynx Edicions.

Wittemyer, G., I. Douglas-Hamilton and W.M. Getz. (2005). "The Socioecology of Elephants: Analysis of the Processes Creating Multitiered Social Structures." *Animal Behaviour* 69(6): 1357–71.

Wittemyer, G., and W.M. Getz. (2007). "Hierarchical Dominance Structure and Social Organization in African Elephants, *Loxodonta africana*." *Animal Behaviour* 73(4): 671–81.

Wrege, P.H., E.D. Rowland, N. Bout and M. Doukaga. (2011). "Opening a Larger Window onto Forest Elephant Ecology." *African Journal of Ecology* 50(2): 176–83.

Chapter 2: The Living Rhinoceroses

Bedini, S.A. (1997). *The Pope's Elephant*. Manchester: Carcanet Press.

Cranbrook, Earl of, and P.J. Piper. (2007). "Short Communications: Javan Rhinoceros *Rhinoceros sondaicus* in Borneo." *Raffles Bulletin of Zoology* 55(1): 217–20.

Dinerstein, E. (2011). "Family Rhinocerotidae (Rhinoceroses)." In D.E. Wilson and R.A. Mittermeier, eds., *Handbook of the Mammals of the World*. Vol. 2, *Hoofed Mammals*, 144–81. Barcelona: Lynx Edicions.

Emslie, R.H., T. Milliken and B. Talukdar. (2013). *African and Asian Rhinoceroses: Status, Conservation and Trade. A Report from the IUCN Species Survival Commission (IUCN-SSC) African and Asian Rhino Specialist Groups and TRAFFIC to the CITES Secretariat Pursuant to Resolution Conf. 9.14 (rev. CoP15)*. CITES CoP16 Doc. 54.2 (Rev. 1) Annex 2.

Feely, J. (2007). "Black Rhino, White Rhino: What's in a Name?" *Pachyderm* 43: 111–15.

Flannery, T. (2012). *After the Future: Australia's New Extinction Crisis*. Quarterly Essay 48 (November).

Hariyadi, A.R., R. Setiawan, D.A. Yayus and H. Purnama. (2010). "Preliminary Behaviour Observations of the Javan Rhinoceros (*Rhinoceros sondaicus*) Based on Video Trap Surveys in Ujung Kulon National Park." *Pachyderm* 47: 93–99.

Menon, V. (1996). *Under Siege: Poaching and Protection of Greater One-horned Rhinoceroses in India*. New Delhi: TRAFFIC India.

Milman, O. (2012). "Javan Rhino Clings to Survival in Last Forest Stronghold." *The Guardian*, September 7.

Rabinowitz, A. (1995). "Helping a Species Go Extinct: The Sumatran Rhino in Borneo." *Conservation Biology* 9(3): 483–88.

Rookmaaker, K. (1997). "Records of the Sunderbans Rhinoceros (*Rhinoceros sondaicus inermis*) in India and Bangladesh." *Pachyderm* 24: 37–45.

———. (2011). "A Review of Black Rhino Systematics Proposed in *Ungulate Taxonomy* by Groves and Grubb (2011) and Its Implications for Rhino Conservation." *Pachyderm* 50: 72–76.

Santiapillai, C. (1990). "Status of the Javan Rhino in Ujung Kulon National Park." *Tigerpaper* 17: 1–8. http://www.asianrhino.nl/English/project/ujung.html.

Sinon, D. (1960). "Sur les noms altaïque de la licorne." *Wiener Zeitschrift für die Kunde des Morgenlandes* (56): 168–76. http://www.rhinoresourcecenter.com/pdf_files/128/1284800952.pdf.

Strien, N.J.v., and K. Rookmaaker. (2010). "The Impact of the Krakatoa Eruption in 1883 on the Population of *Rhinoceros sondaicus* in Ujung Kulon, with Details of Rhino Observations from 1857 to 1949." *JoTT Communication* 2(1): 633–38.

Walker, C., and A. Walker. (2012). *The Rhino Keepers*. Auckland Park, South Africa: Jacana Media.

Wikipedia. "Dürer's Rhinoceros." http://en.wikipedia. org/wiki/Dürer's_Rhinoceros.

WWF. (2013). "Rhino Poaching Crisis Spreads to India." Press release, February 5. http://wwf.panda.org/wwf_news/?207493/Rhino-poaching-crisis-spreads-to-India.

Chapter 3: Ivory and Luxury

African Manager. (2012). "Elephant Ivory Sales Creating 'Deadly New Currency in China.'" June 7. http://www.africanmanager.com/site_eng/detail_article.php?art_id=18506.

Agence France-Presse. (2012). "China's Ivory Thirst Puts Elephants at Risk." May 25.

Alpers, E.A. (1992). "The Ivory Trade in Africa: An Historical Overview." In D. H. Ross, ed., *Elephant: The Animal and Its Ivory in African Culture*, 349–63. Los Angeles: Fowler Museum of Cultural History, UCLA.

Fowler, H.W., and F.G. Fowler, trans. (1905). *The Works of Lucian of Samosata*. Adelaide, Australia: University of Adelaide. http://ebooks.adelaide.edu.au/l/lucian/works/index.html.

Martin, E.B., and D. Stiles. (2002). *The South and South East Asian Ivory Markets*. Nairobi: Save the Elephants.

Martin, R.B., D.H.M. Cumming, G.=C. Craig et al. (2012). *Decision-Making Mechanisms and Necessary Conditions for a Future Trade in African Elephant Ivory: Final Report*. CITES SC62 Doc. 46.4 Annex.

Ross, D.=H. (1992). "Imagining Elephants." In D.=H. Ross, ed., *Elephant: The Animal and Its Ivory in African Culture*, 1–41. Los Angeles: Fowler Museum of Cultural History, UCLA.

Sakamoto, M. (2004). *Black and Grey: Illegal Ivory in Japanese Markets*. 2nd ed. Tokyo: Japan Wildlife Conservation Society.

Shayt, D.H. (1992). "The Material Culture of Ivory Outside Africa." In D.H. Ross, ed., *Elephant: The Animal and Its Ivory in African Culture*. Los Angeles: Fowler Museum of Cultural History, UCLA.

Shepherd, C.R., and V. Nijman. (2008). *Elephant and Ivory Trade in Myanmar*. Selangor, Malaysia: TRAFFIC Southeast Asia.

Shoumatoff, A. (2011). "Agony and Ivory." *Vanity Fair* (August), 121–35.

The Star (Kenya). (2012). "China Key to Elephants' Future in Africa – Experts." May 31.

Stiles, D. (2009). *The Elephant and Ivory Trade in Thailand*. Selangor, Malaysia: TRAFFIC Southeast Asia.

Stiles, D., E.B. Martin and L. Vigne. (2011). "Exaggerated Ivory Prices Can Be Harmful to Elephants." *Swara* 34(4): 18–22.

TRAFFIC. (2012a). "Wildlife Trade on the Agenda at Key Africa–China Meeting." Press release, July 17.

———. (2012b). "Burgeoning Africa–China Wildlife Trade Focus at IUCN Congress Side Event." Press release, September 21.

United States Fish and Wildlife Service. (2010). "Natural Ivory." In *Ivory Identification Guide*. http://www.lab.fws.gov/ivory_natural.php.

Warmington, E.H. (1928). *The Commerce Between the Roman Empire and India*. Cambridge: Cambridge University Press.

Chapter 4: Not an Aphrodisiac

Adams, C. (2011). "Has Viagra Helped Endangered Species by Reducing Demand for Rhino Horn, etc.?" *The Straight Dope*, March 11. http://www.straightdope.com/columns/read/2985/has-viagra-helped-endangered-species-by-reducing-demand-for-rhino-horn-etc.

Cota-Larson, R. (2010). "Yemen No Longer Major Destination for Illegal Rhino Horn." *EcoWorldly*, January 13. http://www.savingrhinos.org/rhino_horn_yemen.html.

Emslie, R.H., and M. Brooks. (1999). *African Rhino: Status Survey and Conservation Action Plan*. Gland, Switzerland: IUCN.

Greenberg, D.A., and D.S. Fudge. (2013). "Regulation of Hard Alpha-keratin Mechanics via Control of Intermediate Filament Hydration: Matrix Squeeze Revisited." *Proceedings of the Royal Society B: Biological Sciences* 280(1750): 2012–2158.

Guggisberg, C.A. W. (1966). *SOS Rhino*. London: Andre Deutsch.

Hieronymus, T.L., L.M. Witmer and R.C. Ridgely. (2006). "Structure of White Rhinoceros (*Ceratotherium simum*) Horn Investigated by X-Ray Computed Tomography and Histology with Implications for Growth and External Form." *Journal of Morphology* 267(10): 1172–76.

Karantza, V. (2011). "Keratins in Health and Cancer: More Than Mere Epithelial Cell Markers." *Oncogene* 30: 127–38.

Leader-Williams, N. (1992). *The World Trade in Rhino Horn: A Review*. Cambridge: TRAFFIC International.

Liu, R., J.A. Duan, M. Wang et al. (2011). "Analysis of Active Components of Rhinoceros, Water Buffalo and Yak Horns Using Two-Dimensional Electrophoresis and Ethnopharmacological Evaluation." *Journal of Separation Science* 34(3): 354–62.

Loh, J., and K. Loh. (1994). "Rhino Horn in Taipei, Taiwan." *TRAFFIC Bulletin* 14(2): 55–58.

Martin, E. B. (1987). "The Yemeni Rhino Horn Trade." *Pachyderm* 8: 13–16.

Martin, E.B., and C. Martin. (1982). *Run Rhino Run*. London: Chatto & Windus.

Martin, E.B., L. Vigne and C. Allan. (1997). *On a Knife's Edge: The Rhinoceros Horn Trade in Yemen*. Cambridge: TRAFFIC International.

Menon, V. (1996). *Under Siege: Poaching and Protection of Greater One-horned Rhinoceroses in India*. New Delhi: TRAFFIC India.

Milliken, T., and J. Shaw. (2012). *The South Africa–Viet Nam Rhino Horn Trade Nexus: A Deadly Combination of Institutional Lapses, Corrupt Wildlife Industry Professionals and Asian Crime Syndicates*. Johannesburg: TRAFFIC.

Nowell, K. (2012). *Assessment of Rhino Horn as a Traditional Medicine*. CITES SC62 Doc. 47.2 Annex (Rev. 2).

Song, B.X., L. Cao, E.Y. Jie et al. (2010). "Research of Antipyretic, Analgesic and Anti-inflammatory Effect of Rhino Horn." *Traditional Chinese Medicine and Clinical Pharmacology*.

Tsai, F.J. (1995). "Antipyretic Effect of Xi Jiao [rhino horn] and Shuiniujiao [water buffalo horn] in Children." *Annual Report of Chinese Medicine and Pharmacy*, 329–37. Taipei, Taiwan: Committee on Chinese Medicine and Pharmacy, Department of Health.

Vigne, L., and E.B. Martin. (2000). "Price for Rhino Horn Increases in Yemen." *Pachyderm* 28: 91–100.

———. (2001). "Closing Down the Illegal Trade in Rhino Horn in Yemen." *Pachyderm* 30: 87–95.

Vigne, L., E. B. Martin and B. Okita-Ouma. (2007). "Increased Demand for Rhino Horn in Yemen Threatens Eastern Africa's Rhinos." *Pachyderm* 43: 73–87.

Yang, S. (2011). "A Review of Rhinoceros Horn." Unpublished paper, Franklin W. Olin College of Engineering, Needham, MA.

Yang, S.Z., trans. (1998). *The Divine Farmer's Materia Medica: A Translation of the Shen Nong Ben Cao Jing*. Boulder, CO: Blue Poppy Press.

Chapter 5: What Makes Poachers Poach?

BBC News. (2004). "Death of a Legendary Bandit." October 18.

Beyers, R.L., J.A. Hart, A.R.E. Sinclair et al. (2011). "Resource Wars and Conflict Ivory: The Impact of Civil Conflict on Elephants in the Democratic Republic of Congo – The Case of the Okapi Reserve." *PLoS ONE* 6(11): e27129.

Blake, S., S.L. Deem, S. Strindberg et al. (2008). "Roadless Wilderness Area Determines Forest Elephant Movements in the Congo Basin." *PLoS ONE* 3(10): e3546.

Bushmeat Crisis Task Force. (1999–2009). *Bushmeat Crisis Task Force*. http://www.bushmeat.org.

The Citizen (Tanzania). (2013a). "Two Police Officers, Civilian Held over Ivory." January 7. http://thecitizen.

co.tz/news/4-national-news/28061-two-police-officers-civilian-held-over-ivory.html.

———. (2013b). "Two Policemen Killed in Ivory Deal Gone Bad." January 7. http://thecitizen.co.tz/news/-/28075-policemen-killed-in-ivory-deal-gone-bad.

Dabany, J.R. (2013). "Poachers Kill 11,000 Gabon Elephants in under a Decade." *Scientific American*, February 6. http://www.scientificamerican.com/article.cfm?id=poachers-kill-11000-gabon-elephants.

Douglas-Hamilton, I., and O. Douglas-Hamilton. (1992). *Battle for the Elephants*. New York: Viking.

Gettleman, J. (2012). "In Gabon, Lure of Ivory Is Hard for Many to Resist." *New York Times*, December 26.

IFAW. (2012). "Three Tonnes of Ivory Vanish as Thieves Loot Southern Africa Stockpiles." Press release, June 22.

Ittaman, Shali. (2006a). "Poacher Takes Over Veerappan Country." Indiatimes News Network, August 9.

———. (2006b). "New Veerappan Dies of Kidney Failure." Indiatimes News Network, August 10.

Koch, E. (1996). "South Africa Environment: Military Implicated in Poaching." Inter Press Service, January 22. http://www.ipsnews.net/1996/01/south-africa-environment-military-implicated-in-poaching/.

Kumleben, M.E. (1996). *Commission of Inquiry into the Alleged Smuggling of and Illegal Trade in Ivory and Rhinoceros Horn in South Africa: Report of the Chairman*. http://www.scribd.com/doc/121327879/Kumleben-Commission-Report.

Maingi, J.K., J.M. Mukeka, D.M. Kyale and R.M. Muasya. (2012). "Spatiotemporal Patterns of Elephant Poaching in South-eastern Kenya." *Wildlife Research* 39(3): 234–49.

Menon, V. (2002). *Tusker! The Story of the Asian Elephant*. New Delhi: Penguin, David Shepherd Wildlife Foundation, Wildlife Trust of India and IFAW.

Mvula, S. (2012). "Masebo Hailed on Safari Hunting Ban." *Zambia Daily Mail*, 31 December. http://www.daily-mail.co.zm/index.php?option=com_k2&view=item&id=1514:masebo-hailed-on-safari-hunting-ban&Itemid=200.

Ngala, N.K. (1995). "Ivory Burning: Kenya's Stockpile on the Pyre Again." *Swara* 18(2): 26–28.

Paulin, P. (2007). "The Baka of Gabon: The Study of an Endangered Language and Culture." In M. David, N. Ostler and C. Dealwis, eds., *Working Together for Endangered Languages: Research Challenges and Social Impacts. Proceedings of the XIth FEL Conference, Kuala Lumpur, Malaysia, October 26–28, 2007*, 163–71. http://www.ddl.ish-lyon.cnrs.fr/fulltext/Paulin/Paulin_2007_FEL.pdf.

Ruggiero, R. (2013). "Minkebe: A Tragedy Revealed and a Lesson to Be Learned." http://newswatch.nationalgeographic.com/2013/02/11/minkebe-a-tragedy-revealed-and-a-lesson-to-be-learned.

Sichikwenkwe, P. (2012). "ZAWA Boss, Four Others Fired." *Times of Zambia*, December 31. http://www.times.co.zm/?p=24819.

Sukumar, R. (2003). *The Living Elephants: Evolutionary Ecology, Behavior and Conservation*. New York: Oxford University Press.

Yackulic, C.B., S. Strindberg, F. Maisels and S. Blake. (2011). "The Spatial Structure of Hunter Access Determines the Local Abundance of Forest Elephants (*Loxodonta africana cyclotis*)." *Ecological Applications* 21(4): 1296–1307.

Wikipedia. "Veerappan." http://en.wikipedia.org/wiki/Veerappan.

Zambian Watchdog. (2013). "Masebo Claims Foreign Planes Entering Zambian Airspace without Being Detected." January 2. http://www.zambianwatchdog.com/?p=48405.

Chapter 6: CITES and the First Ivory Crisis

Aarde, R.v., I. Whyte and S. Pimm. (1999). "Culling and the Dynamics of the Kruger National Park African Elephant Population." *Animal Conservation* 2(4): 287–94.

Bean, M.J. (1977). *The Evolution of National Wildlife Law: Report to the Council on Environmental Quality*. Washington, DC: Council on Environmental Quality.

Boardman, R. (1981). *International Organization and the Conservation of Nature*. Bloomington: Indiana University Press.

Chadwick, D.H. (1992). *The Fate of the Elephant*. San Francisco: Sierra Club.

CITES. Text of the Convention. http://www.cites.org/eng/disc/text.php#texttop.

Committee on Merchant Marine and Fisheries. (1979). "Statement of Craig van Note." *Hearings before the Committee: 96th Congress, 1st session, H.R. 4685, July 25 and 26*, 165–67. http://catalog.hathitrust.org/Record/002949514.

Douglas-Hamilton, I., R.F.W. Barnes, F. Michelmore and K. Beardsley. (1989). *The Ivory Trade and the Future of the African Elephant*. Lausanne: CITES Ivory Trade Review Group.

Douglas-Hamilton, I., and O. Douglas-Hamilton. (1992). *Battle for the Elephants*. New York: Viking.

The Economist. (1989). "Saving the Elephant." July 1.

EIA. (1989). *A System of Extinction: The African Elephant Disaster*. London: EIA.

Eveleth, R. (2011). "Contraception May Save Future Elephants from Culling." *Scientific American*, December 22. http://www.livescience.com/17603-contraception-save-elephants-culling.html.

Gillson, L., and K. Lindsay. (2003). "Ivory and Ecology: Changing Perspectives on Elephant Management and the International Trade in Ivory." *Environmental Science and Policy* 6(5): 411–19.

Luxmoore, R. (1989). "Africa's Elephant Dilemma." *TRAFFIC Bulletin* 11(1): 1.

Shoumatoff, A. (2011). "Agony and Ivory." *Vanity Fair* (August), 121–35.

Timberg, C. (2008). "South Africa to Resume Elephant Culling." *Washington Post* Foreign Service, February 26.

Western, D. (1989). "The Ecological Role of Elephants in Africa." *Pachyderm* 12: 42–45.

Whyte, I. (2004). "Ecological Basis of the New Elephant Management Policy for Kruger National Park and Expected Outcomes." *Pachyderm* 36: 99–108.

Wijnstekers, W. (2011). *The Evolution of CITES: A Reference to the Convention on International Trade in Endangered Species of Wild Fauna and Flora*. 9th ed. Budapest: International Council for Game and Wildlife Conservation. www.cites.org/common/resources/Evolution_of_CITES_9.pdf.

Chapter 7: The Ivory Ban

African Elephant Conservation Coordinating Group [AECCG]. (1992). *The African Elephant Project Database: Summary Information*. 4th ed. Oxford: AECCG.

Bolze, D.A. (1992). "The Ivory Trade and Conserving the African Elephant." *WCI Policy Report* 1. New York: Wildlife Conservation International.

CITES Secretariat. (1995). "The Elephant Dilemma." *CITES/C&M* 2(3): 20–28.

Currey, D., and H. Moore. (1994). *Living Proof: African Elephants and the Success of the CITES Appendix I Ban*. London: EIA.

Dills, A., M. Jacobson and J. A. Miron. (2004). "The Effect of Alcohol Prohibition on Alcohol Consumption: Evidence from Drunkenness Arrests." *Economics Letters* 86(2): 279–84.

Douglas-Hamilton, I. (1992). "In Defence of the Ivory Trade Ban." *Oryx* 26(2): 1–4.

———. (2009). "The Current Elephant Poaching Trend." *Pachyderm* 45: 154–57.

The Economist. (1989). "Saving the Elephant." July 1.

IFAW. (2004). *Elephants on the High Street: An Investigation into Ivory Trade in the UK*. London: IFAW.

Martin, E.B., and D. Stiles. (2003). *The Ivory Markets of East Asia*. Nairobi: Save the Elephants.

———. (2005). *Ivory Markets of Europe*. Kingfold, UK: Care for the Wild International and Save the Elephants.

———. (2008). *Ivory Markets in the USA*. Kingfold, UK: Care for the Wild International and Save the Elephants.

Milliken, T., R.W. Burn and L. Sangalakula. (2002). *Illegal Trade in Ivory and Other Elephant Specimens: Summary Report on the Elephant Trade Information System (ETIS)*. CITES CoP12 Doc. 34.1.

Nash, S.V., ed. (1997). *Still In Business: The Ivory Trade in Asia, Seven Years after the CITES Ban.* Cambridge: TRAFFIC International.

Pfeffer, P. (1992). *Impact de l'interdiction du commerce international de l'ivoire sur le statut des populations d'éléphants d'Afrique.* Paris: Société nationale de protection de la nature.

Schaffer Library of Drug Policy. "Did Alcohol Prohibition Reduce Alcohol Consumption and Crime?" http://www.druglibrary.org/prohibitionresults.htm (accessed January 12, 2013).

Shoshani, J., ed. (2000). *Elephants: Majestic Creatures of the Wild.* 2nd ed. San Francisco: Weldon Owen.

Western, D. (1995). "Elephant and People." *Swara* 18(2): 29.

Chapter 8: Rhinos under Fire

Cheung, J. (1995). "Implementation and Enforcement of CITES: An Assessment of Tiger and Rhinoceros Conservation Policy in Asia." *Pacific Rim Law and Policy Journal* 5(1): 125–59.

CITES. (1987). Resolution 6.10 [repealed].

———. (1994). "Conservation of and Trade in African and Asian Rhinoceroses." Resolution Conf. 9.14 (Rev. CoP15).

———. (2006). *Report on Implementing Resolution Conf. 12.5 of CITES.* CoP14 Doc. 52 Annex 1. People's Republic of China: CITES Management Authority.

Dinerstein, E. (2003). *The Return of the Unicorns: The Natural History and Conservation of the Greater One-horned Rhinoceros.* New York: Columbia University Press.

du Toit, R. (2002). "Black Rhino Crisis in Zimbabwe." *Pachyderm* 32: 83–85.

EIA. (1993). *Taiwan Kills Rhinos with Your Money: Why You Should Boycott Goods Made in Taiwan.* London: EIA.

Emslie, R.H., and M. Brooks. (1999). *African Rhino: Status Survey and Conservation Action Plan.* Gland, Switzerland: IUCN.

Emslie, R.H., S. Milledge, M. Brooks et al. (2007). *African and Asian Rhinoceroses: Status, Conservation and Trade.* CITES CoP14 Doc. 54 Annex 1.

Lang, R. (2012). "A Heart for Rhinos" [interview with Ian Player]. *Africa Geographic* (April), 26–28. http://www.wild.org/wp-content/uploads/2012/03/Ian-Player-interview_April2012.pdf.

Leader-Williams, N. (1992). *The World Trade in Rhino Horn: A Review.* Cambridge: TRAFFIC International.

Martin, E.B. (1998). "Will New Community Development Projects Help Rhino Conservation in Nepal?" *Pachyderm* 26: 88–99.

Martin, E.B., and L. Vigne. (1997). "Good News for Rhinos." *Swara* 20(5): 13–14.

Menon, V. (1996). *Under Siege: Poaching and Protection of Greater One-horned Rhinoceroses in India.* New Delhi: TRAFFIC India.

Milliken, T., K. Nowell and J.B. Thomsen. (1993). *The Decline of the Black Rhino in Zimbabwe: Implications for Future Rhino Conservation.* Pretoria: TRAFFIC East/Southern Africa.

Milliken, T., and J. Shaw. (2012). *The South Africa–Viet Nam Rhino Horn Trade Nexus: A Deadly Combination of Institutional Lapses, Corrupt Wildlife Industry Professionals and Asian Crime Syndicates.* Johannesburg: TRAFFIC. www.traffic.org/species-reports/traffic_species_mammels66.pdf

Mills, J.A. (1994). *Market Under Cover: The Rhinoceros Horn Trade in South Korea.* Cambridge: TRAFFIC International.

———. (1997). *Rhinoceros Horn and Tiger Bone in China: An Investigation of Trade Since the 1993 Ban.* Cambridge: TRAFFIC International.

Nowell, K. (2012). *Assessment of Rhino Horn as a Traditional Medicine.* CITES SC62 Doc. 47.2 Annex (Rev. 2).

New York Times. (1993). "Ivory and Rhinoceros Horns Burned in Public by Taiwan." June 6.

Player, I. (2011). "How to Save the Rhino." *True Green Conservation Alliance.* http://truegreenalliance.ca/2012/03/how-to-save-rhino-dr-ian-player.html.

Rookmaaker, K. (2002). "Miscounted Population of the Southern White Rhinoceros (*Ceratotherium simum simum*) in the Early 19th Century?" *Pachyderm* 32: 22–28.

Thornton, A. (2013). "History Repeating: The Illegal Trade in Rhino Horn." *Environmental Investigation Agency,* February 1. http://www.eia-international.org/history-repeating-the-illegal-trade-in-rhino-horn.

Trade and Environment Database. "US China Rhino and Tiger Dispute." *TED Case Studies.* http://www1.american.edu/ted/uschina.htm (accessed January 19, 2013).

U.S. News and World Report. (1989). "Heavy Artillery for Horns of Plenty." February 20.

Vigne, L., and E.B. Martin. (1989). "Taiwan: The Greatest Threat to the Survival of Africa's Rhinos." *Pachyderm* 11: 23–25.

Walker, C., and A. Walker. (2012). *The Rhino Keepers: Struggle for Survival.* Johannesburg: Jacana Media.

Chapter 9: Re-opening the Trade

Agence France-Presse. (2004). "Ivory Ban Spells Doom for Namibian Tribe's Tradition." *Terra Daily,* October 6. http://www.terradaily.com/2004/041006093726.qmww7r6u.html.

Bond, I. (1994) "Importance of Elephant Hunting to CAMPFIRE Revenue in Zimbabwe." *Traffic Bulletin* 14: 117–19.

Christy, B. (2012). "Ivory Worship." *National Geographic* (October). ngm.nationalgeographic.com/2012/10/ivory/christy-text.

CITES. "CITES MIKE Programme." http://www.cites.org/common/prog/mike/brochure.pdf (accessed January 20, 2013).

———. (2004). *Control System for Worked Ivory in Namibia*. CoP13 Inf. 33.

———. (2008). *Fifty-Seventh Meeting of the Standing Committee, Geneva (Switzerland), 14–18 July 2008: Summary Record*. http://www.cites.org/eng/com/sc/57/E57-SumRec.pdf.

Courouble, M., F. Hurst and T. Milliken. (2003). *More Ivory Than Elephants: Domestic Ivory Markets in Three West African Countries*. Cambridge: TRAFFIC International.

Douglas-Hamilton, I. (1992). "In Defence of the Ivory Trade Ban." *Oryx* 26(2): 1–4.

EIA. (1992). *Under Fire: Elephants in the Front Line*. London: EIA.

———. (1997). *Proceedings of the African Elephant Conference*. London: EIA.

———. (2007). *Made in China: How China's Illegal Ivory Trade Is Causing a 21st Century African Elephant Disaster*. Washington, DC: EIA.

———. (2010). *Open Season: The Burgeoning Illegal Ivory Trade in Tanzania and Zambia*. London: EIA.

Hastie, J., J. Newman and M. Rice. (2002). *Back in Business: Elephant Poaching and the Ivory Black Markets of Asia*. London: EIA.

Hemley, G. (1992). "CITES 1992: Endangered Treaty? Kyoto Decisions Political, Not Practical." *TRAFFIC USA Newsletter* 11(3): 1–3.

IFAW. (2007). *Fatal Flaw: The Inadequacies of Japan's Ivory Trade Controls*. Yarmouth Port, MA: IFAW.

Kiyono, H. (2002). *Japan's Trade in Ivory after the Tenth Conference of the Parties to CITES*. Cambridge: TRAFFIC International.

Martin, E.B., and D. Stiles. (2000). *The Ivory Markets of Africa*. Nairobi: Save the Elephants.

———. (2002). *The South and South East Asian Ivory Markets*. Nairobi: Save the Elephants.

McCarthy, M., and C. Brown. (2008). "Return of Ivory Trade as Britain Backs China." *The Independent*, July 16.

Milliken, T. (1994). "The African Elephant: Another Round at CoP9." *Swara* 17(5): 16–18.

Orenstein, R. (1992). "Ivory Ban Not Just a Response to Western 'Bunnyhuggers.'" Letter to *The Gazette* (Montreal), May 11, B3.

Pitman, D. (1989). *Elephants and People: Zimbabwe's Alternative to the Ivory Trade Bans*. Harare: Zimbabwe Trust.

Poole, J. (1992). "Kenya's Elephants: A Very Different Story to Tell." *Swara* 15(1): 29–31.

Redmond, I. (1991). Unpublished report by the African Ele-Fund, December.

Reeve, R., S. Pope and D. Stewart. (2007). *Ivory, Ekipa and Etosha: The Hidden Cost to Elephants and Rhinos of Namibia's Wildlife Policy*. Cranleigh, UK: David Shepherd Wildlife Foundation.

Rotich, N. (1992). "Total Ban on Ivory Trade Still the Only Way to Save the Elephant." *Swara* 15(1): 6–7.

———. (1994). "The Elephant Is Not Yet Safe!" *Swara* 17(5): 5.

Sakamoto, M. (2004). *Black and Grey: Illegal Ivory in Japanese Markets*. 2nd ed. Tokyo: Japan Wildlife Conservation Society.

Shigwedha, A. (2007). "Govt Mum on Ekipa Scandal." *The Namibian*, May 30.

———. (2008). "Government Bans Ekipa Sales." *The Namibian*, August 21.

Shoshani, J., and R. Orenstein. (1994). "CITES at the Crossroads." *Swara* 17(5): 12–13.

Stiles, D. (2009). "CITES-Approved Ivory Sales and Elephant Poaching." *Pachyderm* 45: 150–53.

't. Sas-Rolfes, M. (1997). "Elephants, Rhinos and the Economics of the Illegal Trade." *Pachyderm* 24: 23–29.

Thompson, C. (2004). "Co-producing CITES and the African Elephant." In S. Jasanoff, ed., *States of Knowledge: The Co-production of Science and the Social Order*, 67–86. London: Routledge.

Townsend, M. (1992). "Zimbabwe's Position on the Ivory Ban." *Swara* 15(1): 13–15

Wasser, S.K., J. Poole, P. Lee et al. (2010). "Elephants, Ivory and Trade." *Science* 327: 1331–32.

Western, D. (1992). "Taking Stock of the Ivory Ban." *Swara* 15(1): 21–23.

Wijnstekers, W. (2011). *The Evolution of CITES: A Reference to the Convention on International Trade in Endangered Species of Wild Fauna and Flora*. 9th ed. Budapest: International Council for Game and Wildlife Conservation. www.cites.org/common/resources/Evolution_of_CITES_9.pdf.

Wu, J., and M. Phipps. (2002). *An Investigation of the Ivory Market in Taiwan*. Cambridge: TRAFFIC International.

Chapter 10: New Markets for Horn

Ammann, K. (2012). "Tiger Cake and Rhino Horn: A Walk on the Asian Wild Side." *Swara* (July–September): 32–37.

Blaine, S. (2012). "Vietnamese Minister Not Available to Sign Memorandum on Rhino Poaching." *Business Day*, October 18. www.bdlive.co.za/national/science/2012/10/18/vietnamese-minister-not-available-to-sign-memorandum-on-rhino-poaching.

CITES. (2004). Resolution Conf. 13.5 (Rev. CoP14).

———. (2012). "CITES Acts to Curb Smuggling of Elephant Ivory and Rhino Horn." Press release, July 31.

Dien, A. (2012). "Officials' Appetite for Rare Animals Hinders Conservation Effort." *Vietweek*, October 12. www.thanhniennews.com/index/pages/20121012-officials-appetite-for-rare-animals-hinders-conservation-effort.aspx.

du Preez, Y. (2012). "Fury as Poaching Charges Dropped." *The Post* (South Africa), April 5. http://www.thepost.co.za/fury-as-poaching-charges-dropped-1.1270893.

du Toit, R. (2002). "Black Rhino Crisis in Zimbabwe." *Pachyderm* 32: 83–85.

Emslie, R.H. (2011a). *Ceratotherium simum*. IUCN Red List of Threatened Species, version 2012.1. www.iucnredlist.org.

———. (2011b). *Diceros bicornis*. IUCN Red List of Threatened Species, version 2012.1. www.iucnredlist.org.

Eurogroup for Animals. (2012). "SA, Vietnam Set to Sign Rhino Deal." Press release, August 21.

Gettleman, J. (2012). "Frenzy for Horns Threatens Rhino's Survival." *New York Times*, January 13.

Jacobs, R. (2012). "AK47s, Quack Medicine and Heaps of Cash: The Gruesome Rhino Horn Trade Explained." *Mother Jones*, August 15. http://www.motherjones.com/environment/2012/08/rhino-horn-trade-explained.

Milliken, T., R.H. Emslie and B. Talukdar. (2009). *African and Asian Rhinoceroses: Status, Conservation and Trade: A Report from the IUCN Species Survival Commission (IUCN-SSC) African and Asian Rhino Specialist Groups and TRAFFIC to the CITES Secretariat Pursuant to Resolution Conf. 9.14 (rev. CoP14) and Decision 14.89*. CITES CoP15 Doc. 45.1 Annex.

Milliken, T., and J. Shaw. (2012). *The South Africa–Viet Nam Rhino Horn Trade Nexus: A Deadly Combination of Institutional Lapses, Corrupt Wildlife Industry Professionals and Asian Crime Syndicates*. Johannesburg: TRAFFIC. www.traffic.org/species-reports/traffic_species_mammals66.pdf.

News24. (2012a). "Vets, Hunter in Court Again." June 12. www.news24.com/SouthAfrica/News/Vets-hunter-in-court-again-20120619.

———. (2012b). "SA, Vietnam Discuss Poaching." August 17. www.news24.com/SciTech/News/SA-Vietwnam-discuss-poaching-20120817.

Potgieter, d.W. (2011). "Noted Vet Held on Rhino Poaching Charges." *The New Age*, November 24. http://thenewage.co.za/35933-1007-53-Noted_vet_held_on_rhino_poaching_charges.

Smillie, S. (2012). "The Evolution of a Rhino Poacher." *IOL Scitech*, December 19. www.iol.co.za/scitech/science/environment/the-evolution-of-a-rhino-poacher-1.1442771#.UOzZF6Wfv2k.

South Africa Department of Environmental Affairs. (2013). "Minister Molewa Updates South Africans on the Rhino Situation and Measures to Thwart Poaching." Media release, January 10. http://www.environment.gov.za/?q=content/molewa_updates_southafricans_rhinosituation_measures.

SouthAfrica.info. (2012). "SA, Vietnam to Sign Anti-poaching Pact." December 3. http://www.southafrica.info/news/international/rhinos-051212.htm#.UQHubqWfv2m.

TRAFFIC. (2012a). "CITES Bares Teeth, But Can It Bite?" Press release, July 27.

———. (2012b). "Viet Nam Acknowledges Severity of Rhino Trade." Press release, September 20.

UNODC. (2012). *Bulletin on Organised Crime in Southern Africa*. Pretoria: UNODC Regional Office for Southern Africa.

Vietcombank Fund Management. "Vietnam Market." http://www.vcbf.com/en/vietnam-market.html (accessed March 21, 2013).

Vietnam, Socialist Republic of. (2013). "Decision on Banning from Export, Import, Purchase and Sale of the Specimens of Some of Wild Fauna Species in Appendices to the Convention on International Trade in Endangered Species of Wild Fauna and Flora." Decision no. 11/2013/QĐ-TTg, January 24.

Vietnam Ministry of Natural Resources and Environment. (2012). "Rhino Horn Claim Unfounded." September 4. http://vea.gov.vn/en/news/news/Pages/Rhino-horn-claim-unfounded.aspx.

Wildlife Extra. (2012). "South Africa Vets & Hunters Involved in Rhino Poaching." July. http://www.wildlife-extra.com/go/news/rhino-m99.html#cr.

WWF. (2012). "New Agreement between South Africa and Vietnam: A Turning Point in Tackling Rhino Poaching Crisis, Say WWF, TRAFFIC." Press release, December 10. www.cisionwire.com/wwf-international/r/new-agreement-between-south-africa-and-vietnam--a-turning-point-in-tackling-rhino-poaching-crisis--,c9347409.

Chapter 11: Behind the Surge

Agence France-Presse. (2012). "Philippines Expands Probe into 'Blood' Ivory." September 28.

Archie, E.A., and P.I. Chiyo. (2012). "Elephant Behaviour and Conservation: Social Relationships, the Effects of Poaching, and Genetic Tools for Management." *Molecular Ecology* 21(3): 765–78.

Associated Press. (2013). "Wildlife Group Wants Thailand to Ban Ivory Trade." January 15.

Bangkok Post. (2013). "Thailand at the Centre of Rising Illegal Ivory Trade." January 13.

Bartholomew, D. (2013). "Father Cristobal Garcia: Priest Fled to the Philippines and Rose in the Church."

Daily News (Los Angeles), January 26. Updated January 29. http://www.dailynews.com/news/ci_22453515/father-cristobal-garcia-priest-fled-philippines-and-rose.

BBC. (2012). "Ivory Wars: Out of Africa." *Panorama*, April 12.

Bouché, P., I. Douglas-Hamilton, G. Wittemyer et al. (2011). "Will Elephants Soon Disappear from West African Savannahs?" *PLoS ONE* 6(6): e20619.

Burn, R.W., F.M. Underwood and J. Blanc. (2011). "Global Trends and Factors Associated with the Illegal Killing of Elephants: A Hierarchical Bayesian Analysis of Carcass Encounter Data." *PLoS ONE* 6(9): e24165.

Cebu Daily News. (2012a). "Is That Ivory New or Antique? Burden of Proof Is on the Owner." September 29.

———. (2012b). "Cardinal Favors 'Persona Non Grata' Status for Journalist." October 2.

Christy, B. (2012). "Ivory Worship." *National Geographic* (October). ngm.nationalgeographic.com/2012/10/ivory/christy-text.

CITES. (2010). *Monitoring of Illegal Killing of Elephants.* CoP15 Doc. 44.2 (Rev. 1).

———. (2012a). *Control of Trade in Ivory in China.* SC62 Inf. 8.

———. (2012b). *Ivory Trade Control in Thailand.* SC62 Doc. 46.2.

———. (2012c). *Supplementary Information on Document Sc62 Doc. 46.1.* SC62 Inf. 1.

———. (2013). *Monitoring the Illegal Killing of Elephants.* CoP16 Doc. 53.1.

Douglas-Hamilton, I. (2009). "The Current Elephant Poaching Trend." *Pachyderm* 45: 154–57.

———. (2012). "Ivory and Insecurity: The Global Implications of Poaching in Africa. Testimony of Iain Douglas-Hamilton, Founder and CEO, Save the Elephants, before the Committee on Foreign Relations, U.S. Senate, May 24, 2012." http://www.elephantsinperil.org/news/ivory-and-insecurity-the-global-implications-of-poaching-in-africa.

Douglas-Hamilton, I., G. Wittemyer and F. Ihwagi. (2010). *Levels of Illegal Killing of Elephants in the Laikipia-Samburu MIKE Site.* CITES CoP15 Inf. 40 (Rev. 1).

EIA. (2012). *Blood Ivory: Exposing the Myth of a Regulated Market.* London: EIA.

Eichenseher, T. (2008). "Poaching May Erase Elephants from Chad Wildlife Park." *National Geographic News*, December 11. http://news.nationalgeographic.com/news/2008/12/081211-zakouma-elephants-missions.html.

Fay, J.M. (2007). "Ivory Wars: Last Stand in Zakouma." *National Geographic* (March).

Fernandez, C. (2012). "Vatican Sacked Cebu Priest Months Ahead of Ivory Scandal, Says Church Exec."

Inquirer Visayas, September 27.

Hance, J. (2012). "Elephant Poachers Kill Unarmed Wildlife Ranger in Kenya." *Mongabay.com*, January 16.

Italy, Ministero delle politiche agricole, alimentari e forestale. (2012). "Si tratta di manufatti rappresentanti soggetti religiosi realizzati in avorio di elefante. Il costo della merce in vendita variava dai 400 ai 40.000 euro, per un valore complessivo oltre 150 mila euro." Press release, Corpo forestale dello stato, October 29.

Martin, E.B., and C. Martin. (2011). "Large and Mostly Legitimate: Hong Kong's Mammoth and Elephant Ivory Trade." *Pachyderm* 50: 37–49.

Martin, E.B., C. Martin and L. Vigne. (2011). "The Importance of Ivory in Philippine Culture." *Pachyderm* 50: 56–67.

Martin, E.B., and L. Vigne. (2011). *The Ivory Dynasty: A Report on the Soaring Demand for Elephant and Mammoth Ivory in Southern China.* London: Elephant Family, Aspinall Foundation and Columbus Zoo and Aquarium.

Milliken, T., R. Burn and L. Sangalakula. (2009). *The Elephant Trade Information System (ETIS) and the Illicit Trade in Ivory: A Report to the 15th Meeting of the Conference of the Parties to CITES.* Unpublished report, CITES CoP15 Annex 1.

Milliken, T., and L. Sangalakula. (2011). "ETIS Update Number Six: Progress in the Implementation of the Elephant Trade Information System (ETIS)." *Pachyderm* 50: 99–104.

The Nation (Thailand). (2012). "Ivory Traders Must Register by January." December 18.

Payne, O. (2013). "Vatican Responds to *National Geographic*'s Correspondence about Religious Use of Ivory." January 22. http://newswatch.nationalgeographic.com/2013/01/22/vatican-responds-to-national-geographics-correspondence-about-religious-use-of-ivory/.

Poilecot, P. (2010). "Le braconnage et la population d'éléphants du parc national de Zakouma (Tchad)." *Bois et forêts des tropiques* 303(1).

Shoumatoff, A. (2011). "Agony and Ivory." *Vanity Fair* (August), 121–35.

Stiles, D. (2008). *An Assessment of the Illegal Ivory Trade in Viet Nam.* Selangor, Malaysia: TRAFFIC Southeast Asia.

———. (2009). *The Elephant and Ivory Trade in Thailand.* Selangor, Malaysia: TRAFFIC Southeast Asia.

———. (2011). "Elephant Meat and Ivory Trade in Central Africa." *Pachyderm* 50: 26–36.

Stiles, D., and E.B. Martin. (2008). "The USA's Ivory Markets: How Much of a Threat to Elephants?" *Pachyderm* 45: 67–76.

Sun Star (Cebu, Philippines). (2012). "Cebu a Transit Point; Ivory Goes to China." October 3.

Vigne, L., and E.B. Martin. (2008). "Survey of the Ivory Items for Retail Sale in Addis Ababa in 2008." *Pachyderm* 44: 65–71.

———. (2010). "Consumer Demand for Ivory in Japan Declines." *Pachyderm* 47: 45–54.

Wasser, S.K., B. Clark and C. Laurie. (2009). "The Ivory Trail." *Scientific American* 301: 68–76.

Wasser, S.K., C. Mailand, R. Booth et al. (2007). "Using DNA to Track the Origin of the Largest Ivory Seizure Since the 1989 Trade Ban." *Proceedings of the National Academy of Sciences of the United States of America* 104(10): 4228–33.

Whaley, F. (2012). "Priest Investigated in Ivory-Smuggling Enquiry in Philippines." *New York Times*, September 26.

Wu, S. (2013). "Kenya: China Has a Zero Tolerance on Illegal Ivory Trade." *The Star* (Kenya), February 8. http://allafrica.com/stories/201302081534.html?viewall=1.

Chapter 12: Rhinos and Prostitutes

ABC News. (2012). "Thai Prostitutes Used to Conceal Ivory Trafficking Ring." November 6. http://www.abc.net.au/news/2012-11-06/an-thai-prostitutes-used-to-stage-fake-rhino-hunts/4355162.

Blaine, S. (2012). "DA Asks Public Protector to Investigate North West Environmental Officials." November 12. http://www.bdlive.co.za/national/science/2012/11/12/da-asks-public-protector-to-investigate-north-west-environmental-officials.

CITES. (2013). "Consideration of Proposals for Amendment of Appendices I and II." CoP 16 Prop. 10. www.cites.org/eng/cop/16/prop/E-CoP16-Prop-10.pdf.

Dube, M. (2012). "South Africa: Hunters to Only Export One Trophy Horn per Year." Government Communication and Information System, April 16.

Gettleman, J. (2012). "Coveting Horns, Ruthless Smugglers Put Rhinos in the Cross Hairs." *New York Times*, December 31.

Gray, D. (2012). "Biggest Asian Wildlife Traffickers Are Untouchable." Associated Press, August 15.

Killing for Profit. (2012a). "Marnus Steyl to Face New Charges over Alleged Rhino 'Pseudo-hunts.'" December 4. http://killingforprofit.com/2012/12/04/marnus-steyl-to-face-new-charges-over-alleged-rhino-pseudo-hunts/.

———. (2012b). "Update: Steyl Granted Bail in 'Pseudo-hunt' Case." December 5. http://killingforprofit.com/2012/12/05/update-steyl-granted-bail-in-pseudo-hunt-case/.

Kogure, T. (2012). "Smugglers Exploit Loophole for Coveted African Rhino Horns." *Asahi Shimbun*, January 15. http://ajw.asahi.com/article/behind_news/social_affairs/AJ201301150094.

Lion Aid. (2012). "Elephant and Rhino Poaching: Big Fish and Little Fish." *Pieter's Blog*, November 20. http://www.lionaid.org/blog/2012/11/

elephant-and-rhino-poaching-big-fish-and-little-fish.htm.

Milliken, T., and J. Shaw. (2012). *The South Africa–Viet Nam Rhino Horn Trade Nexus: A Deadly Combination of Institutional Lapses, Corrupt Wildlife Industry Professionals and Asian Crime Syndicates*. Johannesburg: TRAFFIC. www.traffic.org/species-reports/traffic_species_mammals66.pdf.

News24. (2013). "Two Rhino Killed a Day Since New Year." January 31. http://www.news24.com/Green/News/Two-rhino-killed-a-day-since-New-Year-20130131.

Rademeyer, J. (2012). *Killing for Profit: Exposing the Illegal Rhino Horn Trade*. Cape Town: Zebra Press.

South Africa, Republic of. (2009). "Marking of Rhinoceros Horn and Hunting of White Rhinoceros for Trophy Hunting Purposes." Notice 170. *Government Gazette*, February 13.

South Africa Department of Environmental Affairs. (2013). *Update on the Rhino Poaching Statistics*. February 6. http://www.environment.gov.za/?q=content/rhino_poaching_statistics.

Thanh Nien News. (2012). "$191,000 Rhino Horn Missing from Bank Tycoon's Residence." October 4. http://www.thanhniennews.com/index/pages/20121004-$191,000-rhino-horn-missing-from-bank-tycoon-residence.aspx.

Tuoi Tre News. (2012). "Man Who Gifts Rhino to Banker a Legal Hunter: CITES." October 9. http://www.tuoitrenews.vn/cmlink/tuoitrenews/society/man-who-gifts-rhino-to-banker-a-legal-hunter-cites-1.88277.

———. (2013). "Vietnam Bans Rhino Specimen Imports." January 29. http://www.tuoitrenews.vn/cmlink/tuoitrenews/society/vietnam-bans-rhino-specimen-imports-1.97560#.

Vietnam, Socialist Republic of. (2013). "Decision on Banning from Export, Import, Purchase and Sale of the Specimens of Some of Wild Fauna Species in Appendices to the Convention on International Trade in Endangered Species of Wild Fauna and Flora." Decision no. 11/2013/QĐ-TTg, January 24.

Wildlife Extra. (2012). "South Africa Changes Rules on Rhino Hunts: Halts Vietnamese for Now." July. http://www.wildlifeextra.com/go/news/vietnamese-rhino-hunt.html#cr.

Chapter 13: War on Elephants

Bauer, H. (2007). "Status of Large Carnivores in Bouba Ndjida National Park, Cameroon." *African Journal of Ecology* 45(3): 448–50.

Center for Conservation Biology. (2011). *Elephant Ivory Project*. March. http://elephantivoryproject.org/2011/03/.

Douglas-Hamilton, I. (2012). "Ivory and Insecurity: The Global Implications of Poaching in Africa. Testimony of Iain Douglas-Hamilton, Founder and CEO, Save the

Elephants, before the Committee on Foreign Relations, U.S. Senate, May 24, 2012." http://www.elephantsinperil. org/news/ivory-and-insecurity-the-global-implications-of-poaching-in-africa.

Douglas-Hamilton, I., and O. Douglas-Hamilton. (1992). *Battle for the Elephants*. New York: Viking.

Fay, J.M. (2012). "Elephant Guards Murdered in Chad." *A Voice for Elephants* (blog). *National Geographic Newswatch*, September 28. http://newswatch.nationalgeographic.com/2012/09/28/elephant-guards-murdered-in-chad/.

France 24. (2012). "Okapis, Gorillas, Elephants: The Other Victims of War in Eastern DR Congo." August 28. http://observers.france24.com/content/20120828-okapis-gorillas-elephants-other-victims-war-eastern-democratic-republic-congo-north-kivu-m23-rebels-nature-park.

Gettleman, J. (2012). "Elephants Dying in Epic Frenzy as Ivory Fuels Wars and Profits." *New York Times*, September 4.

Greenfield, R. (1995). "Siad Barre" [obituary]. *The Independent*, January 3. http://www.independent.co.uk/news/people/obituary-mohamed-said-barre-1566452.html.

Hart, T. (2012). *Searching for Bonobo in Congo* (blog). July 3–13. http://www.bonoboincongo.com/2012/07/03/okapi-attack-sends-shock-waves-through-the-ituri-forest/.

IFAW. (2012). "Too Late: Military Intervention Fails to Halt Elephant Slaughter in Cameroon." Press release, March 12.

Invisible Children + Resolve. (2012). *LRA Crisis Tracker: Mid-Year Security Brief (Jan.–June 2012)*. https://salsa.democracyinaction.org/o/2241/images/LRA Crisis Tracker 2012 Mid-Year Security Brief - FINAL.pdf.

Kakabadse, Y. (2011). "The Fight Against Wildlife Crime: Enforcement v. Corruption." *Environmental Policy and Law* 41(3): 123–26.

Kouamo, E. (2012). "Cameroon: Massacre of Elephants." Radio Netherlands Worldwide, April 10.

Llanos, M. (2012a). "Baby Elephant Orphaned in Slaughter Finds a Foster Mom." NBC News, August 3. http://worldnews.nbcnews.com/_news/2012/08/03/13105056-baby-elephant-orphaned-in-slaughter-finds-a-foster-mom?lite.

———. (2012b). "Second Orphaned Elephant Found in Chad after Killings." NBC News, August 7. http://world-news.nbcnews.com/_news/2012/08/07/13167596-second-orphaned-elephant-found-in-chad-after-killings?lite.

Neme, L. (2012). "Dozens of Elephants Massacred in Chad." *Mongabay.com*, July 26.

Nouredine, A. (2012). "Situation du braconnage des éléphants dans le Mayo Rey (secteur du Parc National de Bouba N'Djida, Nord Cameroun)." *Réseau des aires protégées d'Afrique Centrale* [RAPAC], February. http://

www.rapac.org/index.php?option= com_content &view=article&id=390:situation-du-braconnage-des-elephants-dans-le-mayo-rey&atid=50&Itemid=71.

Owono, J. (2012). "The Martyrdom of Elephants: A Sad Tale of Greed." Al Jazeera, March 7.

Platt, J.R. (2012). "Cameroon Elephant Massacre Shows Poaching, Ivory Trade Require an International Response." *Extinction Countdown* (blog). *Scientific American*, March 20. http://blogs.scientificamerican.com/extinction-countdown/2012/03/20/cameroon-elephant-massacre-poaching-ivory-trade/.

Poilecot, P. (2010). "Le braconnage et la population d'éléphants du parc national de Zakouma (Tchad)." *Bois et forêts des tropiques* 303(1).

Shoumatoff, A. (2011). "Agony and Ivory." *Vanity Fair* (August), 121–35.

Winter, S. (2012). "Sickening Elephants' Graveyard Caused by Hatred and Greed." *Express*, April 8. http://www.express.co.uk/news/world/313260/Sickening-elephants-graveyard-caused-by-hatred-and-greed.

WWF. (2012). "Cameroon Increases Elephant Protection after Mass Slaughter." Press release, August 10.

Chapter 14: The Last Rhinos

Agence France-Presse. (2012). "Endangered Sumatran Rhino Gives Birth." June 23. http://news.discovery.com/animals/zoo-animals/sumatran-rhino-birth-10623.htm.

Ahmad Zafir, A.W., J. Payne, A. Mohamed et al. (2011). "Now or Never: What Will It Take to Save the Sumatran Rhinoceros *Dicerorhinus sumatrensis* from Extinction?" *Oryx* 45(2): 225–33.

Asian Rhino Foundation [De Neushoornstichting]. "Sumatran Rhino Sanctuary." *Asian Rhino*. http://www.asianrhino.nl/English/project/srs.html.

Brook, S., P.J.v. Coevorden de Groot, S. Mahood and B. Long. (2011). *Extinction of the Javan Rhinoceros* (Rhinoceros sondaicus) *from Vietnam*. Hanoi: WWF Vietnam.

Campbell, C. (2012). "Asian Rhino Specialist Group Meeting: Assessment Status of Sumatran and Javan Rhino in SE Asia." *The Rhino Print* (Winter): 16–17.

Christy, B. (2010) "Asia's Wildlife Trade: The Kingpin." *National Geographic* (January). http://ngm.nationalgeographic.com/2010/01/asian-wildlife/christy-text.

Cincinnati Zoo and Botanical Garden. (2010). "Sumatran Rhino Born at Cincinnati Zoo Provides Spark of Hope for Indonesia." Press Release, February 18. http://www.prweb.com/releases/Cincinnati_Zoo/Sumatran_Rhino/prweb3616444.htm.

———. (2012). "CREW's Signature Sumatran Rhino Project." http://cincinnatizoo.org/conservation/crew/rhino-signature-project/sumatran-rhino/.

Dinerstein, E. (2011). "Family Rhinocerotidae (Rhinoceroses)." In D.E. Wilson and R.A. Mittermeier, eds., *Handbook of the Mammals of the World*. Vol. 2, *Hoofed Mammals*, 144–81. Barcelona: Lynx Edicions.

Emslie, R.H. (2004). "Rhino Population Sizes and Trends." *Pachyderm* 37: 107–10.

Emslie, R.H., and M. Brooks. (1999). *African Rhino: Status Survey and Conservation Action Plan*. Gland, Switzerland: IUCN-SSC African Rhino Specialist Group.

Emslie, R.H., T. Milliken and B. Talukdar. (2013). *African and Asian Rhinoceroses: Status, Conservation and Trade. A Report from the IUCN Species Survival Commission (IUCN-SSC) African and Asian Rhino Specialist Groups and TRAFFIC to the CITES Secretariat pursuant to Resolution Conf. 9.14 (rev. CoP15)*. CITES CoP16 Doc. 54.2 (Rev. 1) Annex 2.

Goossens, B., and L.N. Ambu (2012). "Sabah Wildlife Department and 10 Years of Research: Towards a Better Conservation of Sabah's Wildlife." *Journal of Oil Palm and the Environment* 3: 38–51.

Groves, C.P., P. Fernando and J. Robovsky. (2010). "The Sixth Rhino: A Taxonomic Reassessment of the Critically Endangered Northern White Rhinoceros." *PLoS ONE* 5(4): e9703.

Hillman Smith, K. (1998). "The Current Status of the Northern White Rhino in Garamba." *Pachyderm* 25: 104–5.

———. (2001). "Status of Northern White Rhinos and Elephants in Garamba National Park, Democratic Republic of Congo, During the Wars." *Pachyderm* 31: 79–81.

IUCN-SSC African Rhino Specialist Group, French Committee, for IUCN-SSC and WWF. (2000). "Conservation Strategy for Cameroon's Western Black Rhino, *Diceros bicornis longipes*." *Pachyderm* 29: 52–53.

Lagrot, I., J.-F. Lagrot and P. Bour. (2007). "Probable Extinction of the Western Black Rhino, *Diceros bicornis longipes*: 2006 Survey in Northern Cameroon." *Pachyderm* 43: 19–28.

Martin, E.B., and L. Vigne. (1997). "Good News for Rhinos." *Swara* 20(5): 13–14.

Milliken, T., R.H. Emslie and B. Talukdar. (2009). *African and Asian Rhinoceroses: Status, Conservation and Trade: A Report from the IUCN Species Survival Commission (IUCN-SSC) African and Asian Rhino Specialist Groups and TRAFFIC to the CITES Secretariat Pursuant to Resolution Conf. 9.14 (Rev. CoP14) and Decision 14.89*. CITES CoP15 Doc. 45.1 Annex.

Milliken, T., and J. Shaw. (2012). *The South Africa–Viet Nam Rhino Horn Trade Nexus: A Deadly Combination of Institutional Lapses, Corrupt Wildlife Industry Professionals and Asian Crime Syndicates*. Johannesburg: TRAFFIC.

Mongabay.com. (2011). "A Final Farewell: The Western Black Rhino Goes Extinct." November 12.

Platt, J.R. (2011). "Rare Northern White Rhino Dies of Old Age: And Then There Were 7 . . ." *Extinction Countdown* (blog). *Scientific American*, June 7. http://blogs.scientificamerican.com/extinction-countdown/2011/06/07/rare-northern-white-rhino-dies-of-old-agemdashand-then-there-were-7/.

Roundtable on Sustainable Palm Oil. (2013). "Sumatran Rhino Crisis Summit." Promotional flyer, March. http://www.rspo.org/file/Sumatran Rhino Crisis Summit 1 Jan 13 flyer.pdf.

Thanh, N.V., and G. Polet. (2007). *Monitoring of Javan Rhinoceros in Cat Tien National Park, Vietnam, July–December 2006*. Areas Technical Report 11. WWF Asian Rhino and Elephant Action Strategy on Vietnam: Cat Tien National Park.

Chapter 15: Corruption, Theft and Organized Crime

Arkell, R. (2012). "Rhino Horn Restrictions to Include All 'Worked' Items." *Antiques Trade Gazette*, March 19. http://www.antiquestradegazette.com/news/2012/mar/19/rhino-horn-restrictions-to-include-all-worked-items/.

BBC News. (2013). "Ivory Haul from Africa Seized in Singapore." January 30.

Brown, L. (2012). "Elephant Graveyard: Customs Officers Seize Vast £2 Million Ivory Haul Weighing Four Tons and Featuring over 1,200 Pieces of Tusk." *Mail Online*, October 20. http://www.dailymail.co.uk/news/article-2220589/Elephant-graveyard-Customs-officers-seize-vast-2million-ivory-haul-weighing-tons-featuring-1-200-pieces-tusk.html?ito=feeds-newsxml.

Cape Times (Cape Town, South Africa). (2011). "Khaki-Collar Crime a Growing Evil." December 14. http://www.highbeam.com/doc/1G1-275348929.html.

CITES. (1997). "Trade in Elephant Specimens." Resolution Conf. 10.10.

———. (2012). *Elephant Conservation, Illegal Killing and Ivory Trade*. SC62 Doc. 46.1 (Rev. 1).

Dube, M. (2012). "Minister Cracks Whip on Horn Stockpiles." *News24*, April 5. http://m.news24.com/news24/SouthAfrica/News/Minister-cracks-whip-on-horn-stockpiles-20120405.

Duggan, B. (2013). "Traveller Crime Gang Held after European Police Raids." *Independent.ie*, January 16. http://www.independent.ie/irish-news/traveller-crime-gang-held-after-european-police-raids-28959048.html.

Europol. (2011). "Europol and Ireland Identify Organized Crime Group Active in Illegal Trading of Rhino Horn." July 7. https://www.europol.europa.eu/content/press/europol-and-ireland-identify-organised-crime-group-active-illegal-trading-rhino-horn-9.

Ferguson, K.K. (2012). "Trophy Hunting in Museums: Rhino Horn Thefts a Growing Problem in Europe." *Spiegel Online*, March 13. http://www.spiegel.de/international/europe/rhino-horn-thefts-a-growing-problem-in-europe-a-821132.html.

Gadling. (2011). "Thieves Steal Rhino Horn from Paris Museum." December. http://www.gadling.com/2011/12/09/thieves-steal-rhino-horn-from-paris-museum.

Gay, M. (2011). "White Rhino, Black Market: Why Old Stuffed Rhinos Now Command Top Dollar." The Atlantic (October). http://www.theatlantic.com/magazine/archive/2011/10/white-rhino-black-market/308632/.

Gray, D.D. (2012). "Biggest Asian Wildlife Traffickers Are Untouchable." Associated Press, August 15. http://www.google.com/hostednews/ap/article/ALeqM5gbB1pzeiEqCsHSsQpy0eVtvr5r7g?docId=edfd4475e-3294a10b1db86f0023aec81.

Hance, J. (2011). "Busted: 1,835 Elephant Tusks Confiscated in Two Seizures Connected by Malaysia." Mongabay.com, August 31.

Humane Society International. (2011). "Rhinoceros Horn Stockpiles: A Serious Threat to Rhinos." September 12. www.hsi.org/assets/pdfs/rhino_horn_stockpiles_report.pdf.

IFAW. (2012a). "China Applies Trade Ban to Wildlife Auctions." Press release, January 11. http://www.ifaw.org/canada/news/china-applies-trade-ban-wildlife-auctions.

———. (2012b). "Three Tonnes of Ivory Vanish as Thieves Loot Southern Africa Stockpiles." Press release, June 22. http://www.sundaystandard.info/article.php?NewsID=13878&GroupID=1.

Jacobs, R. (2012). "AK47s, Quack Medicine, and Heaps of Cash: The Gruesome Rhino Horn Trade Explained." Mother Jones, August 15. http://www.motherjones.com/environment/2012/08/rhino-horn-trade-explained.

Milliken, T., and L. Sangalakula. (2011). "ETIS Update Number Six: Progress in the Implementation of the Elephant Trade Information System (ETIS)." Pachyderm 50: 99–104.

Mozambique News Agency. (2012). "Mozambique: Six Tonnes of Ivory Stolen." July 9. http://allafrica.com/stories/201207091550.html.

O'Keefe, C., and K. Sheridan. (2012). "Traveller Gang Targeted over Stolen Rhino Horns." Irish Examiner, May 11. http://www.irishexaminer.com/ireland/traveller-gang-targeted-over-stolen-rhino-horns-193541.html.

Pitse, R. (2012). "Ivory Stolen from Government Wildlife Depot." Sunday Standard (Botswana), May 7. http://www.sundaystandard.info/article.php?NewsID=13878&GroupID=1.

Rademeyer, J. (2012). "Rhino Butchers Caught on Film at North West Game Farm." Mail and Guardian (Zambia), November 9. http://mg.co.za/article/2012-11-08-rhino-butchers-caught-on-film.

Starkey, J. (2013). "It's War, and in Africa's Killing Fields the Poachers Are Winning." The Times (London), February 1.

Suresh, S. (2012). "UN Members Heed Call to Get Tough on Environmental Crime." EIA, September 28. http://www.eia-international.org/un-members-heed-eia-call-to-get-tough-on-environmental-crime.vixay.

Teh, E.H. (2011). "695 Tusks Found in Port Klang." The Star (Malaysia), September 6.

Thome, W. (2013). "Kenya Fines Ivory Smugglers 340 Dollars as Uganda Proposes 10 Year Jail Term." KenyaBuzz, February 5. http://www.kenyabuzz.com/lifestyle/kenya-fines-ivory-smugglers-340-dollars-as-uganda.

Thornton, A., and D. Currey. (1991). To Save an Elephant: The Undercover Investigation into the Illegal Ivory Trade. London: Doubleday.

UN General Assembly. (2012). "Strengthening the United Nations Crime Prevention and Criminal Justice Programme, in Particular Its Technical Cooperation Capacity." A/C.3/67/L.15/Rev.1. http://www.cites.org/common/news/2012/UNGA_res_wildlife.pdf.

UNODC Southern Africa. (2012). "Rhino Poaching in Southern Africa." Bulletin on Organized Crime in Southern Africa 1.

US Department of State. (2012). "Remarks [by Secretary Clinton] at the Partnership Meeting on Wildlife Trafficking." November 8. http://www.state.gov/secretary/rm/2012/11/200294.htm.

US Senate Committee on Foreign Relations. (2012). "Kerry Statement, Senate Foreign Relations Committee Hearing on Ivory and Insecurity: The Global Implications of Poaching in Africa." May 24. http://www.foreign.senate.gov/press/chair/release/kerry-statement_senate-foreign-relations-committee-hearing-on--ivory-and-insecurity-the-global-implications-of-poaching-in-africa.

Weiss, K. (2012). "Father and Son Plead Guilty in Rhino Horn Smuggling." Los Angeles Times, September 16. http://www.latimes.com/health/la-me-rhino-smugglers-20120916,0,7568821.story.

Zambian Watchdog. (2012). "Ivory Stolen from ZAWA Armoury: Workers Point at Given Lubinda." June 18. http://www.zambianwatchdog.com/2012/06/18/ivory-stolen-from-zawa-armoury-workers-point-at-given-lubinda.

Chapter 16: Coming to Grips with Poaching

Alacs, E.A., A. Georges, N.N. Fitzsimmons and J. Robertson. (2010). "DNA Detective: A Review of Molecular Approaches to Wildlife Forensics." Forensic Science, Medicine and Pathology 6(3): 180–94.

Bennett, E.L. (2011). "Another Inconvenient Truth: The Failure of Enforcement Systems to Save Charismatic Species." Oryx 45(4): 476–79.

CITES. (2011). "The International Consortium on Combating Wildlife Crime." http://www.cites.org/eng/prog/iccwc.php.

———. (2012). "CITES Praises GEF for Approving Innovative Rhino Project." Press release, June 13. http://www.cites.org/eng/news/pr/2012/20120613_rhino_project.php.

———. (2013). "Asia, Africa and North America Join Hands to Crack Down on Wildlife Crime Syndicates." Operation Cobra press release, February 5. http://www.cites.org/eng/news/pr/2013/pr_operation_cobra.pdf.

Coastweek.com. (2012). "Kenya Wildlife Services Arrest Ivory Dealer with Elephant Tusks." September 21–27.

Congo Basin Forest Partnership. (2012). "Major Conclusions of COMIFAC Ministers Extraordinary Session in N'Djamena (Chad)." June 6. http://www.cbfp.org/news_en/items/Conseilministre-Djamena-2012-E.html.

Dinerstein, E. (2011). "Family Rhinocerotidae (Rhinoceroses)." In D.E. Wilson and R. A. Mittermeier, eds., *Handbook of the Mammals of the World.* Vol. 2, *Hoofed Mammals,* 144–81. Barcelona: Lynx Edicions.

Douglas-Hamilton, I. (2012). "Ivory and Insecurity: The Global Implications of Poaching in Africa. Testimony of Iain Douglas-Hamilton, Founder and CEO, Save the Elephants, before the Committee on Foreign Relations, U.S. Senate, May 24, 2012." http://www.elephantsinperil.org/news/ivory-and-insecurity-the-global-implications-of-poaching-in-africa.

Global Times. (2013). "China Leads Crackdown on Trade in Endangered Species." February 18. http://www.globaltimes.cn/content/762127.shtml.

Gupta, S.K., K. Thangaraj and L. Singh. (2011). "Identification of the Source of Ivory Idol by DNA Analysis." *Journal of Forensic Sciences* 56(5): 1343–45.

Hawa, R. (2012). "Kenya: Five Rangers, 78 Elephants Killed by Poachers in a Year." *The Star* (Kenya), May 10. http://allafrica.com/stories/201205111224.html.

Henshall, A. (2012). "Elephants Now Think Twice about Midnight Snacks in Tanzania: Farmers Find a Whiff of Chili Pepper Sends Pachyderms Packing and Saves Corn Crops." *Wall Street Journal,* April 15. http://online.wsj.com/article/SB100014240527023038154045773337 80433251036.html.

IFAW. (2012). "Three Tonnes of Ivory Vanish as Thieves Loot Southern Africa Stockpiles." Press release, June 22. http://www.sundaystandard.info/article.php?NewsID=13878&GroupID=1.

INTERPOL. (2012). "INTERPOL: 200 Arrested in Biggest Crackdown on Elephant Slaughter." Press release, June 19. http://worldnews.msnbc.msn.com/_news/2012/06/19/12303417-interpol-200-arrested-in-biggest-crackdown-on-elephant-slaughter?lite.

———. "Project Wisdom." http://www.interpol.int/Crime-areas/Environmental-crime/Projects/Project-Wisdom (accessed March 20, 2013).

Ishida, Y., N.J. Georgiadis, T. Hondo and A.L. Roca. (2013). "Triangulating the Provenance of African Elephants Using Mitochondrial DNA." *Evolutionary Applications* 6(2): 253–65.

Jadhav, S., and M. Barua. (2012). "The Elephant Vanishes: Impact of Human–Elephant Conflict on People's Wellbeing." *Health Place* 18(6): 1356–65.

Keane, A., J.P.G. Jones, G. Edwards-Jones and E. J. Milner-Gulland. (2008). "The Sleeping Policeman: Understanding Issues of Enforcement and Compliance in Conservation." *Animal Conservation* 11(2): 75–82.

Kiiru, W. (2008) "Human–Elephant Conflicts in Africa: Who Has the Right-of-Way?" In C. Wemmer and C.A. Christen, eds., *Elephants and Ethics: Toward a Morality of Coexistence,* 383–97. Baltimore, MD: Johns Hopkins University Press.

Koross, K. (2012). "We Will Contain Poaching: KWS Director Julius Kipng'etich." *The Star* (Kenya), April 22. http://www.the-star.co.ke/lifestyle/128-lifestyle/72557-we-will-contain-poaching-kws-director-julius-kipngetich.

Liu, R., J. Duan, S. Guo et al. (2012). "Development of a Fingerprint Method for Animal Horn Classification by Liquid Chromatography Coupled with Hierarchical Clustering Analysis." *Journal of Liquid Chromatography and Related Technologies* 35(2): 205–14.

Lusaka Agreement Task Force. *Lusaka Agreement on Co-operative Enforcement Operations Directed at Illegal Trade in Wild Fauna and Flora.* http://www.lusakaagreement.org/about.html (accessed March 20, 2013).

———. (2012). "Poaching Masterminds Arrested During a LATF-ZAWA Joint Operation in Zambia's Southern Province." http://www.lusakaagreement.org/latf_zawa_poaching.html.

Martin, E.B. (2010). "Effective Law Enforcement in Ghana Reduces Elephant Poaching and Illegal Ivory Trade." *Pachyderm* 48: 24–32.

Martin, E.B., and L. Vigne. (2011). "Illegal Ivory Sales in Egypt." *TRAFFIC Bulletin* 23(3): 117–22.

Mlay, C. (1997). "The History of the Tanzania Ivory Trade pre–Appendix I and the International Ivory Trade Ban." In *Proceedings of the African Elephant Conference,* 9–15. London: EIA.

Mwadime, R. (2012). "Kenya: Two KWS Rangers Killed by Poachers in Taita." *Nairobi Star,* March 5. http://allafrica.com/stories/.201203060012.html.

Nowell, K. (2012). *Wildlife Crime Scorecard: Assessing Compliance with and Enforcement of CITES Commitments for Tigers, Rhinos and Elephants.* Gland, Switzerland: WWF.

Ogden, R. (2010). "Forensic Science, Genetics and Wildlife Biology: Getting the Right Mix for a Wildlife DNA Forensics Lab." *Forensic Science, Medicine and Pathology* 6(3): 172–79.

Pioneer News Service. (2012). "Tracey Sniffs Out 32 Kg Ivory in Dalma." February 8. http://dailypioneer.com/nation/41263-tracey-sniffs-out-32-kg-ivory-in-dalma.html.

PRWeb. (2012). "New Hope for Elephants under Threat in Central Africa." Press release, June 6. http://www.prweb.com/releases/world_wildlife_fund/COMIFAC_elephants/prweb9581667.htm.

Sitati, N.W., M.W. Walpole, N. Leader-Williams and P.J. Stephenson. (2012). "Human–Elephant Conflict: Do Elephants Contribute to Low Mean Grades in Schools within Elephant Ranges?" *International Journal of Biodiversity and Conservation* 4(15): 614–20.

Starkey, J. (2013). "It's War, and in Africa's Killing Fields the Poachers Are Winning." *The Times* (London), February 1. http://www.thetimes.co.uk/tto/environment/wildlife/article3674490.ece.

UNEP. (2005). *A Decade of Regional Wildlife Law Enforcement: The Case of the Lusaka Agreement.* http://www.lusakaagreement.org/Documents/Microsoft Word - LATF Evaluation Report.pdf.

Voice of America. (2012). "Interpol Conducts 'War' on Poaching in Africa." November 26. http://www.voanews.com/content/interpol-conducts-war-on-poaching-in-africa/1553523.html.

Walpole, M., and M. Linkie, eds. (2007). "Mitigating Human–Elephant Conflict: Case Studies from Africa and Asia." *Fauna and Flora International Conservation Reports.* Cambridge: Fauna and Flora International.

Wasser, S.K., B. Clark and C. Laurie. (2009). "The Ivory Trail." *Scientific American* 301: 68–76.

Wasser, S.K., W.J. Clark, O. Drori et al. (2008). "Combating the Illegal Trade in African Elephant Ivory with DNA Forensics." *Conservation Biology* 22(4): 1065–71.

Wasser, S.K., C. Mailand, R. Booth et al. (2007). "Using DNA to Track the Origin of the Largest Ivory Seizure since the 1989 Trade Ban." *Proceedings of the National Academy of Sciences of the United States of America* 104(10): 4228–33.

Wijnstekers, W. (2011). *The Evolution of CITES: A Reference to the Convention on International Trade in Endangered Species of Wild Fauna and Flora.* 9th ed. Budapest: International Council for Game and Wildlife Conservation. www.cites.org/common/resources/Evolution_of_CITES_9.pdf.

WWF. (2012). "Countries Fail to Protect Endangered Species from Illegal Trade." Press release, July 23. http://wwf.panda.org/who_we_are/wwf_offices/south_africa/?uNewsID=205743.

Chapter 17: Should Trade Be Legalized?

Bega, S. (2011). "Rhino Poachers Preying on Cancer Sufferers." *Pretoria News*, March 14. http://www.iol.co.za/scitech/science/environment/rhino-poachers-preying-on-cancer-sufferers-1.1041634#.URrwiaWfv2k.

Business Day. (2012a). "SA Mulling Rhino-Horn Trade, Says Minister." May 2. http://www.bdlive.co.za/articles/2012/05/02/sa-mulling-rhino-horn-trade-says-minister;jsessionid=CA74C49BA9954D0D208242A74D4423A1.present2.bdfm.

———. (2012b). "SA to Defer Decision on Rhino Proposal till 2016." October 4.

China Daily. (2013). "Measures Curb Illegal Ivory Trade in China." February 22. http://www.china.org.cn/environment/2013-02/22/content_28027565.htm.

CITES. (2013). "Decision-Making Mechanism for a Process of Trade in Ivory." CoP16 Doc. 36 (Rev. 1). http://www.cites.org/eng/cop/16/doc/E-CoP16-36.pdf.

Cook, D. (2012). "Make It Legal." *The Witness* (Pietermaritzburg, South Africa), October 16.

Cota-Larson, R. (2013). "Rhinos from South Africa to China: A Troubling Timeline." *Annamiticus.* http://annamiticus.com/Reports/TroublingTimeline.pdf.

Dinerstein, E. (2003). *The Return of the Unicorns: The Natural History and Conservation of the Greater One-horned Rhinoceros.* New York: Columbia University Press.

Hartley, W., and S. Blaine. (2012)."Rhino Horn Trade Viable for SA?" *Business Day*, May 4.

Jacobsen, T. (2012). *Rhino and Vicuña: A Parallel.* http://www.rhinoresourcecenter.com/pdf_files/133/1331765741.pdf.

Lichtenstein, G. (2012). "Vicuñas: Does Population Recovery Mean a Success for Sustainable Use?" *SULiNews* 2. http://www.iucn.org/about/union/commissions/sustainable_use_and_livelihoods_specialist_group/sulinews/issue_2/sn2_vicunas/.

Maendaenda, C. (2013). "Tanzania: Govt Probes Poaching Rise." *East African Business Week*, January 27. http://allafrica.com/stories/201301282083.html.

Martin, E.B., and L. Vigne. (2011). *The Ivory Dynasty: A Report on the Soaring Demand for Elephant and Mammoth Ivory in Southern China.* London: Elephant Family, Aspinall Foundation and Columbus Zoo and Aquarium.

Martin, R.B., D.H.M. Cumming, G.C. Craig et al. (2012). "Decision-Making Mechanisms and Necessary Conditions for a Future Trade in African Elephant Ivory: Final Report." CITES SC62 Doc 46.4 Annex.

McAllister, R.R., D. McNeill and I.J. Gordon. (2009). "Legalizing Markets and the Consequences for Poaching of Wildlife Species: The Vicuña as a Case Study." *Journal of Environmental Management* 90(1): 120–30.

Milliken, T., and J. Shaw. (2012). *The South Africa–Viet Nam Rhino Horn Trade Nexus: A Deadly Combination of Institutional Lapses, Corrupt Wildlife Industry Professionals and Asian Crime Syndicates.* Johannesburg: TRAFFIC.

Mkinga, M. (2012). "Dar Drops Bid to Sell Sh89bn Ivory Stockpile." *The Citizen* (Tanzania), December 25. http://thecitizen.co.tz/component/content/article/37-tanzania-top-news-story/27899-dar-drops-bid-to-sell-sh89bn-ivory-stockpile.html.

Moyle, B. (2013). "Brendan Moyle: Legal Ivory Trade Not Cause of Elephant Poaching." *New Zealand Herald*, February 12. http://www.nzherald.co.nz/opinion/news/article.cfm?c_id=466&objectid=10864746.

News24. (2012). "Hunters: Lift Ban on Rhino Trade." March 30. www.news24.com/SciTech/News/Hunters-Lift-ban-on-rhino-trade-20120330.

O' Criodain, C. (2012). "Rhino Poaching: A Contribution to the Debate." *SULiNews* 2. http://www.iucn.org/about/union/commissions/sustainable_use_and_livelihoods_specialist_group/sulinews/issue_2/sn2_rhinodebate/.

En Perú. (2009). "Poachers Return to the Southern Andes Killing Thousands of Vicuñas." October 16. http://enperublog.com/2009/10/16/poachers-return-to-the-southern-andes-killing-thousands-of-vicunas/.

Pillay, K. (2012). "Appeal for One-Off Rhino Horn Auction." *Independent Newspapers*, October 1. http://www.thepost.co.za/appeal-for-one-off-rhino-horn-auction-1.1393594#.UGmsplGOzzw.

Player, I., and A. Fourie. (2011). "How to Win the War Against Poachers." *Daily News* (South Africa), December 16.

Pot-Shot. (2012). "SAHGCA Puts Case for Sustainable Rhino Conservation to Parliament." January 23. www.pacificbreeze353.com/newsletters/index.cfm?y=article&company=17&article=3997&nl=605&click=web&subsection=50&langu=1).

Reuters. (2012). "Legalising Rhino Horn Trade in Focus." April 26.

Saiboko, A. (2012). "Tanzania: Govt Probes Ivory Seized in China." *Tanzania Daily News*, November 1. http://allafrica.com/stories/201211010182.html.

Sethi, N. (2012). "South African Demand for Legal Trade in Rhino Horns Leaves India Jittery." TNN, May 16. http://articles.timesofindia.indiatimes.com/2012-05-16/flora-fauna/31725352_1_trade-in-rhino-horns-indian-rhino-dudhwa-national-park.

't. Sas-Rolfes, M. (2012a). "The Rhino Poaching Crisis: A Market Analysis." http://www.rhino-economics.com/the-rhino-poaching-crisis-a-market-analysis/.

———. (2012b). "Escalation of Rhino Poaching in South Africa: Is the Trade Ban Approach Working?" *SULiNews* 1 (May). http://www.iucn.org/about/union/commissions/sustainable_use_and_livelihoods_specialist_group/sulinews/issue_1/sn1_rhino/.

Tanzania Daily News. (2012). "Tanzania: Poachers Are a Menace, Eliminate Them Now." August 13. http://allafrica.com/stories/201208130077.html.

Time. (2011). "TIME Magazine Exposes Plans for Chinese Rhino 'Farming.'" June 7.

Walker, C., and A. Walker. (2012). *The Rhino Keepers: Struggle for Survival*. Johannesburg: Jacana Media.

Wild, F. (2012). "Horns of a Dilemma." *Washington Post*, May 18.

Xinhua News Agency. (2013). "China Rejects Ivory Poaching Accusations." February 19.

Chapter 18: Dealing with Demand

China Daily. (2013). "Measures Curb Illegal Ivory Trade in China." February 22. http://www.china.org.cn/environment/2013-02/22/content_28027565.htm.

CITES. (2012). *Control of Trade in Ivory in China*. SC62 Inf. 8.

Nowell, K. (2012a). "Assessment of Rhino Horn as a Traditional Medicine." CITES SC62 Doc. 47.2 Annex (Rev. 2).

———. (2012b). *Wildlife Crime Scorecard: Assessing Compliance with and Enforcement of CITES Commitments for Tigers, Rhinos and Elephants*. Gland, Switzerland: WWF.

Omar, C. (2013). "Africa Focus: China Pledges to Back Kenya's Wildlife Conservation Efforts." Xinhua News Agency, February 23. http://www.nzweek.com/world/africa-focus-china-pledges-to-back-kenyas-wildlife-conservation-efforts-50807/.

Radio Free Asia. (2012). "A Champion of Elephants." November 9. http://www.rfa.org/english/women/animal-11092012132430.html.

Starkey, J. (2013). "It's War, and in Africa's Killing Fields the Poachers Are Winning." *The Times* (London), February 1.

't. Sas-Rolfes, M. (1997). "Elephants, Rhinos and the Economics of the Illegal Trade." *Pachyderm* 24: 23–29.

Yang, S.Z. (trans.). (1998). *The Divine Farmer's Materia Medica: A Translation of the Shen Nong Ben Cao Jing*. Boulder, CO: Blue Poppy Press.

Chapter 19: The Future

AEC. (2012). "Elephant Crisis: 25 African Countries Sound the Alarm." Press communiqué, September.

African Wildlife Foundation. (2012). "Rhino Summit Emergency Plan of Action: Toward a Comprehensive Response to the Rhino Poaching Crisis." http://www.awf.org/documents/RhinoActionPlan2.pdf.

Agence France-Presse. (2013). "Charging China Demand Drives Deadly Ivory Trade." February 28. http://globalnation.inquirer.net/65923/charging-china-demand-drives-deadly-ivory-trade#sthash.sHQfF6Uo.dpuf.

Biggs, D., F. Courchamp, R. Martin and H.P. Possingham. (2013). "Legal Trade of Africa's Rhino Horns." *Science* 339 (March 1): 1038–39.

Burn, R.W., F.M. Underwood and J. Blanc. (2011). "Global Trends and Factors Associated with the Illegal Killing of Elephants: A Hierarchical Bayesian Analysis of Carcass Encounter Data." *PLoS ONE* 6(9): e24165.

Ceballos, E. (2013). *Internet Trade of Elephant Ivory in Africa and Asia*. New Westminster, BC: CATCA and ACWF.

CITES. "Action Plan for the Control of Trade in Elephant Ivory." CoP14, Annex 2. http://www.cites.org/eng/dec/valid14/annex2.shtml.

———. (2010). "African Elephant Action Plan." CoP15 Inf. 68.

———. (2011). "African Elephant Fund Launched at CITES Meeting." Press release, August 19. http://www.cites.org/eng/news/pr/2011/20110819_SC61.php.

———. (2013). "Proposed New Resolution Concerning the African Elephant Action Plan and African Elephant Fund (Nigeria and Rwanda)." CoP16 Doc. 53.3 (Rev. 2). http://www.cites.org/eng/cop/16/doc/E-CoP16-53-03.pdf.

Indonesia Ministry of Forestry. (2007). "Strategy and Action Plan for the Conservation of Rhinos in Indonesia." http://www.dephut.go.id/files/badak_1.pdf.

Knight, M. (2012). "The Rhino Dilemma." SULiNews 2. http://www.iucn.org/about/union/commissions/sustainable_use_and_livelihoods_specialist_group/sulinews/issue_2/sn2_rhinodebate/.

Levin, D. (2013). "From Elephants' Mouths, an Illicit Trail to China." New York Times, March 1. http://www.nytimes.com/2013/03/02/world/asia/an-illicit-trail-of-african-ivory-to-china.html?pagewanted=all&_r=0.

Lianxing, L. (2013). "Progress Made in Fight Against Wildlife Crime." China Daily, March 6. http://africa.chinadaily.com.cn/china/2013-03/06/content_16281114.htm.

Nepal Department of National Parks and Wildlife Conservation. (2006). The Greater One-horned Rhinoceros Conservation Action Plan for Nepal (2006–2011). assets.panda.org/downloads/rhino_action_plan_25aug_06_low.pdf.

Sabah [Malaysia] Wildlife Department. (2011). Rhinoceros Action Plan, 2012–2016. http://www.borneotrust.com/BorneoTrust/BCT-%20Rhino%20Action%20Plan%202012.pdf.

South Africa Department of Environmental Affairs. (2010). National Strategy for the Safety and Security of Rhinoceros Populations in South Africa. http://www.rhinoresourcecenter.com/pdf_files/130/1301008151.pdf.

———. (2011). A Study on Dehorning African Rhinoceroses as a Tool to Reduce the Risk of Poaching. https://www.environment.gov.za/sites/default/files/docs/studyon_dehorning_african_rhinoceros.pdf.

———. (2013a). "Biodiversity Management Plan for the Black Rhinoceros (Diceros bicornis) in South Africa, 2011–2020." https://www.environment.gov.za/sites/default/files/gazetted_notices/biodiversity_management_plan_blackrhino.pdf.

———. (2013b). "Media Statement by the Minister of Water and Environmental Affairs, Mrs. Edna Molewa, on Rhino Poaching Intervention and the Position of South Africa to the 16th Conference of Parties of the Convention in International Trade in Endangered Species of Fauna and Flora (CITES)." February 28.

Postscript: The 2013 CITES Meeting

Asian Scientist. (2013). "Thai Buddhist Leaders Call for End to Ivory Use." March 11. http://www.asianscientist.com/topnews/thai-buddhist-leaders-call-ivory-2013/.

CITES. (2013a). "Decision-Making Mechanism for a Process of Trade in Ivory." CoP16 Com. II.18. http://www.cites.org/common/cop/16/com/E-CoP16-Com-II-18.pdf.

———. (2013b). "Draft Revision of Resolution Conf. 10.10 (Rev. CoP15) on Trade in Elephant Specimens." CoP 16 Doc. 26 (Rev. 1). http://www.cites.org/eng/cop/16/doc/E-CoP16-26.pdf.

———. (2013c). "Draft Revision of Resolution Conf. 10.10 (Rev. CoP15) on Trade in Elephant Specimens." Committee II. CoP16 Com. II.26. http://www.cites.org/common/cop/16/com/E-CoP16-Com-II-26.pdf.

———. (2013d). "Elephant Conservation, Illegal Killing and Ivory Trade." SC63 Doc. 18. http://www.cites.org/eng/com/sc/63/E-SC63-18.pdf.

———. (2013e). "Monitoring of Illegal Trade in Ivory and Other Elephant Specimens." CoP16 Com. II. 22. http://www.cites.org/common/cop/16/com/E-CoP16-Com-II-22.pdf.

———. (2013f). "National Ivory Action Plans." SC64 Doc. 2. http://www.cites.org/eng/com/sc/64/E-SC64-02.pdf.

———. (2013g). "Opening Statement by Her Excellency Prime Minister of the Kingdom of Thailand, Yingluck Shinawatra." March 3. Sixteenth Meeting of the Conference of the Parties to the Convention on International Trade in Endangered Species of Wild Flora and Fauna, March 3–14, 2013, Bangkok, Thailand. http://www.cites.org/eng/cop/16/open/th_pm.php.

———. (2013h). "Proposal to Amend the Annotation for Ceratotherium simum simum." Cop 16 Prop. 10. www.cites.org/eng/cop/16/prop/E-CoP16-Prop-10.pdf.

———. (2013i). "Proposal to Amend the Annotation for Loxodonta africana." CoP16 Prop. 12. http://www.cites.org/eng/cop/16/prop/E-CoP16-Prop-12.pdf.

———. (2013j). "Proposed New Resolution Concerning the African Elephant Action Plan and African Elephant Fund." CoP16 Com. II.17. http://www.cites.org/common/cop/16/com/E-CoP16-Com-II-17.pdf.

———. (2013k). "Proposed Revision of Resolution Conf. 10.9 on Consideration of Proposals for the Transfer of African Elephant Populations from Appendix I to Appendix II." CoP16 Com. II.19. http://www.cites.org/common/cop/16/com/E-CoP16-Com-II-19.pdf.

———. (2013l). "Rhinoceroses." Draft Decisions of the Conference of the Parties. Committee II. CoP16 Com. II.24. http://www.cites.org/common/cop/16/

com/E-CoP16-Com-II-24.pdf.

———. (2013m). "Summary Record of the Twelfth Session of Committee II." CoP16 Com. II Rec. 12. http://www.cites.org/common/cop/16/sum/E-CoP16-Com-II-Rec-12.pdf.

———. (2013n). "Summary Record of the 13th Session of Committee II." CoP16 Com. II. Rec. 13. http://www.cites.org/common/cop/16/sum/E-CoP16-Com-II-Rec-13.pdf.

Dabany, J.R. (2013). "Poachers Kill Dozens of Elephants, Including 33 Pregnant Females, in Chad." Reuters, March 19. http://worldnews.nbcnews.com/_news/2013/03/19/17372329-poachers-kill-dozens-of-elephants-including-33-pregnant-females-in-chad?lite.

FREELAND Foundation. (2013). "CITES Missed Opportunities for Tigers, Elephants & Rhinos." Joint press release, EIA, Wildlife Protection Society of India and FREELAND Foundation, March 14. http://freeland.org/eng/news/press-release/278-cites-missed-opportunities-for-tigers-elephants-a-rhinos.

International Institute for Sustainable Development. (2013). *Earth Negotiations Bulletin* 21(73–89). Compiled Reports, CITES Sixteenth Meeting, March 3–14, 2013, Bangkok. http://www.iisd.ca/cites/cop16/compilatione.pdf.

McGrath, M. (2013). "'Gang of Eight' on Ivory Probation." BBC News, March 14. http://www.bbc.co.uk/news/science-environment-21788664.

Reuters. (2013). "Poachers Kill 28 Forest Elephants in Cameroon – WWF." March 13. http://www.chicagotribune.com/sns-rt-cameroon-poachersl6n0c56c3-20130313,0,2016676,full.story.

Sarnsamak, P. (2013). "Tourists Told Not to Buy Any Ivory Products." *The Nation* (Thailand), March 14.

http://www.nationmultimedia.com/national/Tourists-told-not-to-buy-any-ivory-products-30201906.html.

South Africa Department of Environmental Affairs. (2013b). "Media Statement by the Minister of Water and Environmental Affairs, Mrs. Edna Molewa, on Rhino Poaching Intervention and the Position of South Africa to the 16th Conference of Parties of the Convention in International Trade in Endangered Species of Fauna and Flora (CITES)." February 28.

INDEX